McDougal, Littell
Wordskills

Green Level

James E. Coomber
Concordia College
Moorhead, Minnesota

Howard D. Peet
North Dakota State University
Fargo, North Dakota

ML **McDougal, Littell & Company**
Evanston, Illinois
New York   Dallas   Sacramento   Columbia, SC

ISBN: 0-395-97981-1

Copyright © 2000 by McDougal, Littell & Company
Box 1667, Evanston, Illinois 60204
All rights reserved. Printed in the United States of America.

8 9 10 11 12 13 -HWI- 07 06 05 04

CONTENTS

To the Student

Why study vocabulary? Increasing the number of words that you know helps you read, write, and speak better. You'll understand more of what you read with less reliance on the dictionary, and you'll be able to express yourself more accurately. This doesn't mean using twenty-dollar words to amaze others. It just means using the right words to say exactly what you mean.

How to Use This Book

You may notice something unusual about this vocabulary book. Definitions are not given with the word lists. Instead, you are given something more powerful—strategies for determining the meanings of words yourself. You'll find this information in a Special Unit starting on page 1. Then, in the following units, you will master new words using a five step process:

1. First you will infer the word's meaning through context clues.
2. Second you will refine your understanding by studying the word's use in a reading selection.
3. Then your understanding of the words will be reinforced through a variety of exercises.
4. Next you will relate the word to other words in the same family.
5. Finally you will use the word in writing and speaking.

The words in this book are ones you are likely to encounter in your reading. Some you may already know; others may be completely unfamiliar. As you study these words, try to move them into your "active vocabulary," the words you understand well enough to use in your speaking and writing.

A Personal Vocabulary-Building Program

You can apply the vocabulary skills in this book to learning any new words that you encounter. Here are several tips that will help you:

1. Keep a vocabulary notebook. Jot down the new words you encounter. Record the essential information for each word: correct spelling, part of speech, pronunciation, definition.
2. Review the words in your notebook. Take a few minutes each day to study them. Set a realistic goal of learning a certain number of new words per week.
3. Study the words actively. Active study means that you use as many senses as possible in studying the word. Listen to yourself say the word. See it in your mind's eye. Then use the word as soon as possible in speech or in writing. In general, if you use a word twice, it is yours.
4. Invent your own memory devices. Try to associate the word with other similar words you know. Create a mental image that relates to the word and helps you remember its meaning. One student remembered the meaning of the word *pretentious,* "showy, flaunting," by picturing a small boy playing make-believe, *pretending* to be a king.

There is one final reason for studying vocabulary, one that we hope you discover for yourself as you use this book: Words are fascinating! They are as surprising and alive and insightful as the people who use them.

Strategies for Unlocking Word Meaning

What happens when you come across an unfamiliar word in your reading? If you have a dictionary at hand, you can look up the word. If you don't have a dictionary, you still have two excellent strategies that can help you make sense of the word: **context clues** and **word parts analysis.** You will be using these strategies in every unit of this book. With practice you can master these strategies and improve your reading skills.

Part A Determining a Word's Meaning from Context

Skilled readers often use context clues to figure out a word's meaning. **Context** refers to the words or sentences before or after a certain word that help explain what the word means. There are several types of context clues you can look for, including **definition and restatement, example, comparison, contrast,** and **cause and effect.**

Definition and Restatement

Sometimes a writer will directly define a word, especially if the word is a technical term that may be unfamiliar to readers. Here is an example:

> The building was designed in the form of a *hexagon,* a shape having six angles and six sides.

More often, a writer will restate the meaning of a word in a less precise form than a dictionary definition.

> The snowstorm in June was a real *anomaly:* nothing like that had ever happened before.

The meaning of *anomaly*—"a departure from the general rule, an abnormality"—becomes clear from the restatement: "nothing like that had ever happened before." Definition and restatement are often signaled by punctuation (note the comma and the colon in the preceding examples) and by certain key words and phrases.

Words Signaling Definition and Restatement		
which is	or	also known as
that is	in other words	also called

Example

The context in which a word appears may include one or more **examples** that are clues to its meaning. Look at the following sentence.

The *percussion* instruments in the orchestra include various kinds of drums and also cymbals, bells, the triangle, the gong, and the tambourine.

The word *include* followed by a list of examples helps explain what a *percussion* instrument is: "a musical instrument in which the tone is produced when some part is struck or shaken." The following words and phrases often signal an example.

Words Signaling an Example		
like	for example	other
including	for instance	this
such as	especially	these
		these include

Comparison

Another type of context clue is **comparison.** With this clue the writer compares the word in question with other, more familiar words. By noting the similarities between the things described, you can get an idea of the meaning of the unfamiliar word.

Jeff's *compassion* for the earthquake victims, like his feelings of sorrow for the homeless, shows that he cares about others.

The comparison context clue "like his feelings of sorrow" clearly conveys the meaning of *compassion*—"a deep sympathy or pity." Comparisons are often signaled by one of these key words or phrases.

Words Signaling a Comparison		
like	similar to	similarly
as	resembling	also
in the same way	likewise	identical
		related

Contrast

Context may also help reveal the meaning of a word through **contrast,** as in this example:

I thought she would be clumsy with the tools during her first day on the job, but she handled them with great *dexterity*.

In this sentence the word *but* signals a contrast. Therefore, you can assume that *dexterity* means the opposite of *clumsy* (the dictionary defines *dexterity* as "skill in using one's hands"). The following key words and phrases signal a contrast.

Words Signaling a Contrast		
but	on the other hand	instead
although	unlike	different
on the contrary	in contrast to	however

Cause and Effect

Another type of context clue is **cause and effect.** The cause of an action or event may be stated using an unfamiliar word. If, however, the effect is stated in familiar terms, it can help you understand the unfamiliar word. Consider the following example:

Because the old building had become *dilapidated,* we had to spend a lot of time and money on repairs.

In this sentence the cause—a dilapidated building—leads to the effect—doing repairs. Therefore, *dilapidated* must mean "broken down, in need of repair." Certain key words and phrases may signal cause and effect.

Words Signaling Cause and Effect		
because	consequently	so
since	therefore	as a result

Inference from General Context

Often the clues to the meaning of an unfamiliar word are not in the same sentence. In such cases you will need to look at the sentences that surround the word and **infer,** or draw a conclusion about, the word's meaning. A single piece of information several sentences away from the unfamiliar word may unlock the meaning. Study the following example:

Roy used to be a *pugnacious* character, but over the years he seems to have mellowed. He has more self-confidence now and doesn't need to prove himself all the time. But when I first knew him he seemed to have a chip on his shoulder—he was always itching for a fight.

The clues to the meaning of *pugnacious* are found at the end of the paragraph. The details "chip on his shoulder" and "itching for a fight" suggest that *pugnacious* means "eager and ready to fight, quarrelsome."

Sometimes the supporting details in a paragraph must be examined together to help you infer the meaning of an unfamiliar word.

> We had a rather *garrulous* cab driver. He talked about anything that came into his head: sports, politics, traffic, the state of his health. He carried on endlessly about the weather. When we finally left him, he was describing each of his seven grandchildren in detail.

A series of descriptive details follows the unfamiliar word *garrulous*. The details help you draw a conclusion about what a *garrulous* person is—a person who talks too much.

Determining Meaning from Context Each of the following sentences and paragraphs contains an italicized word you may not know. Look for context clues to help you determine the meaning of the word. Write the definition in the blank.

1. In his meeting with the Queen, the Prime Minister was *deferential*. He spoke courteously, listened politely, and showed respect for her judgments and opinions.

   _____

2. The doctor told Audrey that exercise would not improve the condition of her knee; on the contrary, it would probably *aggravate* it.

   _____

3. Although the principal was known for giving strict punishments, this time he was *lenient* with the offending student.

   _____

4. As a result of the *pollutants* in the stream, we could not drink the water or swim.

   _____

5. The osprey's *talon,* which resembles an eagle's claw, is an efficient hunting weapon.

   _____

6. Instead of answering Robin in a flattering or insincere way, Helen decided to be quite *candid* and to tell him just what she thought.

   _____

7. Though not stupid, Andy is rather *gullible;* that is, he believes just about anything we tell him.

   _____

8. Jake managed to *alienate* all of his friends. He refused their offers of help, accused them of interference, and began spreading false rumors about them. In the end, none of them would even speak to him.

   _____

9. The teacher said that *belligerent* actions, such as punching and shoving, would not be permitted.

   _____

10. The child was always *precocious.* She was toddling around at the age of eight months, putting sentences together at age two, and making up tunes on the piano when she was four. She even got chicken pox early.

    _____

11. As a result of the *drought,* the ground was dry and caked, the grass was brown, and the plants were wilted.

    _____

12. Unlike her truck, which was covered with dust and grime, Sharon's car was always *immaculate.*

    _____

13. The *conservatory,* a large, glass-enclosed building filled with flowers and other plants, was a popular tourist attraction.

    _____

14. The river *meandered* back and forth like a snake winding along the ground.

    _____

15. In the same way that a deer runs at the sound of a gunshot, Carlos *sprints* away whenever anyone mentions chores.

    _____

Number correct _____ (total 15)

Understanding Context Clues Choose five of the words below. For each word write a sentence that uses that word. Each of your sentences should contain a different type of context clue—**definition and restatement, example, comparison, contrast,** or **cause and effect.** Then label each sentence according to the type of context clue used.

decree	scrutinize	tepid
impede	spacious	visionary

1. _____

_____

2. _____

_____

3. _____

_____

4. _____

_____

5. _____

_____

Number correct _____ (total 5)

Part B Determining Meaning Through Word Analysis

Words are made up of various combinations of the following parts: *prefix, suffix, base word,* and *root.* Analysis of these parts is another way to determine an unfamiliar word's meaning. The following terms are used in analyzing word parts.

Prefix a word part that is added to the beginning of another word or word part

Suffix a word part that is added to the end of another word or word part

Base word a complete word to which a prefix and/or a suffix may be added

Root a word part to which a prefix and/or a suffix must be added. A root cannot stand alone.

The word *dispassionate* is made up of the prefix *dis-,* the base word *passion,* and the suffix *-ate.* If you know the meanings of these parts, you can determine the meaning of the whole word.

dis- ("not") + *passion* ("emotion") + *-ate* ("having")
dispassionate = not having emotion; calm; impartial

Now look at a word with a root. *Dehydration* is made up of the prefix *de-* ("away from, off"), the Greek root *hydr* ("water"), and the suffix *-ation* ("state of being"). *Dehydration* means "the state of being without water."

Prefixes

The following chart contains prefixes that have only one meaning.

Prefixes That Have a Single Meaning		
Prefix	**Meaning**	**Example**
bene-	good	benefit
circum-	around	circumference
col-, com-, con-, cor-	with, together	collapse, compile construct, correspond
contra-	opposed	contradict
equi-	equal	equidistant
extra-	outside	extraordinary
hemi-	half	hemisphere
inter-	between, among	international
mal-	bad	maltreat, malignant
mid-	halfway	midday
mis-	wrong	misspell
non-	not	nonworking
post-	after in time or space	postpone
pre-	before	predawn
sub-	under, below	subzero

Some prefixes have more than one meaning. Study the common prefixes listed in the following chart.

Prefixes That Have More Than One Meaning		
Prefix	**Meaning**	**Example**
a-, ab-	up, out	arise
	not	abnormal
	away	absent
anti-	against	antiaircraft
	prevents, cures	antidote
de-	away from, off	derail
	down	decline
	reverse action of	defrost
dis-	lack of	distrust
	not	dishonest
	away	disarm
em-, en-	to get into, on	embark
	to make, cause	enable
	in, into	enclose
il-, im-, in-, ir-	not	illegal
	in, into	investigate
pro-	in favor of	profamily
	forward, ahead	propel
re-	again	rethink
	back	repay
semi-	half	semicircle
	twice in a period	semiannual
	partly	semiconscious
super-	over and above	superhuman
	very large	supertanker
trans-	across	transcontinental
	beyond	transcend
un-	not	unhappy
	reverse of	unfasten

Suffixes

Like a prefix, a suffix has a meaning that can provide a strong clue to the definition of a whole word. Suffixes can also determine the part of speech. Certain suffixes make words nouns; others create adjectives, verbs, or adverbs.

Once you know suffixes and their meanings, you can form new words by attaching suffixes to base words or to roots. For instance, the suffix *-er* can be added to the base word *astronomy* to create the word *astronomer*. Notice that the spelling of a base word may change when a suffix is added. In the preceding example, the *y* from *astronomy* was dropped when *-er* was added. For information about spelling rules for adding suffixes, see the **Spelling Handbook,** pages 214–239.

Noun suffixes, when added to a base word or root, form nouns. Become familiar with the following common noun suffixes.

Noun Suffixes That Refer to Someone Who Does Something

Suffix	Examples
-ant	commandant, occupant
-eer	auctioneer
-er	manager
-ician	beautician, statistician
-ist	geologist
-or	counselor

Noun Suffixes That Make Abstract Words

Suffix	Examples
-ance, -ancy, -ence	vigilance, vacancy, independence
-ation, -ion, -ition	imagination, inspection, recognition
-cy	accuracy
-dom	freedom, kingdom
-hood	womanhood, brotherhood
-ice	cowardice, prejudice
-ism	realism, federalism
-ity, -ty	sincerity, frailty
-ment	encouragement, commitment
-ness	kindness, fondness
-ship	ownership, worship
-tude	gratitude, solitude

Adjective suffixes, when added to a base word or root, create adjectives—
words that are used to modify nouns and pronouns.

Adjective Suffixes

Suffix	Meaning	Example
-able, -ible	able to be	readable, convertible
-al	relating to	musical
-ant	relating to	triumphant
-ar	relating to	polar
-ate	having, full of	passionate
-ful	full of	harmful
-ic	pertaining to, like	heroic
-ish	pertaining to, like	foolish
-ive	pertaining to	descriptive
-less	without	senseless
-like	like	lifelike
-ly	like	scholarly
-most	at the extreme	topmost
-ous	full of	furious

Verb suffixes change base words to verbs. The following chart lists four
common verb suffixes.

Verb Suffixes

Suffix	Meaning	Example
-ate	to make	activate
-en	to become	strengthen
-fy	to make	simplify
-ise, -ize	to become	merchandise, computerize

Adverb suffixes change base words to adverbs—words that modify verbs,
adjectives, and other adverbs. The following chart lists the most common
adverb suffixes.

Adverb Suffixes

Suffix	Meaning	Example
-ily, -ly,	manner	happily, quickly
-ward	toward	skyward
-wise	like	clockwise

Roots and Word Families

A word root cannot stand alone but must be combined with other word parts. A great many roots used in our language come from Greek or Latin. A single root can generate many English words. A **word family** is a group of words with a common root. For example, all of the words in the following word family are derived from the Latin root *port,* which means "carry."

import	portable	porter
export	portage	deportee
purport	disport	transportation

Learning word roots will help you develop your vocabulary by enabling you to recognize roots in many related words. The following two charts show some common Greek and Latin roots.

Useful Greek Roots

Root	Meaning	Example
anthrop	human	anthropology
aster, astr	star	asterisk
auto	self, alone	autobiography
bibl, biblio	book	bibliography
bi, bio	life	biology
chron	time	chronology
cracy, crat	rule, government	democracy
dem	people	epidemic
gen	birth, race, kind	generation
geo	earth	geography
gram, graph	write, draw, describe	grammar, paragraph
hydr	water	hydrogen
log	word, reason, study	dialogue, logic, ecology
meter, metr	measure	barometer
neo	new	neoclassical
nom, nym	name, word, law	nominate, antonym
ortho	straight, correct	orthodontist, orthodox
pan	all, entire	panorama
phil	love	philosopher
phob	fear	claustrophobia
phon	sound	phonograph
psych	mind, soul, spirit	psychology
scope	see	telescope
soph	wise	sophisticated
tele	far, distant	television
theo	god	theology
therm	heat	thermometer

Useful Latin Roots

Root	Meaning	Example
capt, cept	take, have	capture, accept
cede, ceed, cess	go, yield, give way	secede, proceed, recess
cred	believe	credit, creed
dic, dict	speak, say, tell	dictate, dictionary
duc, duct	lead	introduce, conductor
fact, fect	do, make	factory, defect
fer	carry	transfer
ject	throw, hurl	eject, inject
junct	join	junction
miss, mit	send, let go	dismiss, admit
mob, mot, mov	move	mobility, motion, movie
par, para	get ready	prepare, parachute
pon, pos, posit	place, put	opponent, deposit
port	carry	porter, portable
puls	throb, urge	pulsate, compulsory
scrib, script	write	prescribe, scripture
spec, spect, spic	look, see	speculate, spectacle, conspicuous
stat	stand, put in a place	statue, state
tain, ten, tent	hold	contain, tenant, attention
tract	pull, move	tractor, retract
ven, vent	come	convention, event
vers, vert	turn	versatile, invert
vid, vis	see	video, vista
voc, vok	voice, call	vocal, invoke
vol	wish	volunteer, malevolent
volv	roll	revolve, involve

Determining Word Meaning Through Prefixes and Suffixes Draw lines to separate each of the following words into three parts—prefix, base word, and suffix. Determine the meaning of the prefix and the suffix. Then, by adding the meanings of the prefix and the suffix to the base word, determine the meaning of the complete word and write the definition in the blank.

1. nonconformist: _____

2. decentralize: _____

3. illogical: _____

4. misrepresentation: _____

5. supernaturalism: _____

6. noncombatant: _____

7. immodesty: _____

8. apolitical: _____

9. semiretirement: _____

10. prehistoric: _____

Number correct _____ (total 10)

Determining Word Meaning Through Prefixes, Suffixes, and Roots Each of the following words consists of a Greek or Latin root and a prefix or suffix. Use your knowledge of roots, prefixes, and suffixes to put together the meanings of the word parts and write a definition for each word. You may check your definitions with a dictionary.

1. prologue: _____

2. intercede: _____

3. deportation: _____

4. invocation: _____

5. restropect: _____

6. dehydration: _____

7. untenable: _____

8. regenerate: _____

9. incredible: _____

10. captivity: _____

Number correct _____ (total 10)

Number correct in unit _____ (total 40)

UNIT 1

Part A   Target Words and Their Meanings

The twenty words that follow will be the focus of this first unit. You will find them in the reading selection and in the exercises in this unit. For a guide to their pronunciations, refer to the **Pronunciation Key** on page 249.

1. associate (ə sō′ shē āt′, -sē-) v. (-it) adj., n.
2. bankrupt (baŋk′ rupt′, -rəpt) adj., v.
3. devoted (di vōt′ id) adj.
4. diverse (dī vʉrs′, də-) adj.
5. drastic (dras′ tik) adj.
6. emotional (i mō′ shən ′l) adj.
7. fictional (fik′ shən ′l) adj.
8. flair (fler) n.
9. flamboyant (flam boi′ ənt) adj.
10. humanitarian (hyōō man′ ə ter′ ē ən) n., adj.
11. humorist (hyōō′ mər ist) n.
12. individualistic (in′ di vij′ ōo wəl is′ tik) adj.
13. inquisitive (in kwiz′ ə tiv) adj.
14. interior (in tir′ ē ər) n., adj.
15. memorable (mem′ ər ə b'l, mem′ rə-) adj.
16. pursue (pər sōo′) v.
17. rural (rōor′ əl) adj.
18. tragedy (traj{ ə dē) n.
19. transform (trans fôrm′) v.
20. unique (yōo nēk′) adj.

Inferring Meaning from Context

For each sentence write the letter of the word or phrase that is closest in meaning to the word or words in italics. Use context clues to help you choose the correct answer. (For information about how context helps you understand vocabulary, see pages 1–6.)

_____ 1. People generally *associate* pyramids with Egypt, windmills with the Netherlands, and the Eiffel Tower with Paris.

a. remember   b. connect   c. examine   d. confuse

_____ 2. When the new supermarket opened in the neighborhood, Jack's Corner Store *went bankrupt* because so much business was lost to the competition.

a. was ruined financially   b. was successful   c. put more money in the bank   d. was not affected

_____ 3. Angie Thompson of Newport, Humberside, England, must be *a devoted* organist. Who else would choose to play the organ for 110 hours straight!

a. a dedicated   b. a religious   c. an unskilled   d. a slow

14

_____ 4. The committee came up with many *diverse* ideas for raising money to build a new school playground, including a car wash, a bake sale, a pizza party, a raffle, and even a dog wash.

a. difficult   b. foolish   c. similar   d. different

_____ 5. The doctor told him that smoking would have *drastic* consequences for his health because of its many harmful side effects.

a. enjoyable   b. minor   c. severe   d. positive

_____ 6. The arrival of the returning soldiers was *an emotional* moment for the waiting families: people were crying, laughing, and cheering.

a. a dull   b. a miserable   c. a stirring   d. a scary

_____ 7. Some people assume Romeo and Juliet were real people. But they were *fictional* characters in one of William Shakespeare's most famous plays.

a. made-up   b. realistic   c. youthful   d. romantic

_____ 8. Ed Johnson of Victoria, British Columbia, demonstrated a real *flair for* climbing when, in 1982, he climbed a one-hundred-foot spar pole and came back down in just over twenty-seven seconds.

a. interest in   b. admiration of   c. talent for   d. dislike for

_____ 9. The rock singer's *flamboyant* costume included a silver shirt, black leather pants, a purple scarf, and silver boots.

a. dignified   b. plain   c. inexpensive   d. flashy

_____ 10. Pearl Buck was not only a famous author but also a *humanitarian;* she gave millions of dollars and countless hours of her time to serve the needy.

a. philosopher   b. writer   c. teacher   d. person who helps others

_____ 11. My history teacher, Ms. Martinez, is *a humorist* who often tells funny stories in class just to make a point or to spark interest in the subject.

a. a serious person   b. an amusing person   c. an unpredictable person   d. a hard grader

_____ 12. The artist advised the students to develop their own *individualistic* styles; she said that true artists are never content to go along with the crowd or to imitate others.

a. ordinary   b. fancy   c. selfish   d. independent

_____ 13. *Inquisitive* children are always asking "How?" or "Why?"

a. troublesome   b. questioning   c. unfortunate   d. rude

_____ 14. The outside of the house was ordinary, but the *interior* was full of lovely antiques.

a. inside   b. yard   c. cellar   d. exterior

15. The most *memorable* part of the story was when the mountain climbers, after days of struggle, finally reached the summit.
   a. boring   b. ordinary   c. easily forgotten   d. easily remembered

16. When the suspect abandoned his car and ran into the alley, the police officer quickly decided to *pursue* him on foot.
   a. chase after   b. guard   c. run away from   d. watch

17. City life is noisy, crowded, and exciting, but *rural* life is quiet and peaceful because there are wide-open spaces and fewer people.
   a. urban   b. family   c. country   d. downtown

18. The death of a favorite pet can be a *tragedy* for its owners, because people often develop such strong affection for their pets.
   a. minor irritation   b. sorrowful event   c. joyous time
   d. expensive lesson

19. The owners hoped that a fresh coat of paint, new furniture, and a thorough cleaning would *transform* the cabin into a pleasant place.
   a. divide   b. enlarge   c. move   d. change

20. Yellowstone Park is *unique* because it has natural wonders found nowhere else on earth.
   a. unlike any other of its kind   b. ordinary   c. expensive
   d. romantic

Number correct _____ (total 20)

Part B Target Words in Reading and Literature

You should now have a general idea of the meaning of each target word. Sharpen your understanding by studying how these words are used in the following selection.

The World of Mark Twain

Howard Peet

Mark Twain is perhaps America's most famous writer, best known for his tales of boyhood, The Adventures of Tom Sawyer *and* The Adventures of Huckleberry Finn. *As this reading selection points out, however, his accomplishments and interests were quite varied.*

The name Mark Twain began as a joke. When the twenty-seven-year-old Samuel Clemens wrote a humorous article, he signed it with a phrase used by Mississippi riverboat pilots to describe water just barely deep enough for safe travel—"Mark Twain." Clemens loved to play games with

Mark Twain, 1897. The Bettmann Archive, New York

his readers, and he had used odd or amusing pen names before. But this name stuck, becoming one of the most famous names in American literature. The life of Samuel Clemens, or Mark Twain, proved to be as interesting and **memorable** as his writing.

He grew up during a time of **drastic** change, when America was being **transformed** from a **rural** nation to an industrial one. New territories, new jobs, new opportunities gave restless dreamers such as Twain plenty of room to move. At an early age, he left his boyhood home of Hannibal, Missouri, to explore the country, ending up in places as **diverse** as Pennsylvania, Iowa, Ohio, Nevada, and California. Because of his adventurous spirit, Twain **pursued** many different careers. He was a printer, a reporter, a writer, an editor, a riverboat pilot, a second lieutenant in a group of Confederate volunteers,[1] and a prospector for silver.

---

[1] Confederate volunteers: those who volunteered to join the Confederate Army during the Civil War

Mark Twain did not lose this **inquisitive** and restless spirit as he grew older. Besides writing books, short stories, and essays, he lectured on various subjects, traveled around the world, invested in a typesetting machine, received honorary degrees from three universities, invented a history game, learned how to ride a bicycle, and ran a publishing company. Twain's bold and busy life captured the imagination of a still young America, and he became a rich celebrity, with admirers around the world. Even when his investment in the typesetting machine failed and his publishing company went **bankrupt,** Twain was not defeated. He just worked harder, eventually paying back every dollar he owed.

Throughout his lifetime, Twain was known for his **flamboyant** and **unique** personality. He packed lecture halls in the United States and Europe with people eager to hear his funny stories and witty comments. Even his manner of dress—the white suit, white hair, bushy mustache, and ever-present cigar or pipe—revealed a certain original **flair,** which audiences loved. Not surprisingly, the architecture and the **interiors** of his home in Hartford, Connecticut, and his study in Elmira, New York, reflect a strong, **individualistic** style. In all aspects of his life, Twain insisted on doing things his own way.

Though Twain was known for his sharp, mocking wit, he formed deep attachments to people. Certain friends, such as Ulysses S. Grant and Helen Keller, meant a great deal to him, and he helped them overcome serious financial problems. Twain was also a **devoted** family man, and several family **tragedies** affected him deeply. After his wife, Olivia ("Livy"), and daughter Susy died, he never fully recovered his **emotional** health.

While his readers recognized him as America's greatest **humorist,** and his friends knew him as a **humanitarian,** Twain did become bitter in his last years. Perhaps because he held such high hopes for his country, he became increasingly critical of its shortcomings. His **fictional** pieces took on a darker outlook as he studied the weaknesses and failings of humanity in his stories. Ironically, the author who will always be **associated** with boyhood innocence—the wooden rafts, barefoot boys, and straw hats made famous by the stories of Tom Sawyer and Huckleberry Finn—no longer believed in the innocence of America. The path of Twain's life, in a sense, reflected the growth of the country itself. In his youth, he shared the unlimited confidence and energy of the young nation. In his old age, he realized that no people, no country, can live up to its dreams. Like the country he wrote about, Twain went through painful changes on his way to full maturity. But he never lost the gift for living an interesting and productive life.

Refining Your Understanding

For each of the following items, consider how the target word is used in the passage. Write the letter of the word or phrase that best completes the sentence.

_____ 1. By *diverse* (line 14) places, the author probably means
a. places at great distances from his home state of Missouri
b. places that differ a great deal from each other   c. places that have little to offer.

_____ 2. A *flamboyant* (line 28) person such as Twain would probably enjoy being   a. ignored by others   b. rude and hurtful   c. the center of attention.

_____ 3. You have a *unique* (line 29) personality because   a. there is no one else in the world just like you   b. you are in a period of change   c. you have positive traits that other people admire.

_____ 4. A person with an "*individualistic* style" (line 35) would probably want to   a. dress like everyone else   b. imitate only the leaders of an age   c. find unique ways of expressing his or her personality.

_____ 5. You would expect a *humanitarian* (line 44) to have   a. a wicked sense of humor   b. concern for others   c. a preference for an exciting life.

Number correct _____ (total 5)

Part C   Ways to Make New Words Your Own

By now you are familiar with the target words and their meanings. This section presents activities that will help you make the words part of your permanent vocabulary.

Using Language and Thinking Skills

Finding Examples Write the letter of the situation that best shows the meaning of the boldfaced word.

Example

_a_   **victory**
a. The challenger beat the champion in last night's chess match.
b. When Gerard missed the free throw, we knew the game was lost.
c. Though Sammy impressed the coach with his enthusiasm, he did not make the team.

_____ 1. **emotional**
   a. The judge told the jury to listen carefully to the testimony.
   b. When the little boy couldn't find his parents, he began to cry uncontrollably.
   c. Coolly and calmly, René worked through the problems on the math test.

_____ 2. **memorable**
   a. Dennis always had the same breakfast: oatmeal, juice, and coffee.
   b. Most people cannot remember what they ate for breakfast.
   c. Last summer our entire family visited the Grand Canyon for the first time.

_____ 3. **inquisitive**
   a. Carly loved to ask her teacher questions.
   b. The musician sat quietly and listened to the recording.
   c. Benetta's mother jogs five miles a day.

_____ 4. **humorist**
   a. The writer's amusing stories entertained readers across the country.
   b. The singer's lack of practice resulted in a poor performance.
   c. Few people could understand the lecture.

_____ 5. **individualistic**
   a. The two sisters sometimes dressed exactly alike.
   b. Some adolescents will do anything to fit in with the crowd.
   c. The artist had a unique style, unlike anything we had ever seen.

_____ 6. **devoted**
   a. The cows searched for grass in the pasture.
   b. Emilia exercised two hours a day, despite the pain, to recover from her injury so that she could rejoin the team.
   c. Hans tries hard only when he is in the right mood.

_____ 7. **flair**
   a. The miner spent years looking for gold but never found it.
   b. Miho received a standing ovation for his first acting performance, and the critics said he had great natural talent.
   c. Isabel always struggled with her spelling of French words.

_____ 8. **humanitarian**
   a. Mother Teresa has gained worldwide respect because of her work with India's poor.
   b. News of the rising crime rate caused a great deal of worry in the neighborhood.
   c. The mayor complained that the citizens were too busy for volunteer work.

_____ 9. **associate**

    a. The smell of the new-mown grass brought back pleasant memories of her carefree childhood.

    b. The crowd cheered wildly when the performer took the stage.

    c. The bank clerk politely but firmly asked the customer to leave.

_____ 10. **transform**

    a. Irrigation turned the desert into productive cropland.

    b. No one expected any change in policy this year.

    c. The new uniforms were baggy but comfortable.

Number correct _____ (total 10)

Practicing for Standardized Tests

Synonyms Write the letter of the word that is closest in meaning to the capitalized word.

_____ 1. FLAMBOYANT: (A) showy (B) floatable (C) fiery (D) boyish (E) quiet

_____ 2. INTERIOR: (A) poor (B) inside (C) curious (D) superior (E) outer

_____ 3. RURAL: (A) urban (B) country (C) suburban (D) grassy (E) exciting

_____ 4. UNIQUE: (A) unequaled (B) common (C) united (D) excellent (E) unfinished

_____ 5. TRAGEDY: (A) anger (B) nobility (C) blessing (D) change (E) misfortune

_____ 6. FICTIONAL: (A) factual (B) made-up (C) showy (D) true (E) natural

_____ 7. PURSUE: (A) rule (B) read (C) run (D) chase (E) arrest

_____ 8. BANKRUPT: (A) penniless (B) lazy (C) cowardly (D) wealthy (E) trustworthy

_____ 9. DRASTIC: (A) modest (B) foolish (C) funny (D) gradual (E) severe

_____ 10. DIVERSE: (A) divided (B) difficult (C) varied (D) poetic (E) similar

Number correct _____ (total 10)

Spelling and Wordplay

Word Maze All the words in the list below are hidden in the maze. The words are arranged forward, backward, up, down, and diagonally. Put a circle around each word as you find it and cross the word off the list. Different words may overlap and use the same letter.

```
I  N  T  E  R  I  O  R  B  B  H  I  M  F
O  N  Y  D  E  G  A  R  T  A  U  N  R  L
E  U  Q  I  N  U  Z  P  S  N  M  D  O  A
X  H  Z  U  G  M  U  I  E  K  O  I  F  I
C  U  G  J  I  R  J  O  V  R  R  V  S  R
D  M  F  X  K  S  W  X  N  U  I  I  N  A
R  A  L  N  H  J  I  K  I  P  S  D  A  M
A  N  A  R  C  H  I  T  E  T  T  U  R  E
S  I  M  L  U  S  O  R  I  L  X  A  T  M
T  T  B  P  U  R  S  U  E  V  K  L  D  O
I  A  O  R  T  U  A  W  M  J  E  I  E  R
C  R  Y  N  W  C  B  L  A  C  J  S  T  A
O  I  A  S  S  O  C  I  A  T  E  T  O  B
L  A  N  O  I  T  C  I  F  G  X  I  V  L
L  N  T  D  I  V  E  R  S  E  H  C  E  E
Y  Z  L  A  N  O  I  T  O  M  E  C  D  G
```

associate
bankrupt
devoted
diverse
drastic
emotional
fictional
flair
flamboyant
humanitarian
humorist
individualistic
inquisitive
interior
memorable
pursue
rural
tragedy
transform
unique

Word's Worth: bankrupt

The word *bank* comes from the Italian word *banca,* meaning "bench." The earliest bankers worked at benches or tables set up in public places. If a banker was not honest or failed to meet obligations, unhappy customers would break the banker's bench, shutting down the business. The Italians used the phrase *banca rotta,* literally meaning "broken bench," to describe a ruined place of business. Now the word refers to people or businesses that cannot pay their debts.

Part D   Related Words

The words below are closely related to the target words. Use your knowledge of the target words and of word parts to determine the meaning of these words. (For information about word parts analysis, see pages 7–13.) Use your dictionary if necessary.

1. association (ə sō' sē ā' shən, -shē-) n.
2. bankruptcy (baŋk' rupt' sē, -rəp sē) n.
3. devotion (di vō' shən) n.
4. diversity (də vʉr' sə tē) n.
5. emotion (i mō' shən) n.
6. exterior (ik stir' ē ər) adj., n.
7. fiction (fik' shən) n.
8. humorous (hyo͞o' mər əs) adj.
9. individualist (in' di vij' o͞o wəl ist) n.
10. inquire (in kwīr') v.
11. inquiry (in' kwə rē, in kwīr' ē) n.
12. memorize (mem' ə rīz') v.
13. nonfiction (nän fik' shən) n.
14. pursuit (pər so͞ot') n.
15. require (ri kwīr') v.
16. tragic (traj' ik) adj.
17. transformation (trans' fər mā' shən) n.
18. unemotional (un' i mō' shən 'l) adj.
19. uninquisitive (un' in kwiz' ə tiv) adj.
20. uniqueness (yo͞o nēk' nes) n.

Understanding Related Words

Sentence Completion Write the related word that best completes the meaning of the sentence.

_____ 1. Jason called the movie theater to __?__ when the next show would begin.

_____ 2. The most __?__ part of the skit was when the clown threw the pie.

_____ 3. I have to __?__ the capitals of the fifty states for a test.

_____ 4. Because of her __?__ to science over many years, Marie Curie made important discoveries.

_____ 5. The police __?__ is sponsoring a fair to raise money.

_____ 6. Even though the __?__ of the house was run-down and shabby, the interior was neat and clean.

_____ 7. The __?__ of a hobby takes time and patience.

_____ 8. Although some novels include real-life occurrences, other novels are works of pure __?__.

_____ 9. The __?__ of this vase makes it very valuable.

_____ 10. Some people show their feelings easily, but others find it difficult to express __?__.

Number correct _____ (total 10)

23

Analyzing Word Parts

The Prefixes *un-* and *non-* The prefixes *un-* and *non-* usually mean "not" or "opposite of." For example, unafraid means "not afraid," while *nonhuman* means "not human." You can create the antonyms of many words simply by adding the prefix *un-* or *non-* to them.

Match each word on the left with its definition on the right. Write the appropriate letter in each blank.

____	1. unemotional	a. forgettable
____	2. nonhumorous	b. without feeling
____	3. unmemorable	c. not funny
____	4. nonfiction	d. not curious
____	5. uninquisitive	e. writing that is not made-up

Number correct _____ (total 5)

The Suffix *-ist* The suffix *-ist* means "a person who does, makes, or practices" or "a person who is skilled in or an expert in." For example, a humorist is a person who engages in the practice of being funny or witty.

In each of the following sentences there is a blank followed by a word in parentheses. Add *-ist* to the word and write it in the blank. Some words will need other spelling changes, which you may want to check in a dictionary.

_____ 1. An _?_ (individual) is a person who insists on living a life that does not imitate others.

_____ 2. The talented _?_ (guitar) played a three-hour concert last night.

_____ 3. You would expect a _?_ (biology) to be an expert in the study of plant and animal life.

_____ 4. A _?_ (psychology) should possess a clear understanding of human behavior and motivations.

_____ 5. The _?_ (revolution) would not be satisfied with promises of gradual changes.

Number correct _____ (total 5)

Number correct in unit _____ (total 65)

Turn to **The Addition of Prefixes** on page 215 of the **Spelling Handbook**. Read the rule and complete the exercises provided.

The Last Word

Writing

Write a short account of a *memorable* event from your childhood. In order to make your account lively and dramatic, describe the background and the characters fully. You might also use dialogue to give the exact words spoken.

Speaking

Prepare a short talk in which you tell a true *humorous* story involving you or someone you know. Make sure that your story conveys the full extent of the humor involved in the incident.

Group Discussion

Being an *individualist* is often difficult. Many people find it easier to follow others than to make their own decisions about what to wear, what music to listen to, or what movies to see. Discuss the following questions:

1. Why is being an individualist so difficult?
2. What advantages are there in being an individualist?
3. What disadvantages are there in being an individualist?

UNIT 2

Part A   *Target Words and Their Meanings*

1. accord (ə kôrd′) n.
2. accurate (ak′ yər it) adj.
3. acquaintance (ə kwānt′ 'ns) n.
4. agent (ā′ jənt) n.
5. clarity (klar′ ə tē) n.
6. communion (kə myōōn′ yən) n.
7. expression (ik spresh′ ən) n.
8. gratitude (grat′ ə tōōd′) n.
9. grave (grāv) adj.
10. instinctive (in stiŋk′ tiv) adj.
11. integrity (in teg′ rə tē) n.
12. intimate (in′ tə mit) adj.
13. physical (fiz′ i k'l) adj.
14. possess (pə zes′) v.
15. purity (pyoor′ ə tē) n.
16. quality (kwāl′ ə tē) n.
17. responsibility (ri spän′ sə bil′ ə tē) n.
18. simplicity (sim plis′ ə tē) n.
19. sufficient (sə fish′ 'nt) adj.
20. treacherous (trech′ ər əs) adj.

Inferring Meaning from Context

For each sentence write the letter of the word or phrase that is closest in meaning to the word or words in italics. Use context clues to help you choose the correct answer. (For information about how context helps you understand vocabulary, see pages 1–6.)

_____ 1. After the two sides in the civil war failed to reach an *accord* during the truce, the fighting started again.

a. an agreement   b. a place   c. an explanation
d. a legal complaint

_____ 2. At track meets the timing must be *accurate,* measured precisely to parts of a second. For example, when Steve Cram of Great Britain ran the mile in 1985, his time was officially recorded as 3 minutes, 46.32 seconds.

a. exact   b. checked   c. fast   d. believable

_____ 3. The politician had a wide range of *acquaintances;* she knew many people throughout the five-county area.

a. people whom she knew slightly   b. enemies   c. best friends
d. voters

_____ 4. Since Alice was going to be out of town, she asked Jim to be her *agent* in the sale of her car.

a. friend   b. representative   c. opponent   d. guest

_____ 5. Thanks to modern technology, a telephone conversation with someone a thousand miles away can have just as much *clarity* as a phone conversation with your neighbor next door.

a. friendliness   b. interest   c. economy   d. clearness

_____ 6. Living in a cabin in the woods, Henry David Thoreau experienced a *communion with* nature; he felt very close to the living creatures around him.

a. transformation of   b. separation from   c. knowledge of
d. deep relationship with

_____ 7. "Shelf life" is the *expression* grocers use in describing how long a product can remain on the shelves for sale.

a. advertising gimmick   b. word or phrase   c. sales approach
d. pronunciation

_____ 8. The best way you can show *gratitude* to your parents and teachers is to tell them how much you appreciate them.

a. intelligence   b. humor   c. thankfulness   d. responsibility

_____ 9. The problem of world poverty is *grave:* one-fourth of the world's people live on less than two hundred dollars a year—not enough to provide adequately for themselves and their families.

a. easily solved   b. exaggerated   c. avoidable   d. serious

_____ 10. The will to live is *instinctive* in all animals; they don't have to be taught to fight for survival.

a. easily broken   b. rare   c. learned   d. natural

_____ 11. Kate's strongest character trait is her *integrity;* that is why people trust her.

a. willpower   b. stubbornness   c. honesty   d. positive personality

_____ 12. The Hollywood columnist reported that the relationship between the two movie stars was *intimate* and that they were even talking about marriage. Actually, however, their relationship was only a casual one.

a. close   b. businesslike   c. difficult   d. unique

_____ 13. The doctors decided that Jared's illness was not *physical* but mental.

a. serious   b. memorable   c. of the body   d. fictional

_____ 14. Greyhounds have no sense of smell, but they *possess* the best eyesight of any dog.

a. develop   b. need   c. have   d. lack

_____ 15. An important aspect of public water supplies is *purity;* the water must be free of bacteria and other organisms before it is safe to drink.

a. depth   b. cleanness   c. taste   d. temperature

16. Strength was a *quality* of the oldest known tree, a bristlecone pine that grew on Mt. Wheeler in eastern Nevada and lived for over two thousand years.

    a. requirement   b. characteristic   c. development
    d. drawback

17. A student shows *responsibility* by completing assignments and handing them in on time.

    a. intellectual ability   b. kindness   c. dependability
    d. individuality

18. *Simplicity* should be a key feature in all street and highway signs. Motorists must be able to read and understand them quickly, without puzzling over what they mean.

    a. lack of complexity   b. complexity   c. originality   d. cleverness

19. Janet Harris of Selsey, England, set a record for the number of peas eaten with chopsticks in sixty seconds. She ate 7,175 peas, which must have seemed *sufficient*.

    a. enough   b. inadequate   c. tasty   d. easy

20. The narrow mountain road, with its many curves and dips, is *treacherous;* drivers must be very careful.

    a. scenic   b. long   c. dangerous   d. old

Number correct _____ (total 20)

Part B   Target Words in Reading and Literature

You should now have a general idea of the meaning of each target word. Sharpen your understanding by studying how these words are used in the following selection.

A Mother in Mannville

Marjorie Kinnan Rawlings

This is an excerpt from a story about a writer who rents a cabin in the Carolina mountains in order to have the quiet and solitude she needs to do her work. The writer gets to know one of the children from a nearby orphanage, a boy who does chores for her.

His name was Jerry; he was twelve years old, and he had been at the orphanage since he was four. I could picture him at four, with the same **grave** gray-blue eyes and the same—independence? No, the word that comes to me is **"integrity."**

The word means something very special to me, and the **quality** for which I use it is a rare one. My father had it—there is another of whom I am almost sure—but almost no man of my **acquaintance possesses** it with the **clarity,** the **purity,** the **simplicity** of a mountain stream. But the boy Jerry had it. It is bedded on courage, but it is more than brave. It is honest, but it is more than honesty. The ax handle broke one day. Jerry said the woodshop at the orphanage would repair it. I brought money to pay for the job, and he refused it.

"I'll pay for it," he said. "I broke it. I brought the ax down careless."

"But no one hits **accurately** every time," I told him. "The fault was in the wood of the handle. I'll see the man from whom I bought it."

It was only then that he would take the money. He was standing back of his own carelessness. He was a free-will **agent** and he chose to do careful work; and if he failed, he took the **responsibility** without subterfuge.[1]

And he did for me the unnecessary thing, the gracious thing, that we find done only by the great of heart. Things no training can teach, for they are done on the instant, with no predicated experience. He found a cubbyhole beside the fireplace that I had not noticed. There, of his own **accord,** he put kindling and "medium" wood, so that I might always have dry fire material ready in case of sudden wet weather. A stone was loose in the rough walk to the cabin. He dug a deeper hole and steadied it, although he came, himself, by a short cut over the bank. I found that when I tried to return his thoughtfulness with such things as candy and apples, he was wordless. "Thank you" was, perhaps, an **expression** for which he had had no use, for his courtesy was **instinctive.** He only looked at the gift and at me, and a curtain lifted, so that I saw deep into

[1] subterfuge: action used to avoid difficulty or blame.

the clear well of his eyes, and **gratitude** was there, and affection, soft over the firm granite of his character.

He made simple excuses to come and sit with me. I could no more have turned him away than if he had been **physically** hungry. I sug- 35 gested once that the best time for us to visit was just before supper, when I left off my writing. After that, he waited always until my typewriter had been some time quiet. One day I worked until nearly dark. I went outside the cabin, having forgotten him. I saw him going up over the hill in the twilight toward the orphanage. When I sat down on my stoop, a place was 40 warm from his body where he had been sitting.

He became **intimate,** of course, with my pointer, Pat. There is a strange **communion** between a boy and a dog. Perhaps they possess the same singleness of spirit, the same kind of wisdom. It is difficult to explain, but it exists. When I went across the state for a weekend, I left 45 the dog in Jerry's charge. I gave him the dog whistle and the key to the cabin, and left **sufficient** food. He was to come two or three times a day and let out the dog, and feed and exercise him. I should return Sunday night, and Jerry would take out the dog for the last time Sunday afternoon and then leave the key under an agreed hiding place. 50

My return was belated, and fog filled the mountain passes so **treacherously** that I dared not drive at night. The fog held the next morning, and it was Monday noon before I reached the cabin. The dog had been fed and cared for that morning.

Refining Your Understanding

For each of the following items, consider how the target word is used in the passage. Write the letter of the word or phrase that best completes the sentence.

_____ 1. To become *intimate* (line 42) with the dog, Jerry probably
a. acted roughly   b. treated the dog kindly   c. spoke in a bossy voice.

_____ 2. Your *acquaintances* (line 7) include   a. all the people you know
b. only very good friends   c. other members of your family.

_____ 3. If a person is his own *agent* (line 17), it means that he   a. acts for himself   b. praises himself   c. makes excuses for himself.

_____ 4. If you do something of your own *accord* (line 24), you do it   a. quickly   b. boastfully   c. willingly.

_____ 5. "His courtesy was *instinctive*" (line 30) means that courtesy   a. was taught him by his parents and teachers   b. was not one of his strong points   c. came to him naturally.

Number correct _____ (total 5)

Part C   Ways to Make New Words Your Own

By now you are familiar with the target words and their meanings. This section presents activities that will help you make the words part of your permanent vocabulary.

Using Language and Thinking Skills

True-False Decide whether each statement is true (**T**) or false (**F**).

_____ 1. *Accurate* is a word an advertiser might use in writing a commercial for a watch.

_____ 2. An animal with an *instinctive* fear of fire has learned that fear from some other creature.

_____ 3. *Please* is a word that expresses *gratitude*.

_____ 4. A person who represents or acts for someone else is that person's *agent*.

_____ 5. To describe a *quality* of an object, you would list one of its essential features; for example, hardness is one quality of a brick.

_____ 6. You might use an *expression* to wish someone good luck or to say goodbye.

_____ 7. People who refuse to speak to one another are in *communion* with each other.

_____ 8. Lying and cheating are two signs of a person's *integrity*.

_____ 9. By voting on election day, citizens show *responsibility*.

_____ 10. A person who is poor may *possess* a great deal of money.

Number correct _____ (total 10)

Word's Worth: accord

What does *accord* have in common with *courageous?* Both words come from the same Latin root, *cor,* which means "heart." Originally, the word *accord* meant "to act with one heart," as two close friends might do. Now the term generally has a more formal meaning: an agreement reached between two countries or those on either side of a conflict.

Practicing for Standardized Tests

Antonyms Write the letter of the word that is most nearly opposite in meaning to the capitalized word.

_____ 1. TREACHEROUS: (A) tragic (B) safe (C) ignorant
(D) dangerous (E) humorous

_____ 2. ACQUAINTANCE: (A) associate (B) stranger (C) agent
(D) enemy (E) crowd

_____ 3. CLARITY: (A) clearness (B) stinginess (C) stupidity
(D) beauty (E) fogginess

_____ 4. PURITY: (A) beauty (B) innocence (C) ambition
(D) uncleanness (E) disgust

_____ 5. SIMPLICITY: (A) ease (B) youth (C) directness
(D) complexity (E) ignorance

_____ 6. ACCORD: (A) bankruptcy (B) dishonor (C) harmony
(D) disagreement (E) knowledge

_____ 7. GRAVE: (A) cheerful (B) deadly (C) legal (D) heavy
(E) memorable

_____ 8. PHYSICAL: (A) visible (B) mental (C) strong (D) healthy
(E) wise

_____ 9. INTIMATE: (A) emotional (B) deep (C) unfamiliar
(D) quiet (E) friendly

_____ 10. SUFFICIENT: (A) enough (B) quick (C) inadequate
(D) wealthy (E) plenty

Number correct _____ (total 10)

Turn to **The Prefix _in-_** on page 219 of the **Spelling Handbook.** Read the rule and complete the exercise provided.

Spelling and Wordplay

Crossword Puzzle Read the clues and print the correct answer to each in the proper squares. There are fourteen target words in this puzzle.

ACROSS

1. A known person
9. Abbr. University of Alaska
10. Clearness
13. A support
14. Make a knot
15. To tear apart
16. A sudden, hostile attack
18. Serious
20. Abbr. apartment
21. Ma's mate
22. Petroleum
23. Earth's light source
25. Attempt
26. Past tense of "eat"
28. Abbr. Selective Service System
29. An earnest request
30. 3.14159265
32. Second tone on the scale
33. Abbr. room
35. Also
36. Agreement
39. Abbr. United States Navy
40. Prefix meaning "of the earth"
41. The __ __ __ __ of March
44. Abbr. steamship
45. Thankfulness
47. Informal greeting
48. Negative word
50. Abbr. credit note
51. A set of clothes
52. Dangerous
53. Possessive pronoun

DOWN

1. Careful and exact
2. A characteristic
3. Abbr. United Arab Republic
4. Close and familiar
5. Toward
6. Neither, __ __ __
7. Sayings
8. One's duty
11. Pronoun: that thing
12. Biblical "you"
13. Quality of being pure
17. Abbr. April
18. What the green light means
19. Short for Alex
21. More pale
24. Objective case of "we"
27. Organ for hearing
29. Short for "professional"
30. To have
31. High card
34. To come together
35. Abbr. Tuesday
36. F. B. I. __ __ __ __ __
37. Tooth on a gear
38. Long, narrow trench in the earth
42. To eat
43. Abbr. State University
46. Abbr. Rural Electrification Administration
47. Objective case of "he"
49. Word of choice

Part D Related Words

The words below are closely related to the target words. Use your knowledge of the target words and of word parts to determine the meaning of these words. (For information about word parts analysis, see pages 7–13.) Use your dictionary if necessary.

1. accuracy (ak′ yər ə sē) n.
2. acquaint (ə kwānt′) v.
3. clarify (klar′ ə fī′) v,
4. commune (kə myo͞on′) v.
5. community (kə myo͞o′ nə tē) n.
6. express (ik spres′) v.
7. insufficient (in′ sə fish′ ənt) adj.
8. intimacy (in′ tə mə sē) n.
9. irresponsible (ir′ i spän′ sə b'l) adj.
10. physics (fiz′ iks) n.
11. possession (pə zesh′ ən) n.
12. possessive (pə zes′ iv) adj.
13. responsible (ri spän′ sə b'l) adj.
14. suffice (sə fīs′) v.

Understanding Related Words

Sentence Completion Write the related word from the list below that best completes the meaning of the sentence.

accuracy   clarify   insufficient   physics   responsible
acquaint   express   irresponsible   possessive   suffice

_____ 1. Several centuries ago most clocks had only the hour hand. Later, the minute hand was added, showing that, as the years passed, _?_ became more important.

_____ 2. Little children tend to be quite _?_ ; they want to hold on to their own toys and not share them.

_____ 3. Drivers who do not stop for stop signs are _?_ ; their carelessness is likely to cause an accident someday.

_____ 4. It took the students some time to _?_ themselves with their new classmates.

_____ 5. Employers are _?_ for the safety of the work place; they must also make sure that workers have retirement and health-and-accident plans.

_____ 6. When the mayor learned that his comments had been misunderstood, he scheduled a press conference so that he could _?_ what he meant.

_____ 7. The restaurant owner said that three large pizzas would _?_ for a party of that size.

_____ 8. People go bankrupt because their supply of money is _?_ .

_____ 9. ? is the science of physical materials and energy.

_____ 10. The poet explained that her new poetry would
 ? sorrows and joys that many people have felt.

Analyzing Word Parts

The Suffix -ity Did you notice that the suffix *-ity* appears at the end of six target words in this unit? This suffix suggests a state or condition. For example, *purity* is "a state of being pure," and *simplicity* is "a state of being simple."

Match each *-ity* word on the left with its definition on the right. Write the appropriate letter in each blank.

____ 1. necessity   a. the condition of lacking intelligence

____ 2. possibility   b. the condition of being able to happen

____ 3. community   c. the state of merriment

____ 4. stupidity   d. the state of being needed

____ 5. jollity   e. the state of living together as a group

The Last Word

Writing

Create a magazine advertisement for one of the following items:
(1) a new video game, (2) a mystery novel about spies, or (3) a home entertainment system featuring a television, radio, and tape or compact disc player. Include in your ad at least three target or related words. Use the words naturally and underline them.

Speaking or Group Discussion

Develop one or more of the following topics in a speech or class discussion. Give examples from your own experience to support your opinion.
1. What *expressions* are the most overused by adolescents today, and why?
2. Should parents be held *responsible* if their child commits a crime?
3. Are white lies a violation of *integrity*?
4. Is it wrong to be *possessive*?

UNIT 3

Part A Target Words and Their Meanings

1. aloof (ə lo͞of′) adj., adv.
2. barbaric (bär ber′ ik) adj.
3. bough (bou) n.
4. bound (bound) adj., v., n.
5. casually (kazh′ o͞o wəl lē) adv.
6. courteous (kʉr′ tē əs) adj.
7. dense (dens) adj.
8. dismay (dis mā′) n.
9. energetic (en′ ər jet′ ik) adj.
10. inanimate (in an′ ə mit) adj.
11. keen (kēn) adj.
12. languid (laŋ′ gwid) adj.
13. long (lôŋ) v., adj.
14. offensive (ə fen′ siv) adj.
15. patronizing (pā′ trə nīz′ iŋ) adj.
16. position (pə zish′ ən) n., v.
17. realistic (rē′ ə lis′ tik) adj.
18. reluctant (ri luk′ tənt) adj.
19. sullenness (sul′ ən nis) n.
20. surge (sʉrj) n., v.

Inferring Meaning from Context

For each sentence write the letter of the word or phrase that is closest in meaning to the word or words in italics. Use context clues to help you choose the correct answer. (For information about how context helps you understand vocabulary, see pages 1–6.)

_____ 1. The doctor's *aloof* manner made her patients uneasy; she seldom spoke to them and did little to make them feel comfortable.
a. sarcastic b. caring c. distant d. honest

_____ 2. The prisoners of war were forced to live in *barbaric* conditions, without any of the basic comforts of modern life.
a. forced b. strange c. crude and uncivilized d. pleasant

_____ 3. The *boughs* of the Tule tree in Mexico stretch out as far as sixty feet. It is the world's widest tree.
a. leaves b. branches c. tops d. twigs

_____ 4. Many of the wagons crossing Utah and Nevada in the 1850's carried fortune hunters *bound for* the California gold country to the west.
a. headed for b. fleeing from c. forced to go to d. prevented from going to

_____ 5. Wearing blue jeans and a faded sweatshirt, Mara feared she may have dressed too *casually* for the mayor's dinner.
a. well b. warmly c. fashionably d. informally

36

_____ 6. A *courteous* person always says "please" and "thank you," showing others that he or she cares about them.

a. courageous   b. fearful   c. polite   d. individualistic

_____ 7. The forest was so *dense with* trees that little sunlight found its way through the leaves.

a. emptied of   b. thin with   c. rotten with   d. crowded with

_____ 8. The young child's look of *dismay* showed her frustration and her fear that she would never learn to ride her bike.

a. discouragement   b. satisfaction   c. envy   d. curiosity

_____ 9. The fourteen University of Seattle students were indeed tireless and *energetic* as they leapfrogged more than six hundred miles in about five days.

a. healthy   b. full of energy   c. struggling to find energy
d. lacking in energy

_____ 10. From a distance, the large turtle appeared *inanimate,* showing no signs of life or movement.

a. lively   b. lifeless   c. slow   d. diseased

_____ 11. William Tell must have had *keen* eyesight and an incredible aim to shoot the apple off his son's head without hurting him.

a. young   b. sharp   c. normal   d. quick

_____ 12. The director complained about the *languid* rehearsal, which had none of the crispness or energy of the previous ones.

a. ambitious   b. sluggish   c. long   d. challenging

_____ 13. As a child, Mark Twain *longed* to be a pilot on a Mississippi steamboat. Some years later his wish came true when he took command of his own riverboat.

a. wished very much   b. studied   c. never wanted   d. claimed

_____ 14. Since many people find cigarette smoking *offensive* and unhealthy, it has been banned on long-distance air flights.

a. irritating   b. unusual   c. unfriendly   d. glamorous

_____ 15. The lawyer's way of speaking to witnesses was *patronizing.* He treated them like inferiors.

a. interesting   b. fancy   c. intelligent   d. snobbish

_____ 16. Aunt Rita found herself in an uncomfortable *position;* she had to tell my parents about the trouble my brother had caused at her house.

a. period of waiting   b. state of excitement   c. situation
d. compromise

_____ 17. The teacher set *realistic* goals for her students. She never expected too little or too much.

a. ridiculous   b. harmful   c. impossible   d. practical

_____ 18. When news of the great leader's death was announced, the shocked audience seemed *reluctant* to believe it, as if such a tragedy could not have happened.

a. eager   b. willing   c. pleased   d. unwilling

_____ 19. When Anne finally realized that her *sullenness* hurt no one but herself, she tried to be more pleasant and positive.

a. humor   b. gloominess   c. curiosity   d. forgetfulness

_____ 20. When the movie star was discovered in the stands of the baseball stadium, a *surge* of fans gathered to ask for her autograph, almost knocking her over in their excitement.

a. sudden rush   b. pair   c. tiny group   d. dozen

Number correct _____ (total 20)

Part B   *Target Words in Reading and Literature*

You should now have a general idea of the meaning of each target word. Sharpen your understanding by studying how these words are used in the following selection.

Red Dress–1946

Alice Munro

In this excerpt from a famous story by the contemporary Canadian writer Alice Munro, a teenage girl remembers her first high school dance. The narrator and her friend Lonnie have just entered the gym where the dance is being held. This story takes place in 1946.

The gymnasium smelled of pine and cedar. Red and green bells of fluted[1] paper hung from the basketball hoops; the high, barred windows were hidden by green **boughs.** Everybody in the upper grades seemed to have come in couples. Some of the Grade Twelve and Thirteen[2] girls had brought boyfriends who had already graduated, who were young businessmen around the town. The girls stood beside them, resting their hands **casually** on male sleeves, their faces bored, **aloof,** and beautiful.

5

---

[1] fluted: with long grooves, often for decoration
[2] In Ontario, Canada, at this time, high school went through thirteenth grade.

I **longed** to be like that. They behaved as if only they—the older ones—
were really at the dance, as if the rest of us, whom they moved among
and peered around, were, if not invisible, **inanimate;** when the first dance   10
was announced—a Paul Jones[3]—they moved out **languidly,** smiling at
each other as if they had been asked to take part in some half-forgotten
childish game. Holding hands and shivering, crowded up together, Lonnie
and I and the other Grade Nine girls followed.

I didn't dare look at the outer circle as it passed me, for fear I should   15
see some unmannerly hurrying-up. When the music stopped, I stayed
where I was, and half-raising my eyes I saw a boy named Mason
Williams coming **reluctantly** toward me. Barely touching my waist and
my fingers, he began to dance with me. My legs were hollow; my arm
trembled from the shoulder; I could not have spoken. This Mason   20
Williams was one of the heroes of the school; he played basketball and
hockey and walked the halls with an air of royal **sullenness** and **barbaric**
contempt. To have to dance with a nonentity like me was as **offensive** to
him as having to memorize Shakespeare. I felt this as **keenly** as he did
and imagined that he was exchanging looks of **dismay** with his friends.   25
He steered me, stumbling, to the edge of the floor. He took his hand from
my waist and dropped my arm.

"See you," he said. He walked away.

It took me a minute or two to realize what had happened and that he
was not coming back. I went and stood by the wall alone. The Physical   30

---

3 Paul Jones: a dance in which the participants weave in and out of a circle. When the
music stops, the two people closest to each other are dance partners.

Education teacher, dancing past **energetically** in the arms of a Grade Ten boy, gave me an inquisitive look. She was the only teacher in the school who made use of the words *social adjustment,* and I was afraid that if she had seen or if she found out, she might make some horribly public attempt to make Mason finish out the dance with me. I myself was not angry or surprised at Mason; I accepted his **position,** and mine, in the world of school, and I saw that what he had done was the **realistic** thing to do. He was a Natural Hero, not a Student Council type of hero **bound** for success beyond the school; one of those would have danced with me **courteously** and **patronizingly** and left me feeling no better off. Still, I hoped not many people had seen. I hated people seeing. I began to bite the skin on my thumb.

When the music stopped, I joined the **surge** of girls to the end of the gymnasium. Pretend it didn't happen, I said to myself.

The band began to play again. There was movement in the **dense** crowd at our end of the floor; it thinned rapidly. Boys came over, girls went out to dance. Lonnie went. The girl on the other side of me went. Nobody asked me.

Refining Your Understanding

For each of the following items, consider how the target word is used in the passage. Write the letter of the word or phrase that best completes the sentence.

_____ 1. The narrator believes that a "Student Council type of hero" would have treated her *patronizingly* (line 40) in order to   a. show his interest   b. show his gratitude   c. show that he was superior.

_____ 2. The teacher who dances *energetically* (line 31) is probably
a. feeling old   b. lively and spirited   c. trying to embarrass her students.

_____ 3. You would expect a person who moves *languidly* (line 11) to
a. enjoy work that requires great speed   b. be prone to accidents
c. walk slowly.

_____ 4. The girl telling the story felt *keenly* (line 24) that Mason Williams found her offensive. By *keenly* she meant   a. strongly   b. wrongly
c. disappointingly.

_____ 5. If a friend rested a hand *casually* (line 7) on your sleeve, you might view such an action as a sign of   a. anger   b. impatience
c. a relaxed mood.

Number correct _____ (total 5)

Part C   *Ways to Make New Words Your Own*

By now you are familiar with the target words and their meanings. This section presents activities that will help you make the words part of your permanent vocabulary.

Using Language and Thinking Skills

Understanding Multiple Meanings Each box in this exercise contains a boldfaced word with its various definitions. Read the definitions and then the sentences that use the word. Write the letter of the definition that applies to each sentence.

---

keen
a. having a sharp edge or point
b. sharp and quick in seeing, hearing, thinking, and so on
c. strong or intense, especially in regard to feelings

_____ 1. Blair sharpened his knife until it had a *keen* point.

_____ 2. Even though she is over ninety, great-grandmother has a *keen* mind.

_____ 3. The old miner revealed his secret: hard work and a *keen* pickax.

_____ 4. Nearly everyone felt *keen* emotions when the blind girl made her way to the speaker's stand and gave the graduation address.

_____ 5. Bloodhounds' *keen* sense of smell makes them valuable in searches for missing persons.

---

bound
a. going to a specific place or headed in a particular direction
b. a limit or border
c. confined to an area or tied up

_____ 1. The last song in the show was "We're *Bound* for the Rio Grande."

_____ 2. The referee blew the whistle when the ball went out of *bounds*.

_____ 3. The first police officer on the scene found three bank employees *bound* and lying on the floor, waiting to be released.

_____ 4. That jet taxiing down the runway is *bound* for Atlanta.

_____ 5. With his talent, Juan's future in business should have no *bounds*.

Number correct _____ (total 10)

Word's Worth: barbarian

The ancient Greeks were understandably proud of their own culture. However, they were not very tolerant or understanding of other cultures. They mocked their foreign neighbors, whose languages sounded like the meaningless syllables "bar bar" to their ears. So the Greeks invented a word, *barbaros,* from those syllables as a term for foreigners. The English word *barbarian* is now used to describe a person or group of people who are considered inferior or lacking in culture and refinement.

Practicing for Standardized Tests

Synonyms Write the letter of the word that is closest in meaning to the capitalized word.

_____ 1. CASUALLY: (A) informally (B) formally (C) reasonably (D) politely (E) neatly

_____ 2. OFFENSIVE: (A) separate (B) humorous (C) annoying (D) sensible (E) proven

_____ 3. INANIMATE: (A) lively (B) lengthy (C) spirited (D) difficult (E) motionless

_____ 4. RELUCTANT: (A) incapable (B) enthusiastic (C) hesitant (D) challenging (E) disobedient

_____ 5. SULLENNESS: (A) honesty (B) gloominess (C) carefulness (D) punishment (E) cheerfulness

_____ 6. KEEN: (A) funny (B) unusual (C) intense (D) surprising (E) unclear

_____ 7. ENERGETIC: (A) naughty (B) lively (C) revolving (D) slow (E) fortunate

_____ 8. REALISTIC: (A) bright (B) worried (C) silly (D) sensible (E) impatient

_____ 9. BARBARIC: (A) civilized (B) poor (C) primitive (D) strong (E) wealthy

_____ 10. LANGUID: (A) watery (B) wordy (C) fast (D) weak (E) dirty

Number correct _____ (total 10)

Spelling and Wordplay

Spell the Right Word This exercise requires that you pay careful attention to the spellings and sounds of the target words. Use each clue to identify one of the target words. Then write the word in the blank.

_____ 1. This word sounds similar to *dents*.

_____ 2. This word has a syllable that repeats itself.

_____ 3. You have to listen or read closely to know whether this word is *bow* or _?_ .

_____ 4. This word rhymes with a word that means "circular."

_____ 5. This word rhymes with *proof*.

_____ 6. This word includes *court* and describes how you should be when you are there.

_____ 7. Add one letter to *urge*.

_____ 8. This word contains a word meaning "someone you marry."

_____ 9. This word contains the name of a month.

_____ 10. Change one letter in *song*.

Number correct _____ (total 10)

Part D Related Words

The words below are closely related to the target words. Use your knowledge of the target words and of word parts to determine the meaning of these words. (For information about word parts analysis, see pages 7–13.) Use your dictionary if necessary.

1. aloofness (ə lo͞of′ nis) n.
2. animate (an′ ə māt′, -mit) v., adj.
3. animated (an′ ə māt′ id) adj.
4. animation (an′ ə mā′ shən) n.
5. animator (an′ ə mā′ tər) n.
6. animosity (an′ ə mäs′ ə tē) n.
7. barbarian (bär ber′ ē ən) n.
8. energize (en′ ər jīz′) v.
9. languor (laŋ′ gər) n.
10. offend (ə fend′) v.
11. patron (pā′ trən) n.
12. reality (rē al′ ə tē) n.
13. reluctance (ri luk′ təns) n.
14. sullen (sul′ ən) adj.

43

Understanding Related Words

Sentence Completion Write the word from the list that best completes the meaning of the sentence.

aloofness   barbarian   languor   patron   reluctance
animation   energize   offend   reality   sullen

_____ 1. With great ? , Shawanna agreed to take on the unpleasant chore of mopping the floor.

_____ 2. The ancient Romans would call anyone who did not share their language and culture a ? .

_____ 3. The Japanese have long known on-the-job exercise can ? employees and help them work more efficiently.

_____ 4. The publishers agreed not to include any material that might ? sensitive young readers.

_____ 5. ? is the process of making cartoon drawings into a motion picture.

_____ 6. The child's ? , the doctor said, was a side effect of the medication.

_____ 7. Ria was in a dark and ? mood after she lost the debate.

_____ 8. When the athlete tried unsuccessfully to return to competition after major surgery, she had to face the hard ? that her career was finally over.

_____ 9. Dr. Rose, who has given thousands of dollars to the symphony, is truly a ? of the arts.

_____ 10. Some settlers on the western frontiers became lonely; but others, because of their ? , enjoyed being alone in the wide spaces.

Number correct _____ (total 10)

> Turn to **Words Ending in -ize and -ise** on page 227 of the **Spelling Handbook.** Read the rule and complete the exercise provided.

Analyzing Word Parts

The Latin Root anim The root *anim* means "life" or "spirit." Words with this root refer to liveliness in behavior, speech, even personality. The target word *inanimate* in this unit is an example. With the negative *in-* prefix, it means literally "without life or spirit."

Write the word from the list that best completes the meaning of the sentences. Use your dictionary, if needed.

animal   animate   animated   animator   reanimation

_____ 1. The most famous _?_ was Walt Disney, whose genius brought cartoon characters to life on the screen.

_____ 2. The coach's effort at _?_ was successful; the team played with great spirit in the second half.

_____ 3. The Greeks believed that even an _?_ has a soul.

_____ 4. The speaker was very _?_ ; he waved his arms, paced back and forth, and often shouted.

_____ 5. *Frankenstein* is the story of a scientist who learns how to _?_ a dead person.

Number correct _____ (total 5)

Number correct in unit _____ (total 70)

The Last Word

Writing

In the reading selection from "Red Dress," Alice Munro describes an embarrassing experience from her teen years. Write about an experience in which you have felt ill at ease or observed someone else feeling out of place. First get your story down on paper, giving it as much detail as you can. Then revise your story, using target words from this unit as they seem appropriate.

Speaking

Think of a person you know whose life, personality, or actions best illustrates one of the following words: *courteous, aloof, realistic, offensive, energetic.*

Prepare and give a brief speech, either serious or humorous, that explains how this person illustrates the word you chose. Be sure to use vivid examples.

Group Discussion

As you know, "Red Dress" is told from a girl's point of view. What if it had been told by a boy? How might the story have been similar or different? Are boys and girls in their teens equally sensitive and ill at ease? Explain.

UNIT 4: Review of Units 1–3

Part A Review Word List

Unit 1 Target Words

1. associate
2. bankrupt
3. devoted
4. diverse
5. drastic
6. emotional
7. fictional
8. flair
9. flamboyant
10. humanitarian
11. humorist
12. individualistic
13. inquisitive
14. interior
15. memorable
16. pursue
17. rural
18. tragedy
19. transform
20. unique

Unit 1 Related Words

1. association
2. bankruptcy
3. devotion
4. diversity
5. emotion
6. exterior
7. fiction
8. humorous
9. individualist
10. inquire
11. inquiry
12. memorize
13. nonfiction
14. pursuit
15. require
16. tragic
17. transformation
18. unemotional
19. uninquisitive
20. uniqueness

Unit 2 Target Words

1. accord
2. accurate
3. acquaintance
4. agent
5. clarity
6. communion
7. expression
8. gratitude
9. grave
10. instinctive
11. integrity
12. intimate
13. physical
14. possess
15. purity
16. quality
17. responsibility
18. simplicity
19. sufficient
20. treacherous

Unit 2 Related Words

1. accuracy
2. acquaint
3. clarify
4. commune
5. community
6. express
7. insufficient
8. intimacy
9. irresponsible
10. physics
11. possession
12. possessive
13. responsible
14. suffice

Unit 3 Target Words

1. aloof
2. barbaric
3. bough
4. bound
5. casually
6. courteous
7. dense
8. dismay
9. energetic
10. inanimate
11. keen
12. languid
13. long
14. offensive
15. patronizing
16. position
17. realistic
18. reluctant
19. sullenness
20. surge

Unit 3 Related Words

1. aloofness
2. animate
3. animated
4. animation
5. animator
6. animosity
7. barbarian
8. energize
9. languor
10. offend
11. patron
12. reality
13. reluctance
14. sullen

Inferring Meaning from Context

For each sentence write the letter of the word or phrase that is closest in meaning to the word or words in italics.

_____ 1. The leaders of the community may politely disagree about specific measures, but they are *in accord* about long-term goals.
a. in agreement   b. in a meeting   c. in a deadlock   d. far apart

_____ 2. Sally is so *aloof* that she has few friends.
a. thrifty   b. intelligent   c. angry   d. unapproachable

_____ 3. Dr. Sanchez is a *humanitarian* who donates one week each year to taking care of poor children in need of dental work.
a. tireless person   b. charitable person   c. fatherly figure
d. dedicated laborer

_____ 4. Lucia offered *a unique* solution to the problem.
a. a fast   b. a typical   c. an unusual   d. an exciting

_____ 5. The famous mountain climber expressed no fear or worry about the *treacherous* journey he was about to begin.
a. dangerous   b. thrilling   c. lonely   d. challenging

_____ 6. The teacher encouraged *diverse* opinions in the class.
a. forceful   b. carefully supported   c. differing   d. politely expressed

_____ 7. When Tanya's parents told her that her cat had disappeared during the night, her reaction was understandably *emotional*.
a. angry   b. marked by strong feelings   c. panicky   d. reserved

_____ 8. Sherlock Holmes is still the most famous and popular *fictional* detective.
a. analytical   b. historical   c. private   d. imaginary

_____ 9. When the team lost, everybody looked *grave*.
a. surprised   b. relieved   c. frustrated   d. solemn

_____ 10. Our family doctor is *a humorist* who puts us at ease.
a. a serious person   b. a friendly person   c. an amusing person
d. a practical person

_____ 11. The sleeping dog was so still that he looked like he was *inanimate*.
a. dreaming   b. contented   c. barely living   d. not alive

_____ 12. Inez had *an instinctive* flair for art and design, but she paid surprisingly little attention to fashion.
a. a fearful   b. a natural   c. a violent   d. a greedy

____ 13. The engineer took great pride in the *purity* of the water produced by her filtration process.

a. cleanliness   b. taste   c. virtue   d. appearance

____ 14. Mary's mother was *reluctant* to go swimming because she had just had her hair styled.

a. relieved   b. foolish   c. unwilling   d. anxious

____ 15. The impressionists often painted *rural* scenes.

a. flowery   b. country   c. realistic   d. city

Number correct _____ (total 15)

Using Review Words in Context

Using context clues, determine which word from the list below best fits in each blank. Write the word in the blank. Each word will be used only once.

associate	courteous	gratitude	physical	responsibility
barbaric	devoted	integrity	possess	sufficient
bound	flair	memorable	pursue	transform

The Courtesy of Knights

The modern world often seems to _____ courtesy with minor actions, such as opening doors for others or saying thank-you. In the Middle Ages, however, courtesy represented a whole way of life.

The first knights of the Middle Ages were warriors who were _____ by ties of loyalty to a lord. After the knights proved their loyalty in battle, the lord would show his _____ by giving them land, money, gifts, or special privileges. These early knights were valued primarily for their _____ qualities, such as strength and fighting skill. Their main _____ in life was fighting.

Because church officials and other educated leaders worked to _____ the often brutal and _____ warriors into civilized Christians, knighthood gradually changed. Knights were expected to live a moral life and to _____ Christian ideals, although they often fell short of those ideals. A knight was required to be charitable toward the weak, generous with those less fortunate, and _____ toward his opponents. The list of virtues needed for knighthood came to include _____, or honesty, as well as fairness and kindness. A knight was also supposed to be the _____ servant of a noble woman, whom he loved and served.

48

While knights still needed to _____ military skills, they also had to master skills in other areas. They learned the arts of dancing and gentle conversation and typically learned to play at least one musical instrument. They often developed a _____ for romance and skill in the language of love, keeping countless poets in steady business.

These poets created _____ songs that celebrated what knights did for the sake of glory and the love of a lady. Courage and success in battle were no longer _____ for establishing a knight's reputation: his manners, virtues, knowledge, and social skills were also essential elements of greatness. The qualities one needed in a noble's court—summarized by the word *courtesy*—became the mark of true greatness in a knight.

While acts of courtesy today are not viewed as signs of greatness, they do show our debt to the knights of old and the ideals that motivated them.

Number correct _____ (total 15)

Part B *Review Word Reinforcement*

Using Language and Thinking Skills

Matching Examples Write the word from the list below that is most clearly related to the situation described in each sentence.

| agent | bough | flamboyant | patronizing | surge |
| bankrupt | expression | interior | quality | tragedy |

_____ 1. Heavy storms left many large branches in the streets.

_____ 2. The lifeguards closed the beach because of the danger of the swiftly moving current and sudden changes in the water level.

_____ 3. The designer of the Eiffel Tower in Paris, Alexandre Eiffel, also designed the inner structure of the Statue of Liberty in New York Harbor.

_____ 4. Disabled people object to being treated like children who cannot take care of themselves.

_____ 5. The performer was known for his unusual and colorful costumes.

_____ 6. Robert Todd Lincoln, son of Abraham Lincoln, was present at the assassinations of three presidents. They were President Garfield, President McKinley, and Robert's own father.

_____ 7. The young author hoped to find someone who could deal with publishers for her.

_____ 8. Ellen feared that her growing debts would lead to serious financial difficulty.

_____ 9. There is a saying in Yugoslavia that three things cannot be hidden: poverty, a cough, and love.

_____ 10. The violins made by Antonio Stradivari in the 1700's are still regarded as the finest in the world.

Number correct _____ (total 10)

Practicing for Standardized Tests

Synonyms Write the letter of the word that is closest in meaning to the capitalized word.

____ 1. ACCURATE: (A) memorable (B) honest (C) exact (D) incorrect (E) slow

____ 2. CASUALLY: (A) informally (B) clearly (C) lazily (D) quickly (E) rigidly

____ 3. DENSE: (A) light (B) bright (C) crowded (D) loose (E) diverse

____ 4. INQUISITIVE: (A) annoying (B) smart (C) tough (D) uninterested (E) curious

____ 5. DRASTIC: (A) bare (B) weak (C) kind (D) deliberate (E) extreme

____ 6. ACQUAINTANCE: (A) interest (B) friend (C) expert (D) relative (E) inheritance

____ 7. INDIVIDUALISTIC: (A) private (B) secretive (C) independent (D) lively (E) cooperative

____ 8. COMMUNION: (A) graciousness (B) sharing (C) honesty (D) feast (E) beauty

____ 9. LONG: (A) refuse (B) suffer (C) strengthen (D) yearn (E) cry

____ 10. POSITION: (A) evidence (B) logic (C) disagreement (D) criticism (E) place

Number correct _____ (total 10)

Antonyms Write the letter of the word that is most nearly opposite in meaning to the capitalized word.

_____ 1. INTIMATE: (A) forced (B) close (C) fearful (D) open (E) distant

_____ 2. CLARITY: (A) cloudiness (B) accuracy (C) loudness (D) carelessness (E) silence

_____ 3. ENERGETIC: (A) tireless (B) active (C) beneficial (D) inactive (E) strong

_____ 4. REALISTIC: (A) cheap (B) ordinary (C) impractical (D) expensive (E) believable

_____ 5. SULLENNESS: (A) dirtiness (B) gloominess (C) anger (D) cheerfulness (E) pleasure

_____ 6. OFFENSIVE: (A) evil (B) powerful (C) honest (D) pushy (E) pleasing

_____ 7. SIMPLICITY: (A) easiness (B) fear (C) wisdom (D) stupidity (E) complexity

_____ 8. LANGUID: (A) lively (B) graceful (C) sleepy (D) dry (E) funny

_____ 9. DISMAY: (A) clarity (B) alarm (C) relief (D) curiosity (E) interest

_____ 10. KEEN: (A) matchless (B) sharp (C) dull (D) fierce (E) ready

Number correct _____ (total 10)

Spelling and Wordplay

Crossword Puzzle Read the clues and print the correct answers in the proper squares.

ACROSS

1. Uncivilized
8. To have
14. Distant
15. Unity
16. Abbr. northeast
17. A writing instrument
18. Abbr. gross ton
19. Abbr. Minnesota
21. Sharp or eager
23. Toward
24. A tree's juice
26. To exist
28. To wish for; lengthy
30. Having no equal
33. Greater in number
36. Chem. symbol for iron
37. To rotate
38. Of the body
41. Abbr. trade union
43. Insurance _ _ _ _ _
44. To get free of
45. More pale
47. A small bay or cove
50. Abbr. High German
53. An informal greeting
54. Ready, set, _ _!
55. Side away from the wind
56. _ _ _ _ _ Majesty
57. Not down
59. A golf _ _ _
60. A natural talent
61. Pa's mate
62. Numerous
64. A smooth and level surface
65. First number
66. Dissimilar
71. Abbr. naval intelligence
72. To _ _ _ _ a book
73. Informally
74. Abbr. Saint
77. Gloomy and withdrawn
82. Unhappy
83. Headed for
86. A disaster
87. To chase

DOWN

1. Out of money
2. To the leeward side
3. Abbr. Royal Observatory
4. Brought into life
5. Abbr. Air Force
6. Frozen water
7. Scorn or hatred
8. Abbr. provost marshal general
9. Six allowed each inning
10. Abbr. serial number
11. Lack of complexity
12. A long period of time
13. Abbr. serial number
17. Abbr. press agent
20. A part of a book
22. To revise for publication
25. A sudden, strong increase
27. An attempt
29. A professional football league
31. A characteristic
32. Having much energy
34. An exclamation of surprise
35. A plural suffix
39. Anger
40. An advertisement
42. Not down
46. Open wide and say "_ _"
47. Sick
48. Abbr. National Education Association
49. A Hawaiian flower necklace
50. People
51. Thankfulness
52. A comedian
58. Window glass
60. Costs for services
63. Same as 48 Down
64. To cook in a pan
67. A delivery truck
68. Out in the country
69. Abbr. South America
70. Santa's helper
75. A spelling contest
76. A large motor coach
78. An ancient Sumerian city
79. Abbr. Los Angeles
80. Abbr. left guard
81. Abbr. North Dakota
83. Abbr. bushel
84. A word indicating choice
85. Abbr. name unknown

52

Part C   Related Word Reinforcement

Using Related Words

Forming Words Write a related word for each target word below. The related word you form should be the part of speech shown in parentheses.

Example   tragedy   (adj.)   tragic

1. accurate   (n.)   _____
2. possess   (adj.)   _____
3. fictional   (n.)   _____
4. clarity   (v.)   _____
5. languid   (n.)   _____
6. unique   (n.)   _____
7. memorable   (v.)   _____
8. devoted   (n.)   _____
9. responsibility   (adj.)   _____
10. inquisitive   (v.)   _____

Number correct _____ (total 10)

Reviewing Word Structures

The Prefixes _un-_ and _in-_ and the Suffixes _-ion, -ity,_ and _-ive_ For each word below, form a related word by using one of the prefixes or suffixes given. Follow the directions in parentheses, and choose from these prefixes and suffixes: _un-, in-, -ion, -ity, -ive._ Write the new word in the blank. To check your spelling, refer to the list on page 46.

1. emotional (form an adjective): _____

2. associate (form a noun): _____

3. sufficient (form an adjective): _____

4. possess (form an adjective): _____

5. diverse (form a noun): _____

Number correct _____ (total 5)

Number correct in unit _____ (total 75)

Vocab Lab 1

FOCUS ON: **Literary Terms**

By now the words you learned in previous units should be part of your active vocabulary. You can expand your vocabulary even further by becoming familiar with the following words, which are used in the study of literature.

antagonist (an tag′ ə nist) n. the character who opposes the main character. ● The Sheriff of Nottingham is the *antagonist* of Robin Hood.

characterization (kar′ ik tər ə zā′ shən) n. the way in which a writer reveals the nature of a character. ● Writers often use dialogue and physical description as means of *characterization.*

climax (klī′ maks) n. the high point of interest or suspense in a story or play. ● At the *climax* of the story, Rosa quickly puts her plan into action and escapes.

exposition (eks′ pə zish′ ən) n. the part of a story or play that provides background information and introduces the setting and main characters. ● In the story about Superman, the *exposition* reveals that he came from the planet Krypton.

flashback (flash′ bak′) n. an interruption in the sequence of a story to describe an event that took place earlier. ● Atsuki's fear of water is explained by a *flashback* to the time when he nearly drowned as a child.

foreshadowing (fôr shad′ ō iŋ) n. the technique of giving hints about events that have not yet happened. ● Edgar Allan Poe uses *foreshadowing* to build suspense in his stories.

imagery (im′ ij rē) n. words and phrases that appeal to the reader's senses. ● The poem contains *imagery* of autumn: deep colors, cool winds, and burning leaves.

mood (mo͞od) n. the feeling or atmosphere that a writer creates for the reader. ● Some of Wordsworth's nature poems convey a very peaceful *mood.*

parody (par′ ə dē) n. a work that comically imitates another work. ● Woody Allen's movie *Play It Again, Sam* is a *parody* of *Casablanca.*

plot (plät) n. what happens in a story: the sequence of events. ● The *plot* of *The Miracle Worker* centers on Annie Sullivan's struggle to teach Helen Keller.

point of view the perspective or vantage point from which a story is told. ● *Great Expectations* is told from the *point of view* of Pip, who describes his life.

protagonist (prō′ tag′ ə nist) n. the main character in a story. ● Tom Sawyer is the *protagonist* in Twain's *The Adventures of Tom Sawyer.*

satire (sa′ tīr) n. making fun of people's foolishness or weaknesses in a work of literature. ● Swift's description of Lilliput in *Gulliver's Travels* is a *satire* of small-minded people.

setting (set′ iŋ) n. the particular time and place where the action of a literary work takes place. ● The *setting* of *The Red Badge of Courage* is a battlefield of the American Civil War.

theme (*th*ēm) n. the main idea or message of a work of literature. ● The *theme* of *The Miracle Worker* centers on the great difficulties of communication.

Sentence Completion Complete each sentence below by writing the appropriate focus word.

_____ 1. The plot moves ahead quickly except for a brief ? that shows the main character in an earlier crisis.

_____ 2. The ? of Pearl Buck's novel *The Good Earth* is early twentieth-century China.

_____ 3. The ? of the story occurs when the detective finally puts all the clues together and solves the mystery.

_____ 4. Mark Twain's *Huckleberry Finn* is written from the ? of the boy Huck, an innocent and a wise observer.

_____ 5. Many admire Jack London's use of dialogue and description of physical appearance as means of ? .

_____ 6. The ? in this story is a boy who is stranded in the wilderness and must struggle to survive.

_____ 7. The ? in the poem "Crossing" includes a clanging bell, a waving engineer, and freight cars flashing by.

_____ 8. The humorous Sherlock Hemlock puppet on *Sesame Street* is a ? of Sherlock Holmes.

_____ 9. The ? of *The Old Man and the Sea* is simple: an old fisherman in a small boat catches a huge fish and must defend his catch from sharks.

_____ 10. *Animal Farm,* a story of barnyard animals who revolt against the farmer, is really a ? of communism.

_____ 11. The witches' prediction that Macbeth will be King of Scotland is a ? of what happens later in the play.

_____ 12. The dialogue in the opening scene provides useful ? that helps the audience understand what is going on.

_____ 13. The ? of "Autumntime," a story set in the future, is that life without natural things would be ugly and unhappy.

_____ 14. In "Little Red Riding Hood" the ? is the wolf.

_____ 15. "The Tell-Tale Heart," which describes a murder and its effects, creates a ? of tension and anxiety.

Number correct _____ (total 15)

FOCUS ON: *Analogies*

Various activities—such as synonym, antonym, and sentence completion exercises—help build vocabulary skills. An analogy exercise is another way to enrich your understanding of words. An **analogy** shows a relationship between words. A typical analogy problem looks like this:

> Determine the relationship between the capitalized words. Then decide which other word pair expresses a similar relationship. Write the letter of this word pair.
>
> ____ 1. COLLIE : DOG :: (A) fish : water   (B) bird : eagle
> (C) airplane : fly   (D) hammer : tool   (E) train : railroad

The analogy can also be stated this way:
A *collie* is to a *dog* as a __?__ is to a __?__ .

Use the following four steps to find the answer to an analogy problem.

1. Determine the relationship between the first two words.
2. Make up a sentence using the two words: A *collie* is a type of *dog*.
3. Decide which of the choices given has a similar type of relationship.
4. Test your choice by substituting the pair of words for the original pair in the sentence you made up.

It becomes obvious that (D) is the best answer to this problem when you use the test: A *hammer* is a type of *tool*.

Below are a few of the types of relationships used in analogies.

Type of Analogy	Example
cause to effect	virus : cold :: carelessness : errors
pain to whole	finger : hand :: spoke : wheel
object to purpose	broom : sweep :: knife : cut
action to object	dribble : basketball :: fly : kite
item to category	trout : fish :: corn : vegetable
type to characteristic	deer : swift :: turtle : slow
word to synonym	nice : pleasant :: gratitude : thankfulness
word to antonym	nice : unpleasant :: cowardly : brave
object to its material	shoe : leather :: necklace : gold
product to source	apple : tree :: milk : cow
worker and creation	composer : symphony :: author : novel
worker and tool	carpenter : hammer :: surgeon : scalpel
time sequence	sunrise : sunset :: winter : spring
word and derived form	act : action :: image : imagine

Analogies Determine the relationship between the capitalized words. Then decide which other word pair expresses a similar relationship. Write the letter of this word pair.

_____ 1. TEETH : CHEW :: (A) race : win (B) television : watch
(C) nose : smell (D) dance : practice (E) argument : fight

_____ 2. WHEEL : CAR :: (A) room : house (B) garden : flower
(C) food : table (D) air : steam (E) book : chapter

_____ 3. HERO : BRAVE :: (A) lawyer : illegal (B) food : hungry
(C) joke : funny (D) honesty : honest (E) morning : nightly

_____ 4. PAINTER : BRUSH :: (A) plumber : wrench (B) hen : rooster
(C) bicycle : travel (D) hike : trail (E) tongue : mouth

_____ 5. SAIL : SEA :: (A) peel : pear (B) run : exercise
(C) walk : shoe (D) skate : ice (E) play : volleyball

_____ 6. SULLEN : GLOOMY :: (A) warm : boiling (B) long : short
(C) uncivilized : barbaric (D) selfish : generous
(E) unhappy : happy

_____ 7. BREAD : BAKERY :: (A) milk : dairy (B) hammer : carpenter
(C) valentine : pharmacy (D) garage : car (E) farmer : farm

_____ 8. SCULPTOR : STATUE :: (A) pilot : airplane (B) story : author
(C) mechanic : auto (D) doctor : pill (E) painter : portrait

_____ 9. RAFT : WOOD :: (A) electricity : energy (B) paper : book
(C) furnace : coal (D) shirt : cotton (E) basketball : sport

_____ 10. BANKRUPT : PROSPEROUS :: (A) interior : exterior
(B) desperate : hopeless (C) pedestrian : ordinary
(D) economical : thrifty (E) universal : worldwide

Number correct _____ (total 10)

Number correct in Vocab Lab _____ (total 25)

UNIT 5

Part A *Target Words and Their Meanings*

1. application (ap′ lə kā′ shən) n.
2. artery (är′ tər ē) n.
3. consume (kən soom′, -syoom′) v.
4. contend (kən tend′) v.
5. corrosion (kə ro′ zhən) n.
6. diameter (dī am′ ət ər) n.
7. domestic (də mes′ tik) adj., n.
8. economical (ē′ kə näm′ i k'l, ek′ ə-) adj.
9. efficiently (ə fish′ ənt lē, i-) adv.
10. existence (ig zist′ əns) n.
11. injection (in jek′ shən) n.
12. innovation (in′ ə vā′ shən) n.
13. isolate (ī′ sə lat′, is′ ə-) v., n.
14. obstacle (äb′ sti k'l) n.
15. procedure (prə sē′ jər, prō-) n.
16. refinery (ri fīn′ ər ē) n.
17. system (sis′ təm) n.
18. technological (tek′ nə läj′ i k'l) adj.
19. terminal (tur′ mə n'l) adj., n.
20. volume (väl′ yoom, -yəm) n.

Inferring Meaning from Context

For each sentence write the letter of the word or phrase that is closest in meaning to the word or words in italics. Use context clues to help you choose the correct answer. (For information about how context helps you understand vocabulary, see pages 1–6.)

_____ 1. Sunburn is best prevented by the *application* of sunblock lotion, which protects the skin from harmful rays.

a. removal   b. putting on   c. storage   d. washing off

_____ 2. The heart specialist said that the patient had a clogged *artery*. As a result of the clog, the flow of blood was dangerously reduced.

a. windpipe   b. nerve ending   c. blood vessel   d. sinus cavity

_____ 3. Fresh fruit needs to be shipped to the city quickly so that it can be *consumed* before it spoils.

a. grown   b. wasted   c. used   d. thrown away

_____ 4. It was bad enough facing the freezing temperatures and bitter winds, but we also had to *contend with* deep snowdrifts that blocked the trail.

a. struggle against   b. enjoy   c. take advantage of   d. describe

_____ 5. The *corrosion* caused by the salty sea spray ate a hole in the left front panel of our car.

a. moisture   b. rust   c. fog   d. mud

_____ 6. The *diameter* of the earth from the North Pole to the South Pole is a straight line 7,900 miles long.

    a. distance through   b. rotation of   c. total area of
    d. circle around

_____ 7. To help support American industry, the family decided their next car would not be foreign but *domestic*.

    a. sporty   b. made in this country   c. inexpensive   d. imported

_____ 8. Buying large sizes of products you use is likely to be more *economical* than buying the products in small sizes.

    a. expensive   b. wasteful   c. thrifty   d. interesting

_____ 9. Our reorganized work space allowed us to work more *efficiently;* we got more done and were less tired at the end of the day.

    a. slowly   b. effectively   c. unhappily   d. nervously

_____ 10. Hank knew of the *existence* of black holes in outer space, but he knew nothing else about them.

    a. weight   b. purpose   c. size   d. presence

_____ 11. Tony hoped that the *injection* of humor in his speech would give his audience a few laughs and perhaps improve his grade.

    a. lack   b. introduction   c. organization   d. dismissal

_____ 12. The use of concrete was an important *innovation* that made it possible for the Romans, beginning around 200 B.C., to construct much larger buildings.

    a. disadvantage   b. new method   c. philosophy   d. problem

_____ 13. Prison officials decided to *isolate* the troublesome prisoner, so they separated him from other prisoners.

    a. set apart   b. scold   c. reward   d. share their concerns with

_____ 14. Nora found that her youth and inexperience were *obstacles* in her search for a job. After two months, she still was looking for work.

    a. advantages   b. barriers   c. responsibilities   d. agents

_____ 15. The principal told Randall that the usual *procedure* for adding a class was to talk to the teacher first.

    a. method   b. excuse   c. reason   d. expression

_____ 16. The raw sugar was shipped to a *refinery,* where it was made into the pure white product we buy at the supermarket.

    a. warehouse   b. market   c. finishing school
    d. processing plant

_____ 17. River transportation is important in Paraguay because the country lacks a good *system* of roads or railroads.

    a. position   b. network   c. example   d. idea

_____ 18. The developing African country hoped to receive *technological* assistance from the United States in the form of computers, machinery, factory equipment, and telephone systems.
a. scientific and industrial   b. educational   c. political
d. health and public safety

_____ 19. When our train finally arrived at the *terminal,* we knew the long journey was over.
a. end of the line   b. track   c. crossing   d. signal

_____ 20. The governor received a significant *volume* of protest mail after he announced a new tax increase; thousands of citizens were outraged.
a. reduction   b. quantity   c. delay   d. announcement

Number correct _____ (total 20)

Part B   *Target Words in Reading and Literature*

You should now have a general idea of the meaning of each target word. Sharpen your understanding by studying how these words are used in the following selection.

Moving Oil and Gas

Howard Peet

How much do you know about pipelines? You may have heard of those that carry oil in places like Alaska, but you probably do not know how widespread the pipeline has become in today's world. From the following selection you will learn more about this method of moving goods and how it supplies a nation with fuel and energy.

Somewhere underground, every day, around the clock, huge **volumes** of crude oil products and natural gas are moving, carried by a **system** that works so silently and **efficiently** that you may not even be aware of its **existence.** What has made all this possible is the development of the pipeline.

Moving substances over distances through pipes is an old idea. The   5
ancient Romans used pipelines—and the force of gravity—to supply cities with water. Their system worked only if water could flow downward toward its destination. It was in sixteenth-century London that people first thought of putting pumps in pipelines to keep their water flowing. In 1865, the world's first successful oil pipeline carried eight hundred barrels of oil a day from an   10
oil field in Pennsylvania to a railroad five miles away. A few years later, a wooden pipeline carried natural gas 25 miles to customers in Rochester, New York, and in 1879 a pipeline began carrying ten thousand barrels of oil a day from Coryville to Williamsport, Pennsylvania, a distance of 110 miles.

In the 1920's, a **technological innovation** took place that eventually 15 made it possible for gas and oil companies to build pipelines thousands of miles long. This was the development of seamless, electrically welded pipe that was strong enough to move much greater quantities of goods than ever before. This invention also made it possible to increase the size of the pipes. The **diameter** of an oil pipeline these days is often forty 20 inches; in a natural gas pipeline it can be four feet or more. As a result of the improved technology, pipelines became the most **economical** way to transport fuel. It is now much cheaper, for example, to send a gallon of oil from Texas to New York than to send a postcard the same distance.

Oil must make a long journey from where it comes out of the ground to 25 where it is **consumed,** and pipelines are needed for at least part of that journey. First the natural gas must be separated from the crude oil and sent off to be processed and marketed. Then the crude oil is transported, perhaps by a tanker at a waterside **terminal.** Eventually the oil goes to a **refinery,** a plant that converts crude oil into various useful products, such 30 as gasoline, kerosene, aviation fuel, or heating oil. Finally these products must be transported to markets by tanker, truck, railroad tank car, or pipeline.

A large pipeline is a kind of **artery** for the nation—it is able to carry more than a million barrels of oil a day. Today, a network of pipelines with 35 a total length of about 227,000 miles carries petroleum products to every part of the United States. At the same time, natural gas is being moved in in a million-mile network. Pipelines are also being used to ship many things besides gas, oil, and water. Now you can send just about anything from coal to food through a tube. In fact, pipelines rank third among types 40 of **domestic** freight carriers in the amount of tonnage they handle.

Pipelines are normally buried about three feet underground. To meet safety standards, they must be put through careful testing **procedures.**

Valves are installed along the line in order to limit and **isolate** any damage that might result from an accident. Since **corrosion** can be a problem, pipelines are often protected by the **application** of a low-voltage electric current that keeps corrosion away almost indefinitely. Although most pipelines are made of steel, plastic pipes are also used; for example, plastic lines are used for the **injection** of water into the ground to force oil and gas to the surface.

Pipelines go almost anywhere—through swamps and forests, across deserts, under rivers and lakes, and over mountain ranges. Sometimes ditches must be dug through solid rock; in some cases, the pipeline may lie on the surface. The builders of the Trans-Alaska Pipeline, which taps the oil reserves of Alaska's North Slope region, had to **contend** with a number of **obstacles** but overcame them all. In its 800-mile course, the pipeline crosses twenty large rivers, three hundred streams, three mountain ranges, and nearly 400 miles of frozen land.

The next time you use natural gas or an oil product—whether to fuel a motor, cook a meal, or heat a building—think about where the gas or oil comes from and the distance it travels. Also consider how pipelines contribute to the quality and convenience of your daily life.

Refining Your Understanding

For each of the following items, consider how the target word is used in the passage. Write the letter of the word or phrase that best completes the sentence.

_____ 1. Though the word *volume* (line 1) can refer to the amount of space occupied by an object or substance, in this selection its meaning is the same as   a. quantity   b. weight   c. price.

_____ 2. If an oil company applies more *efficient procedures* (lines 3 and 43) to the process of getting oil out of the ground, it will probably a. save money   b. spend more money   c. lose money.

_____ 3. *Domestic* consumers (line 41) of American petroleum are a. foreigners who import the oil   b. Americans who use the oil c. Americans who export the oil.

_____ 4. An *obstacle* to *innovation* (lines 56 and 15) in the oil industry would be   a. an interest in improvement   b. a desire to experiment c. a fear of new ideas.

_____ 5. The author calls a large pipeline an *artery* (line 34) because   a. the flow of oil is crucial for the life of our country   b. pipelines look like human blood vessels   c. pipelines damage the environment.

Number correct _____ (total 5)

Part C Ways to Make New Words Your Own

By now you are familiar with the target words and their meanings. This section presents activities that will help you make the words part of your permanent vocabulary.

Using Language and Thinking Skills

Sentence Completion Write the word from the list below that best completes the sentence.

artery	corrosion	domestic	refinery	terminal
consume	diameter	procedure	technological	volume

_____ 1. As her bus pulled into the _?_, Teresa looked through the window for the people who were supposed to pick her up.

_____ 2. If you want to keep your bicycle free of _?_, remember to keep it out of the rain.

_____ 3. A(n) _?_ is an industrial plant that removes impurities from a product like oil or sugar.

_____ 4. The flood closed the highway, which was the main _?_ into town.

_____ 5. Despite efforts at conservation, we continue to _?_ our natural resources at an alarming rate.

_____ 6. Andrew's thermos bottle holds a large _?_ of soup, which he eats for lunch on cold days.

_____ 7. The _?_ of a circle is a line segment that passes through the center point with both ends on the boundary.

_____ 8. The conference of engineers, scientists, and public officials dealt with recent _?_ advances that can help control pollution.

_____ 9. I took an auto repair course to learn the proper _?_ for changing the oil.

_____ 10. The _?_ policy of a president deals with issues and problems within the country's borders.

Number correct _____ (total 10)

Practicing for Standardized Tests

Synonyms Write the letter of the word that is closest in meaning to the capitalized word.

_____ 1. ECONOMICAL: (A) wealthy (B) bankrupt (C) emotional (D) inquisitive (E) cheap

_____ 2. EFFICIENTLY: (A) skillfully (B) loosely (C) wastefully (D) courteously (E) watchfully

_____ 3. SYSTEM: (A) accord (B) law (C) position (D) disorganization (E) organization

_____ 4. OBSTACLE: (A) agent (B) accident (C) reduction (D) barrier (E) reminder

_____ 5. INJECTION: (A) disease (B) insertion (C) replacement (D) tool (E) rejection

_____ 6. INNOVATION: (A) flair (B) declaration (C) benefit (D) invention (E) knowledge

_____ 7. ISOLATE: (A) separate (B) invite (C) devote (D) punish (E) display

_____ 8. CONTEND: (A) satisfy (B) express (C) battle (D) languish (E) run

_____ 9. APPLICATION: (A) dismay (B) use (C) position (D) expression (E) surge

_____ 10. EXISTENCE: (A) quality (B) being (C) transformation (D) communion (E) benefit

Number correct _____ (total 10)

Word's Worth: corrode

Mice and rust have something in common: they both gnaw away at things. The Latin word _rodére_ means "to gnaw," so mammals that gnaw, like rats, squirrels, and beavers, are called _rodents_. If you add the prefix _cor-_ to _rodere_, it makes the meaning stronger: _corrodere_ means "to gnaw to pieces." This is the origin of the English word _corrode_. When you think about it, something that has been corroded by rust does look as if it has been gnawed to pieces.

Spelling and Wordplay

Word Maze All the words in the list below are hidden in the maze. The words are arranged forward, backward, up, down, and diagonally. Put a circle around each word as you find it and cross the word off the list. Different words may overlap and use the same letter.

```
L A R T E R Y K L G H P E I
C O P R O C E D U R E L M N
O B J P Z X W T J D I I U N
R S V O L U M E E F N S S O
R T R E F I N E R Y J O N V
O A Z Y J R C G H D E L O A
S C R E T E M A I D C A C T
I L A N I M R E T V T T O I
O E Z M E T S Y S I I E N O
N B D O M E S T I C O O T N
B E C N E T S I X E N N E R
C E C O N O M I C A L Z N A
D Y L T N E I C I F F E D X
T E C H N O L O G I C A L Z
```

application
artery
consume
contend
corrosion
diameter
domestic
economical
efficiently
existence
injection
innovation
isolate
obstacle
procedure
refinery
system
technological
terminal
volume

Part D Related Words

The words below are closely related to the target words. Use your knowledge of the target words and of word parts to determine the meanings of these words. (For information about word parts analysis, see pages 7–13.) Use your dictionary if necessary.

1. apply (ə plī′) v.
2. arterial (är tir′ ē əl) adj.
3. consumer (kən soo′ mər, -syoo′) n.
4. contention (kən ten′ shən) n.
5. corrode (kə rōd′) v.
6. corrosive (kə rōs′ iv) adj.
7. dejected (di jek′ tid) adj.
8. economy (i kän′ ə mē) n.
9. efficiency (ə fish′ ən sē, i-) n.
10. efficient (ə fish′ ənt) adj.
11. eject (i jekt′, ē-) v.
12. exist (ig zist′) v.
13. inject (in jekt′) v.
14. isolation (ī′ sə lā′ shən, is′ ə-) n.
15. proceed (prə sēd′, prō-) v.
16. project (prə jekt′) v., (präj′ ekt) n.
17. refine (ri fīn′) v.
18. refinement (ri fīn′ mənt) n.
19. reject (rē′ jekt) n., (ri jekt′) v.
20. systematic (sis′ tə mat′ ik) adj.

Understanding Related Words

Matching Ideas Write the word from the list below that is most clearly related to the situation described by the group of sentences.

apply   consumer   corrosive   isolation   refine
arterial   contention   efficiency   proceed   systematic

_____ 1. As the measles outbreak worsened, college officials took steps to prevent the disease from spreading. They set aside a special dormitory for the students with measles in order to keep them away from healthy students.

_____ 2. The search for the missing child was very thorough. Volunteers were organized into three groups. Twenty searchers combed the woods, ten more waded down the stream, and five people questioned other campers and hikers.

_____ 3. Many businesses try to find out what their customers would be willing to buy. They investigate customers' likes and dislikes and try to predict what products will be purchased.

_____ 4. Gold, as it is found in nature, is often mixed with other metals in the form of ore. Special equipment is needed to separate the gold from the other metals and to purify the gold so that it can be used.

_____ 5. Getting accepted by a college requires a lot of work. There is a long form to fill out, and you may have to write an essay about yourself and collect letters of recommendation from your teachers.

_____ 6. Salt has been used to melt ice on many northern roads. But car owners find that the salt, when mixed with water, eats away at a car's finish. After a while, the bottom of the car rusts out.

_____ 7. The color green in any traffic signal—whether on a city street, an airport runway, or a railroad track—means one thing: When the light turns green, the traffic can move ahead.

_____ 8. It is Anna's firm belief that pit bulls do not belong in town. She feels so strongly about this that she will argue with her neighbors and with anyone else who will listen.

_____ 9. In a large city, traffic engineers identify certain streets that carry most of the city traffic. These streets are built wide so that they can have as many as six lanes of traffic.

_____ 10. Machines can complete some tasks more quickly and accurately than human beings can.

Number correct _____ (total 10)

> Turn to **Words Ending in y** on page 221 of the **Spelling Handbook.** Read the rule and complete the exercises provided.

True-False Decide whether each statement is true or false. Write **T** for True or **F** for False.

____ 1. An imaginary creature, such as a unicorn, does not actually _exist_.

____ 2. If you knew a chemical would _corrode_ metal, you would use it to protect the finish of a new car.

____ 3. A person with great _refinement_ has crude habits and unpolished manners.

____ 4. A good manager tries to hire _efficient_ workers.

____ 5. People who study the _economy_ pay careful attention to the production, selling, and buying of goods and services.

Number correct _____ (total 5)

Analyzing Word Parts

Suffix Additions Each of the words listed below is a target word. Spell the matching related word by filling in the blanks before each suffix. Note that some words have spelling changes when a suffix is added.

1. artery: _ _ _ _ _ _ al

2. consume: _ _ _ _ _ _ _ er

3. contend: _ _ _ _ _ _ _ ion

4. corrosion: _ _ _ _ _ _ _ ive

5. isolate: _ _ _ _ _ _ ion

Number correct _____ (total 5)

The Latin Root *jacere* The target word *injection* comes from the Latin root *jacere*, meaning "to throw." The following words also come from this root:

dejected   eject   inject   project   reject

Look up the words in a dictionary and use them to complete these sentences.

_____ 1. The veterinarian decided to _?_ a painkiller into the dog's cut paw to relieve the discomfort.

_____ 2. When a product does not meet required standards, an inspector is supposed to _?_ it.

_____ 3. The _?_ team left the court slowly after losing the painfully close contest.

_____ 4. A good ventriloquist can _?_ his or her voice so that a cat sitting across the room seems to be talking.

_____ 5. The speaker asked the police to _?_ the troublemakers.

Number correct _____ (total 5)

Number correct in unit _____ (total 70)

The Last Word

Writing

Imagine that you are looking for a summer job. You find this want ad:

Wanted: Responsible teenager to care for our house while we are on vacation. Duties include lawn and garden care, watering house plants, and feeding our cat and fish. Apply by letter, stating your qualifications, to Box 99.

Write an *application* letter for this job, describing your qualifications.

Speaking

Doing a job in a *systematic* way often helps you do the job *efficiently*. Think of a job you do often that illustrates the truth of this statement. Prepare a short talk explaining your *system* for doing this job and telling how it increases your *efficiency*. For example, you might talk about how you study for a test, clean your room, cook dinner, wash your family car, or bathe your dog.

Group Discussion

As a class, discuss the following questions: How are teenage *consumers* important to the American economy? What products and advertisements are aimed primarily at teenagers? How can teenagers be responsible *consumers*?

UNIT 6

Part A Target Words and Their Meanings

1. abandon (ə ban′ dən) v.
2. assembly (ə sem′ blē) n.
3. considerable (kən sid′ ər ə b′l) adj.
4. converge (kən vʉrj′) v.
5. debt (det) n.
6. decline (di klīn′) v., n.
7. definitely (def′ ə nit lē) adv.
8. despite (di spīt′) prep., n.
9. destination (des′ tə nā′ shən) n.
10. dislodge (dis läj′) v.
11. elusive (i lo͞o′ siv) adj.
12. extract (ik strakt′) v. (eks′ trakt) n.
13. fixture (fiks′ chər) n.
14. obviously (äb′ vē əs lē) adv.
15. populate (päp′ yə lāt′) v.
16. portion (pôr′ shən) n., v.
17. scour (skour) v.
18. sheer (shir) adj.
19. survive (sər vīv′) v.
20. trace (trās) n., v.

Inferring Meaning from Context

For each sentence write the letter of the word or phrase that is closest in meaning to the word or words in italics. Use context clues to help you choose the correct answer. (For information about how context helps you understand vocabulary, see pages 1–6.)

_____ 1. We *abandoned* the idea of taking the trip when we discovered that it would cost far more than we could afford.

a. agreed to   b. remembered   c. gave up   d. considered

_____ 2. All the students in the school were required to attend the *assembly* in the gym; the new principal was going to introduce himself.

a. board meeting   b. contest   c. drama   d. gathering

_____ 3. Alyssa's father had *considerable* experience as a track coach; he had spent fifteen years as head coach and eight years as assistant coach.

a. a great deal of   b. little   c. an average amount of
d. successful

_____ 4. Coming from four corners of the gym, the cheerleaders *converged* at the center of the court to form a pyramid, then they separated and ran back to their corners.

a. shouted   b. separated   c. came together   d. tumbled

_____ 5. The young lawyer had many *debts* because he had to take out a number of loans to pay for law school.

a. questions   b. achievements   c. bills   d. regrets

_____ 6. When Calvin Coolidge, the thirtieth President of the United States, was asked to run for reelection, he *declined* the offer, saying, "I do not choose to run."

a. refused   b. accepted   c. considered   d. postponed

_____ 7. When heavy rains are forecast, one should *definitely* take a raincoat.

a. seldom   b. certainly   c. never   d. sometimes

_____ 8. *Despite* the stormy weather, we had our picnic.

a. Because of   b. As a result of   c. In honor of   d. In spite of

_____ 9. Our *destination* was Los Angeles, but along the way the plane would stop at Chicago and Denver.

a. home base   b. place of arrival   c. starting point
d. temporary stop

_____ 10. It took three people using boards as levers to *dislodge* the boulder from the road so that traffic could get through.

a. raise   b. destroy   c. repair   d. remove

_____ 11. In his flight from the law, the thief remained *elusive;* he drove around the police blockade and switched to a different car.

a. careful   b. hard to catch   c. dangerous   d. embarrassed

_____ 12. Dentists today will *extract* a bad tooth only if nothing else can be done; whenever possible, they try to save the tooth.

a. repair   b. clean   c. fill   d. pull out

_____ 13. New sinks, water fountains, lighting tracks, and other *fixtures* were installed throughout the school.

a. designs   b. movable objects   c. permanent objects
d. decorations

_____ 14. With a strong wind, a blue sky, and an excellent forecast, it was *obviously* a fine day for sailing.

a. not at all   b. clearly   c. possibly   d. probably

_____ 15. Astronomers wonder whether creatures like humans *populate* other planets besides the earth and, if so, whether communication with these creatures would be possible.

a. invade   b. need   c. live on   d. study

_____ 16. Each *portion* of the brain controls a different activity of the body; for example, one section controls speech, another controls sight.

a. organ   b. part   c. movement   d. cell

_____ 17. After the robbery, the detectives *scoured* the bank for clues. They looked for fingerprints, went through every file, and left no stone unturned in their investigation.

a. photographed b. watched c. considered
d. thoroughly searched

_____ 18. In some places, the distance from the top of the Grand Canyon to the bottom is a *sheer* one-mile drop, making it impossible to climb.

a. casual b. slight c. unique d. very steep

_____ 19. People cannot *survive* without water for more than a few days, but they can live for much longer without food.

a. exist b. travel c. eat d. feel good

_____ 20. We found no *trace* of pollution in the clear, clean mountain stream.

a. evidence b. cause c. memory d. regulation

Number correct _____ (total 20)

Part B *Target Words in Reading and Literature*

You should now have a general idea of the meaning of each target word. Sharpen your understanding by studying how these words are used in the following selection.

Gold Fever

Vic Kondra

The "forty-niners," the people who traveled to California by the thousands in 1849 to search for gold, have not been the only ones to experience gold fever. In the following reading selection, a contemporary group of Boy Scouts on a camping trip to California gold rush territory finds that panning for gold is a fascinating pastime.

Gold fever **obviously** had spread through the Scouts in Troop 121 of Merced, California, and it grew stronger with each mile they trekked into gold rush country. In their excitement, a few noticed how narrow the trail became as it threaded its way along a five-hundred-foot **sheer** cliff above the Merced River, once a magnet for thousands of gold seekers in the mid-1800's.   5

At their **destination** the fifteen-member troop and five adult leaders quickly made camp, held **assembly,** and raised the Stars and Stripes. Shovels and pans were the order of the day as the group **converged** on the river. Doug Boyster, one of the adult leaders, had **considerable**   10 experience gold panning so he was able to show the boys the most likely spots. Pant legs rolled up and heads bowed, the Scouts panned for those **elusive** bits of bright yellow metal that in 1849 started one of the greatest stampedes of treasure hunters the world has ever seen.

The ghosts of those old miners probably were chuckling in their beards 15 as they watched this excited group of young men in search of riches. Gold fever really hit when Kevin Vance found a tiny flake of gold in the bottom of his pan, but by late afternoon the fever cooled, and most of the troop **abandoned** the search in favor of a swim in the river. Only a few of the more determined continued to dig and pan. 20

Scoutmasters Art Hood and Bill Jackson later rounded up the swim-mers and took them on a tour of Hites Cove, an area once rich in gold and heavily **populated** with forty-niners in search of fortunes. Few found gold; many were lucky even to **survive.** Most of the early gold seekers worked under unbelievable hardships and were rewarded with little but 25 hunger and disease. Often what little gold they did find was used to pay their **debts,** spent quickly, or stolen from them. Few became rich in the gold fields.

Traces of the gold rush period were all around Troop 121's campsite. Huge cast-iron and steel **fixtures** from an ore mill lay abandoned, and 30 parts of a giant steam engine were rusting away. Just above the camp, columns made of flat sections of granite supported a roadbed along the mountainside where mule-drawn cars had brought gold ore from some-where far upriver. **Portions** of buildings made from more of the granite slabs were still standing. No mortar was used in the buildings, yet after 35 more than 120 years the walls remain upright.

The next morning the troop discovered a group of modern gold miners hard at work about a mile upstream from the camp. Four men were **scouring** the river with a floating dredge. In the bottom of a deep pool a scuba diver used a four-inch suction hose to **extract** gold-bearing gravel and mud from the river bottom. The suctioned material was pumped to a floating platform and through a sluice box[1] designed to wash away the gravel and trap the gold. **Despite** eager questions, the four modern miners **declined** to say how much gold they had found but did admit to taking a few small nuggets.

It was not until the trip home that visions of a gold strike arose again. One of the Scouts mentioned that winter snows and high water frequently **dislodge** large pockets of nuggets and ore. That did it. Gold fever was running high as plans were made for a spring trip back into Hites Cove. This time they would **definitely** need more shovels, and maybe they could build a sluice box and maybe rent a dredge. Just wait until next year!

40

45

50

---

[1] sluice box: a trough through which water is channeled

Refining Your Understanding

For each of the following items, consider how the target word is used in the passage. Write the letter of the word or phrase that best completes each sentence.

_____ 1. When the Scout leaders called *assembly* (line 8), the Scouts were expected to   a. gather together   b. put together their equipment   c. clean the grounds.

_____ 2. Group members "*converged* on the river" (lines 9–10) because they a. wanted to go separate ways   b. all wanted to do the same thing   c. wanted to move away from the river.

_____ 3. If most of the troop "*abandoned* the search" (line 19), they a. were ready to do something else   b. reluctantly quit panning c. took a short break from panning.

_____ 4. Some "*traces* of the gold rush period" (line 29) were still around because   a. people use exactly the same equipment today b. the years had not totally destroyed the equipment   c. written records were kept.

_____ 5. If "winter snows and high water frequently *dislodge* large pockets of nuggets and ore" (lines 47–48), we would expect   a. more gold in the streams   b. less gold in the streams   c. gold of poorer quality.

Number correct _____ (total 5)

Part C Ways to Make New Words Your Own

By now you are familiar with the target words and their meanings. This section presents activities that will help you make the words part of your permanent vocabulary.

Using Language and Thinking Skills

Finding the Unrelated Word Write the letter of the word or phrase that is not related in meaning to the other words in the set.

_____ 1. a. apparent b. clear c. elusive d. definite

_____ 2. a. consent b. decline c. refuse d. reject

_____ 3. a. obviously b. plainly c. quickly d. clearly

_____ 4. a. scour b. search c. investigate d. glance

_____ 5. a. despite b. because of c. regardless of d. in spite of

_____ 6. a. meeting b. assembly c. isolation d. gathering

_____ 7. a. prize b. bill c. debt d. obligation

_____ 8. a. trace b. surplus c. speck d. hint

_____ 9. a. part b. portion c. total d. piece

_____ 10. a. inhabit b. occupy c. desert d. populate

Number correct _____ (total 10)

Word's Worth: abandon

It is interesting that a word that today means "giving up control" comes from an old French phrase that meant just the opposite. Centuries ago, *mettre á bandon* meant "to put under somebody's control." Part of this phrase passed into English; thus *abandon* originally meant "complete control." A feudal lord was said to hold his powerless subjects *in abandon*. Today a person who acts *with abandon* acts without restraint or control. It just shows how some words can abandon their original meanings.

Finding Antonyms Each sentence below contains an italicized target word and an antonym of the target word. Write the antonym in the blank.

Example

__**stingy**__   Colleen was a *generous* friend, unlike her stingy roommate, Katie, who never gave anything away.

_____ 1. Anthony was tempted to accept Mr. Scott's offer, but he decided to *decline* and keep his present job.

_____ 2. A crowd of curious onlookers moved quickly to *converge* on the scene of the disaster until the officers ordered them to scatter.

_____ 3. Jamarr had to *abandon* his dream of becoming a professional baseball player when injuries would not allow him to continue playing.

_____ 4. When Mr. Ryan learned that a family of raccoons had managed to establish a home in the attic, he knew he would have to *dislodge* them.

_____ 5. With modern equipment, today's mountaineers can *survive* at altitudes that once would have caused climbers to perish.

_____ 6. Yolanda will *definitely* make the basketball team; Lindsay may possibly make the team if she improves enough.

_____ 7. The poet's influence on other writers was *considerable*, but reviewers paid only slight attention to her work.

_____ 8. The north face of the mountain was too *sheer* to climb, but the south face had a gentle slope, which made climbing easier.

_____ 9. When an oral surgeon *extracts* a molar, he often installs a temporary bridge.

_____ 10. The glider flight had its origin at the municipal airport, but its *destination* turned out to be a cornfield on the outskirts of town.

Number correct _____ (total 10)

Practicing for Standardized Tests

Analogies Determine the relationship between the pair of capitalized words. Then decide which other word pair expresses a similar relationship. Write the letter of this word pair.

_____ 1. ABANDON : MAINTAIN :: (A) race : win (B) freeze : harden (C) demand : insist (D) extract : insert (E) avoid : fear

_____ 2. CONSIDERABLE : MANY :: (A) pleasurable : harmful (B) possible : certain (C) cold : cool (D) abundant : scarce (E) grave : serious

_____ 3. CONVERGE : SEPARATE :: (A) plant : sow (B) argue : yell (C) plan : build (D) pause : stop (E) deny : accept

_____ 4. FOX : ELUSIVE :: (A) athlete : fit (B) stone : alive (C) clarity : puzzling (D) air : earthly (E) humorist : tragic

_____ 5. FIXTURE : FAUCET :: (A) assembly : individual (B) integrity : traitor (C) game : tennis (D) gold : silver (E) career : study

_____ 6. STUDENT : ASSEMBLY :: (A) boss : conference (B) aircraft : wing (C) chalkboard : eraser (D) technology : invention (E) sailor : anchor

_____ 7. DECLINE : INVITATION :: (A) dance : ballroom (B) consume : preservation (C) cut : scissors (D) steer : car (E) teach : instruction

_____ 8. PORTION : WHOLE :: (A) page : book (B) savings : bank (C) obstacle : wall (D) happiness : sullenness (E) fuel : wood

_____ 9. DEFINITELY : CERTAINLY :: (A) courteously : rudely (B) warmly : feverishly (C) quickly : quietly (D) gravely : humorously (E) efficiently : effectively

_____ 10. EXTRACT : TOOTH :: (A) build : carpenter (B) dream : reality (C) compete : competition (D) erase : pencil (E) lift : weights

Number correct _____ (total 10)

Spelling and Wordplay

Crossword Puzzle Read the clues and print the correct answer to each in the proper squares. There are fourteen target words and one related word in this puzzle.

ACROSS

1. In spite of
6. Things owed
9. A small bay
11. Region
12. Very steep
14. Temporary canvas shelter
16. Abbr. artificial intelligence
17. Abbr. avenue
18. Abbr. Illinois
19. Quite evident
21. Abbr. Northwestern University
22. Exclamation of fear or awe
24. Abbr. agricultural engineer
25. Like
26. Midday
27. Similar to a mitten
29. Short for Timothy
31. A __ __ __ __ ranch
34. Not down
35. Suffix meaning "related to" or "having the nature of"
36. Bragged (like a bird)
37. Abbr. Old English
38. Pa's mate
40. Abbr. lieutenant
42. Groups of cattle
44. Relating to lines
47. To eat
48. Abbr. Bachelor of Arts
49. To pull out
53. Abbr. December
54. Large or important

DOWN

1. Goal
2. To glance at hastily
3. A piece of something
4. Contraction of "I have"
5. Coffee or __ __ __?
6. Removed by force
7. Honey-making insect
8. To outlive
10. To operate a car
13. Abbr. each
15. Hard to grasp
16. Deserts
20. To search thoroughly
23. Santa's laugh
28. Abbr. vice-president
30. Objective case of "I"
32. Abbr. underwriter
33. A dip
36. An automobile
38. Short for metropolitan
39. The first number
40. An identifying tag
41. A very small amount
43. Plural form of "Doc"
45. Not out
46. Chopping tool
49. Abbr. eastern time
50. Abbr. teachers college
51. Indefinite article
52. Seventh tone of the scale
53. Abbr. decibel

Part D **Related Words**

The words below are closely related to the target words. Use your knowledge of the target words and of word parts to determine the meaning of these words. (For information about word parts analysis, see pages 7–13.) Use your dictionary if necessary.

1. abandonment (ə ban′ dən mənt) n.	11. elude (i lo͞od′) v.
2. assemblage (ə sem′ blij) n.	12. extraction (ik strak′ shən) n.
3. assemble (ə sem′ b'l) v.	13. inclination (in′ klə nā′ shən) n.
4. consider (kən sid′ ər) v.	14. incline (in′ klīn) n. (in klīn′) v.
5. considerate (kən sid′ ər it) adj.	15. indebted (in det′ id) adj.
6. define (di fīn′) v.	16. lodge (läj) n., v.
7. definite (def′ ə nit) adj.	17. obvious (äb′ vē əs) adj.
8. destined (des′ tind) v.	18. population (päp′ yə lā′ shən) n.
9. destiny (des′ tə nē) n.	19. recline (ri klīn′) v.
10. disassembly (dis′ ə sem′ blē) n.	20. survivor (sər vī′ vər) n.

Understanding Related Words

Matching Definitions Match each word on the right with its definition on the left. Write the letter of the matching word in the blank.

_____ 1. a sloped surface

_____ 2. to avoid or escape by quickness or cunning

_____ 3. clear or easily understood

_____ 4. a going away from a person or thing without intending to return

_____ 5. the act of taking something out by force or effort

_____ 6. all the people of a country or community

_____ 7. one who continues to live, perhaps in spite of something

_____ 8. to house; to place or deposit for safekeeping

_____ 9. a taking apart

_____ 10. a group of persons gathered together

a. abandonment
b. assemblage
c. disassembly
d. elude
e. extraction
f. incline
g. lodge
h. obvious
i. population
j. survivor

Number correct _____ (total 10)

> Turn to **The Final Silent *e*** on page 223 of the **Spelling Handbook.** Read the rule and complete the exercises provided.

Sentence Completion Write the related word from the list below that best completes the meaning of the sentence.

assemble   considerate   definite   destiny   indebted
consider   define   destined   inclination   recline

_____ 1. The actress said she was greatly ? to her drama coach for all the help he had given her.

_____ 2. Whenever the topic of politics came up, you could always count on Mrs. Jackson to have forceful and ? opinions.

_____ 3. Renata's grandparents said that they knew they were ? for a life together when they first met each other forty-eight years ago.

_____ 4. The lawyer asked the members of the jury to ? all the evidence carefully before they made up their minds.

_____ 5. The Scout leader asked the troop to ? on the playground at 6 A.M. because they would be taking buses to the campground.

_____ 6. For homework, we had to ? each word and use it in a sentence.

_____ 7. The nurse advised the sick student to ? on the couch until his dizzy spell passed.

_____ 8. Throughout the ages many civilizations have believed that ? controls what happens in a person's life.

_____ 9. Carly had many good friends because she was such a thoughtful, kind, and ? person.

_____ 10. Carlos had a(n) ? for spicy foods, so we all went to the Mexican restaurant for dinner.

Number correct _____ (total 10)

Analyzing Word Parts

The Latin Root *cline* The target word *decline* comes from the Latin root *cline,* meaning "to bend" or "to lean." Related words that come from this same Latin root include *inclination, incline, and recline.*

Keeping in mind the meaning of *cline,* match each of the four words listed below with its correct definition. (One word will be used twice.) Use a dictionary if needed.

decline   inclination   incline   recline

_____ 1. to bend forward

_____ 2. to turn down

_____ 3. a slope

_____ 4. to lie back or lie down

_____ 5. a tendency, liking, or preference

Number correct _____ (total 5)

Number correct in unit _____ (total 80)

The Last Word

Writing

Write a thank-you note to someone to whom you feel you are *indebted.* The person you write to might be a parent or other relative, a teacher, or a friend. You might be grateful to this person for doing you some special favor or for being *considerate* of your feelings. In your note explain what the person did to deserve your thanks.

Speaking

Prepare a short talk about your favorite vacation *destination.* You might talk about a place you have already visited or about a place you would like to visit someday. Illustrate your talk with pictures or maps to help explain where this place is and what there is to see and do there.

Group Discussion

There are many words we use every day that are difficult to *define.* Many of these are words that name personal qualities. For instance, consider the words *courage, loyalty,* and *patriotism.* What do they mean? Make a list of other words that name personal qualities. Discuss what the words mean and why they are so difficult to define. Then discuss what techniques might help you to define such words. For instance, you might find that using examples or anecdotes helps you explain their meanings.

UNIT 7

Part A   Target Words and Their Meanings

1. achievement (ə chēv′ mənt) n.
2. acquire (ə kwīr′) v.
3. defect (dē′ fekt) n. (di fekt′) v.
4. desperate (des′ pər it, -prit) adj.
5. duplicate (dōō′ plə kāt′) v.
   (dōō′ plə kit) adj., n.
6. eligible (el′ i jə b′l) adj.
7. exclusive (iks klōō′ siv) adj.
8. falter (fôl′ tər) v.
9. financial (fə nan′ shəl, fī-) adj.
10. maintenance (mān′ t′n əns) n.
11. monopolize (mə näp′ ə līz′) v.
12. outlook (out′ look′) n.
13. pedestrian (pə des′ trē ən) adj., n.
14. prominent (präm′ ə nənt) adj.
15. relish (rel′ ish) v., n.
16. requirement (ri kwīr′ mənt) n.
17. typical (tip′ i k′l) adj.
18. universal (yōō′ nə vʉr′ s′l) adj.
19. vagabond (vag′ ə bänd′) adj., n.
20. veto (vē′ tō) n., v.

Inferring Meaning from Context

For each sentence write the letter of the word or phrase that is closest in meaning to the word or words in italics. Use context clues to help you choose the correct answer. (For information about how context helps you understand vocabulary, see pages 1–6.)

____ 1. Maria regarded learning to swim as a major *achievement*, the most important thing she had done all summer.

a. problem   b. failure   c. accomplishment   d. skill

____ 2. It takes years of schooling and training to *acquire* the skills needed to become a good doctor.

a. obtain   b. find   c. lose   d. desire

____ 3. The only *defect* in David's golf swing was a slight bend of his left arm, which decreased his accuracy.

a. strength   b. fault   c. habit   d. virtue

____ 4. As she hung from the airplane's wing, the stuntwoman feared she was in *a desperate* situation.

a. a hopeless   b. a strange   c. an athletic   d. a graceful

____ 5. Ted was able to *duplicate* the old drawing, matching the original in every detail.

a. read over   b. copy   c. change   d. print

_____ 6. The law sets a minimum age for candidates for president of the United States. To be *eligible,* you must be at least thirty-five years old.

a. interested   b. intelligent enough   c. qualified   d. famous

_____ 7. The club was very *exclusive;* only those students who spoke a foreign language could join.

a. large   b. selective   c. exciting   d. expensive

_____ 8. After her illness, Carla was so weak that she *faltered* and fell against the stair rail.

a. jumped up   b. ran over   c. yelled   d. stumbled

_____ 9. When Ms. Carlotti inherited a large sum of money from her aunt, her banker gave her *financial* advice.

a. employment   b. final   c. money-related   d. health-related

_____ 10. The *maintenance* of the Cleasons' car involved replacing the filters and changing the spark plugs.

a. driving   b. upkeep   c. selling   d. licensing

_____ 11. Eileen loved to talk so much that she tried to *monopolize* every conversation.

a. record   b. wait patiently during   c. take turns in   d. control

_____ 12. Gail's *outlook on* life is positive. She believes she can accomplish anything she puts her mind to, and she is naturally optimistic.

a. view of   b. criticism of   c. study of   d. writing about

_____ 13. The use of *pedestrian* language can make a composition seem lifeless. Interesting writing requires fresh and original language.

a. fascinating   b. unusual   c. dull   d. thoughtful

_____ 14. The clown's most *prominent* feature was his electrified red nose.

a. handsome   b. homely   c. outstanding   d. neglected

_____ 15. Tom spends many hours reading biographies and adventure stories at the library; he obviously *relishes* reading.

a. enjoys   b. abuses   c. dislikes   d. regrets

_____ 16. A passing grade on the unit test is the main *requirement* for going on to the next unit of the book.

a. problem   b. condition   c. examination   d. excuse

_____ 17. Sandy beaches and palm trees are a *typical* sight on the Florida coastline. Each year thousands of tourists come to enjoy them.

a. rare   b. forgettable   c. normal   d. believable

_____ 18. Love and encouragement are *universal* needs, necessary for the healthy development of every child in every culture and country.

a. limited   b. timely   c. foreign   d. worldwide

_____ 19. In the Middle Ages, *vagabond* minstrels would make their way from town to town, singing songs and telling stories.

a. criminal   b. wandering   c. ignorant   d. violent

_____ 20. The president's *veto* of a bill may prevent it from becoming law. A veto can be overturned only if two thirds of each House of Congress votes in favor of the bill.

a. rejection   b. misunderstanding   c. approval   d. description

Number correct _____ (total 20)

Part B   *Target Words in Reading and Literature*

You should now have a general idea of the meaning of each target word. Sharpen your understanding by studying how these words are used in the following selection.

Thomas Edison: The Early Years of Genius

Howard Peet

Most Americans have heard of Thomas Edison, but many people have never heard of his early struggles and disappointments. The author tells about Edison's youth and first efforts as an inventor.

Perhaps no other person has had a greater effect on modern life than Thomas Alva Edison (1847–1931), whose inventions include the electric light bulb, the phonograph, and the movie projector. In his lifetime he **acquired** 1,093 patents for his inventions. The vast number of his **achievements** brought him **universal** fame and made his name a   5
household word. But such success was not easily won.

As a boy, Edison showed a tireless curiosity. His experience in public school was not a happy one, however. When he became **eligible** to attend school at the age of seven, his endless questions annoyed his teacher. The frustrated, impatient teacher even told his mother that her   10
son was retarded. Outraged at the teacher's negative **outlook,** the mother pulled her son out of school after only three months of formal education. Luckily, she was a gifted teacher herself, and she took responsibility for his learning. Soon he began to learn so fast that his mother could not keep up with him. Through wide reading and his own experi-   15
ments, young Edison was discovering the excitement of modern science.

His family's **financial** difficulties forced Edison to take his first job at the age of twelve. He sold newspapers on a railway and used his spare time to conduct chemical experiments. Due to a **defect** in one of his experiments, a fire accidentally started in the baggage car. As punishment, the   20 ment, the conductor boxed his ears and threw him and his chemicals off the train. The conductor's slaps may have contributed to the development of Edison's deafness, which became almost total in his later years.

Edison continued working in **pedestrian** jobs during his adolescent years. Though the jobs did not match his ability or potential, he put his free time to good use by continuing his self-education. Eventually, he traveled around the country while working as a **vagabond** telegrapher; the little money he made was spent mostly on equipment or books for his experiments.

While in his early twenties, Edison was awarded his first patent. He designed a voting machine to be used by an **exclusive** group—the United States Congress. A member of Congress could sit with this machine at his or her seat and push a yes or a no button. The member's vote would immediately be **duplicated** on a large board at the front of the congressional chamber. Edison went to Washington, D. C., to convince Congress to purchase his machine. The representatives treated him as a **prominent** person, allowing him to speak before a committee.

However, the invention was turned down because it recorded results too quickly. The members of Congress wanted to preserve the forty-five minutes it took to record a roll call vote. This gave them time to trade votes or prepare for any possible **veto** by the president. Following his rejection, Edison said, "I will never again invent anything nobody wants." He set one **requirement** for all his future inventions: they must meet "the **desperate** needs of the world."

Edison's determination did not **falter**. Even though he was so poor that he had to sleep in the office where he worked, he continued to explore

Thomas Edison sits next to one of his most famous inventions, the phonograph
1878, MATHEW BRADY
The Granger Collection

ways of inventing or improving machines. While working for a company in New York City, he studied the operation of the ticker, a telegraphic device used to record changes in the stock market prices. One day the ticker broke down and none of the repair people could fix it. To the amazement of the office manager, Edison fixed the machine himself. He was then given the job of supervising the **maintenance** of the ticker. With his **typical** experimental approach, he proceeded to find ways of making the machine more reliable and efficient. 50

Edison received several patents for his improvements of the stock ticker. The president of the company that employed him bought the rights to these patents for $40,000, an enormous sum at that time. Edison turned around and invested his money in a laboratory workshop, where he could pursue his research around the clock. 55

For more than fifty years Edison continued to explore the mysteries of science and machines. This work that he loved **monopolized** his life to the point that he rarely got more than four hours of sleep a night. He **relished** his investigations so much that he had little time left for family or friends. Yet what he accomplished eventually changed the way ordinary people lived their lives. No inventor ever gave more to the world. 60, 65

Refining Your Understanding

For each of the following items, consider how the target word is used in the passage. Write the letter of the word or phrase that best completes the sentence.

_____ 1. If work "*monopolized* his life" (line 61), we can gather that Edison
a. tried to avoid work b. spent most of his waking hours at work
c. worked quickly and efficiently.

_____ 2. To meet the "*desperate* needs of the world" (line 44), Edison probably tried to a. find out what people needed most in their lives b. estimate how much money people would spend
c. invent new luxuries for the wealthy.

_____ 3. The fact that Edison was a "*vagabond* telegrapher" (line 27) indicates he a. never worked hard b. did not dress well or take care of his appearance c. traveled to find work.

_____ 4. "*Universal* fame" (line 5) suggests that Edison was known
a. locally b. throughout the country c. throughout the world.

_____ 5. Edison held *pedestrian* (line 24) jobs as a youth, which means that they a. required walking b. were ordinary and dull
c. were understandable by the average person.

Number correct _____ (total 5)

Part C   *Ways to Make New Words Your Own*

By now you are familiar with the target words and their meanings. This section presents activities that will help you make the words part of your permanent vocabulary.

Using Language and Thinking Skills

Understanding Multiple Meanings   Each box in this exercise contains a bold-faced word with its definitions. Read the definitions and then the sentences that use the word. Write the letter of the definition that applies to each sentence.

---

pedestrian
a. a person who is walking (n.)
b. unimaginative; dull (adj.)
c. of or for people who are walking (adj.)

____   1. The *pedestrian* bridge was crowded with sightseers and shoppers returning home.

____   2. In contrast to Bill's *pedestrian* answer, Christine's solution had originality.

____   3. Cars must yield the right of way to a *pedestrian*.

---

defect
a. a fault or imperfection (n.)
b. to desert one's country; to abandon a cause or group, often to support another (v.)

____   4. The foreign visitor went to the embassy and said he wanted to *defect* to the United States.

____   5. The only *defect* in Bob's plan was that he could not get his car started.

____   6. The new choir director was so strict that several singers wanted to *defect* to the glee club.

---

relish
a. a distinctive or appetizing flavor (n.)
b. great enjoyment or pleasure (n.)
c. a food such as pickles or olives (n.)
d. to enjoy; to like (v.)

_____ 7. Larry asked Betty to bring *relishes* to the barbecue.

_____ 8. People who *relish* their jobs usually do them well.

_____ 9. Mr. Oliver listened with *relish* as his piano students performed at the recital.

_____ 10. There was a *relish* of garlic in Marco's spaghetti sauce.

Number correct _____ (total 10)

Practicing for Standardized Tests

Synonyms Write the letter of the word that is closest in meaning to the capitalized word.

_____ 1. VAGABOND: (A) thief (B) liar (C) resident (D) worker (E) wanderer

_____ 2. DEFECT: (A) loss (B) decline (C) result (D) fault (E) blame

_____ 3. RELISH: (A) hurry (B) refine (C) enjoy (D) tolerate (E) decorate

_____ 4. DUPLICATE: (A) create (B) present (C) copy (D) lie (E) control

_____ 5. ELIGIBLE: (A) athletic (B) handsome (C) qualified (D) improper (E) expensive

_____ 6. FALTER: (A) corrode (B) pursue (C) destroy (D) stumble (E) cancel

_____ 7. FINANCIAL: (A) considerable (B) needy (C) common (D) wealthy (E) monetary

_____ 8. OUTLOOK: (A) destiny (B) viewpoint (C) honesty (D) discussion (E) quality

_____ 9. REQUIREMENT: (A) rule (B) reluctance (C) obstacle (D) choice (E) end

_____ 10. UNIVERSAL: (A) worldwide (B) large (C) national (D) instinctive (E) unusual

Number correct _____ (total 10)

Antonyms Write the letter of the word that is most nearly *opposite* in meaning to the capitalized word.

_____ 1. DESPERATE: (A) optimistic (B) tired (C) annoyed (D) wishful (E) popular

_____ 2. EXCLUSIVE: (A) common (B) shy (C) understandable (D) silent (E) intimate

_____ 3. MAINTENANCE: (A) destruction (B) purity (C) procedure (D) remodeling (E) innovation

_____ 4. MONOPOLIZE: (A) control (B) share (C) simplify (D) change (E) dislodge

_____ 5. PEDESTRIAN: (A) ordinary (B) fascinating (C) lasting (D) childish (E) quiet

_____ 6. PROMINENT: (A) inconsiderate (B) superior (C) unnoticeable (D) insufficient (E) false

_____ 7. ACHIEVEMENT: (A) act (B) sorrow (C) failure (D) thrill (E) weakness

_____ 8. TYPICAL: (A) considerable (B) sheer (C) technological (D) unusual (E) easy

_____ 9. ACQUIRE: (A) lose (B) get (C) express (D) forget (E) allow

_____ 10. VETO: (A) deny (B) elude (C) approve (D) forbid (E) join

Number correct _____ (total 10)

Word's Worth: _veto_

The tribunes of ancient Rome were officials responsible for protecting the interests of the common people. They were given the power to cancel certain laws and decrees simply by saying _veto_, which means "I forbid." In this way, tribunes were supposed to protect ordinary citizens from laws that might harm them. The founders of the United States had the tribunes in mind when they gave the president the power to veto, or cancel, laws passed by Congress.

Spelling and Wordplay

Proofreading Find the ten misspelled target words in the following letter and write them correctly on the lines below the letter.

My Greatest Achievement

Last year at summer camp I found myself in a desparate situation. Because I had passed all my swimming requirements, I became eligable for the Annual Race to the Raft. That meant I would have to swim a half mile to the raft floating in the middle of the lake. I had never swum that distance, or even come close, and I was scared that I might falter. However, the temptation of financal reward proved too great. A prominant local banker had donated $50 to be given to the winner. So I decided to try my luck.

On the day of the race, an excluesive group of campers gathered by the lake. Only eight campers had aquired the right to participate. These boys and girls, unlike me, seemed totally confident, free from any weakness or defect. During the last three years one boy, Douglas McElroy, had monopalized the event. With tipical boldness, he told us that he would dupelicate his previous victories. Of course, the others disagreed violently with his outlook. While they argued with him, I just stood there, looking at the raft that seemed miles away. I did not relesh the thought of drowning.

The race began with everyone diving into the water from the pier. At first, Douglas took the lead, and I settled in at a comfortable pace in last place. Unfortunately, Douglas did win as expected, and I did finish last. For many people, that would be a disappointing ending to the story. However, I felt great when I touched the raft. I felt even better when I called my parents with the news of my triumph—a half mile without stopping! That race was my greatest achievement.

1. _____
2. _____
3. _____
4. _____
5. _____

6. _____
7. _____
8. _____
9. _____
10. _____

Number correct _____ (total 10)

Part D Related Words

The words below are closely related to the target words. Use your knowledge of the target words and of word parts to determine the meaning of these words. (For information about word parts analysis, see pages 7–13.) Use your dictionary if necessary.

1. achieve (ə chēv′) v.
2. acquisition (ak′ wə zish′ ən) n.
3. atypical (ā tip′ i k′l) adj.
4. defective (di fek′ tiv) adj.
5. despair (di sper′) v., n.
6. desperation (des′ pə rā′ shən) n.
7. duplication (doo′ plə kā′ shən) n.
8. eligibility (el′ i jə bil′ i tē) n.
9. exclude (iks klood′) v.
10. finance (fə nans′, fī′ nans) n., v.
11. financier (fin ən sir′) n.
12. include (in klood′) v.
13. ineligible (in el′ i jə b′l) adj.
14. inquire (in kwīr′) v.
15. maintain (mān tān′) v.
16. monopoly (mə näp′ ə lē) n.
17. prominence (präm′ ə nens) n.
18. require (ri kwīr′) v.
19. typify (tip′ ə fī′) v.
20. universe (yoo′ nə vʉrs′) n.

Understanding Related Words

Sentence Completion Write the word from the list below that best completes the meaning of the sentence.

achieve   defective   inquire   monopoly   require
acquisition duplication maintain   prominence   typify

_____ 1. Many schools ? that new students have physical exams before they start classes.

_____ 2. Jim wrote to ? when we would be going to Seattle to visit him.

_____ 3. Until the breakup of AT&T, the company had a(an) ? on telephone service in the United States.

_____ 4. The toaster Maria bought was ? , so she had to exchange it for one that worked.

_____ 5. The art collector paid a great deal of money for the ? of a famous painting.

_____ 6. Before their rise to ? , many famous actors held a variety of low-paying jobs and went through periods of unemployment.

_____ 7. Yolanda worked hard to ? her goal of learning to swim before camp was over.

_____ 8. In order to play on the soccer team, you must _?_ a C average in your major subjects.

_____ 9. Because of a(an) _?_ on the mailing list, Marty got two copies of the computer magazine he ordered.

_____ 10. Cacti, scrub trees, and sand _?_ the scenery of much of the Southwest.

Number correct _____ (total 10)

Close Relatives Each of the sentences below needs to be completed by a pair of words that are very closely related in meaning. Write the two related words that best complete each sentence.

atypical   despair   eligibility   exclude   finance
typical   desperation   ineligible   include   financier

1. The Honor Society voted to _____ students who had B averages and to _____ students whose averages were lower.

2. Bobby is a(an) _____ ten-year-old who has to be urged to practice the piano; however, his friend Jimmy is somewhat _____, because he loves to practice and never needs to be reminded.

3. Stocks, bonds, and other aspects of the world of _____ are often confusing to someone who is not a professional _____.

4. The athletic association, which rules on the _____ of high school basketball players, declared that players over twenty years old were _____.

5. Some of the stranded Scouts began to _____ of ever getting back to the campsite, but their leader wisely warned them that _____ and panic would only make their problems worse.

Number correct _____ (total 5)

Turn to **Words with _ie_ and _ei_** on page 229 of the **Spelling Handbook.** Read the rule and complete the exercises provided.

Analyzing Word Parts

The Latin Root *uni* The Latin root *uni* means "one." This root is found in the target word *universal* as well as in the related word *universe*. Other words, such as *unicycle, uniform, unit,* and *unite,* also contain this root. In the blank, write the word that best completes each sentence. Use a dictionary if needed.

unicycle   uniform   unit   united   universe

_____ 1. Whether in Maine or California, stoplights are __?__ throughout the country—always red on top, yellow in the middle, and green on the bottom.

_____ 2. In order to ride a __?__ without falling over, the rider must have a very good sense of balance.

_____ 3. In Ms. Cato's geography class, the __?__ on Argentina lasted for one week.

_____ 4. Canada is a collection of ten provinces __?__ into one country.

_____ 5. The Milky Way Galaxy is one of the many galaxies in our __?__ .

Number correct _____ (total 5)

The Greek Root *mono* The Greek root *mono* comes from the Greek word *monos,* which means "single" or "alone." The target word *monopolize* and the related word *monopoly* contain this root. The root can also be found in the words listed below. In the blank, write the word that best completes each sentence. Use a dictionary if needed.

monarch   monoplane   monorail   monotone   monotony

_____ 1. King Olaf V, the __?__ of Norway, has reigned since 1957.

_____ 2. Imagine the __?__ of eating nothing but bread and water for a whole week!

_____ 3. A biplane has two wings; a __?__ has one wing.

_____ 4. A train riding on a __?__ carried visitors from downtown Seattle to the World's Fair in 1962.

_____ 5. Public speakers are urged not to talk in a __?__ but to vary the pitch of their voice.

Number correct _____ (total 5)

Number correct in unit _____ (total 90)

92

The Last Word

Writing

There are many words we use to describe a person's *outlook* on life. For example, we say a person is optimistic if he or she tends to take a hopeful view of things. We say a person is pessimistic if he or she tends to take a gloomy view of things. Write a short description of your outlook on life. Tell whether you are generally optimistic or pessimistic. Include specific examples of things that you have said or done that demonstrate your outlook.

Speaking

Think of a *prominent* person whose *achievements* you admire. For example, you might think of a sports star, a political leader, or other public figure. Prepare a short talk about the person, doing library research if needed. Describe his or her achievements and explain why you admire this person.

Group Discussion

A time capsule is a container filled with objects *typical* of the time when it is buried. It is usually put in the foundation of a building for discovery in the future. Imagine that your class has been asked to make such a capsule to be buried in the foundation of a new school. Discuss what objects you would include that would be typical of present-day life.

UNIT 8: Review of Units 5–7

Part A Review Word List

Unit 5 Target Words

1. application
2. artery
3. consume
4. contend
5. corrosion
6. diameter
7. domestic
8. economical
9. efficiently
10. existence
11. injection
12. innovation
13. isolate
14. obstacle
15. procedure
16. refinery
17. system
18. technological
19. terminal
20. volume

Unit 5 Related Words

1. apply
2. arterial
3. consumer
4. contention
5. corrode
6. corrosive
7. dejected
8. economy
9. efficiency
10. efficient
11. eject
12. exist
13. inject
14. isolation
15. proceed
16. project
17. refine
18. refinement
19. reject
20. systematic

Unit 6 Target Words

1. abandon
2. assembly
3. considerable
4. converge
5. debt
6. decline
7. definitely
8. despite
9. destination
10. dislodge
11. elusive
12. extract
13. fixture
14. obviously
15. populate
16. portion
17. scour
18. sheer
19. survive
20. trace

Unit 6 Related Words

1. abandonment
2. assemblage
3. assemble
4. consider
5. considerate
6. define
7. definite
8. destined
9. destiny
10. disassembly
11. elude
12. extraction
13. inclination
14. incline
15. indebted
16. lodge
17. obvious
18. population
19. recline
20. survivor

Unit 7 Target Words

1. achievement
2. acquire
3. defect
4. desperate
5. duplicate
6. eligible
7. exclusive
8. falter
9. financial
10. maintenance
11. monopolize
12. outlook
13. pedestrian
14. prominent
15. relish
16. requirement
17. typical
18. universal
19. vagabond
20. veto

Unit 7 Related Words

1. achieve
2. acquisition
3. atypical
4. defective
5. despair
6. desperation
7. duplication
8. eligibility
9. exclude
10. finance
11. financier
12. include
13. ineligible
14. inquire
15. maintain
16. monopoly
17. prominence
18. require
19. typify
20. universe

Inferring Meaning from Context

For each sentence write the letter of the word or phrase that is closest in meaning to the word or words in italics.

_____ 1. Interstate highways are the *arteries* of automobile and truck travel in the United States.
   a. main routes   b. most dangerous roads   c. great achievements
   d. expensive means

_____ 2. The *assembly* was made up of three representatives from each participating country.
   a. auditorium   b. gathering   c. monopoly   d. government

_____ 3. Eight teams are going to *contend* for the championship in the holiday tournament.
   a. gather   b. apply   c. compete   d. volunteer

_____ 4. The accident happened when two cars *converged* at the intersection.
   a. failed to stop   b. went too fast   c. spun out   d. came together

_____ 5. The *elusive* kitten ran around the yard and up a tree before we could catch it.
   a. quick-witted   b. desperate   c. hard to catch   d. timid

_____ 6. Some *exclusive* restaurants require men to wear jackets and ties.
   a. domestic   b. selective   c. ordinary   d. downtown

_____ 7. Many plastic products are made by the *injection* of plastic resins into molds; the resins harden into the shape of the mold.
   a. insertion   b. shaping   c. hammering   d. pressing

_____ 8. The film critic said that the movie suffered from a *pedestrian* plot.
   a. violent   b. complicated   c. uninteresting   d. strange

_____ 9. Henry took the responsibility for the most difficult *portion* of the team assignment.
   a. construction   b. part   c. solution   d. requirement

_____ 10. Collecting money from customers was one job the newspaper carrier did not *relish*.
   a. take   b. learn   c. finish   d. enjoy

_____ 11. Keith *scoured* the library for a book about extraterrestrial beings, but he could not find one.
   a. called   b. went to   c. asked   d. thoroughly searched

_____ 12. When the bus pulled out of the *terminal*, Iris remembered that she had left her package on the bench.
   a. city   b. garage   c. station   d. intersection

___ 13. Poverty, disease, and malnutrition are *universal* problems.
  a. worldwide b. serious c. growing d. solvable

___ 14. Uncle Al is a *vagabond* at heart; he moves every two or three years.
  a. pedestrian b. wanderer c. sick person d. lonely person

___ 15. The governor's *veto of* the tax bill stopped it from becoming law.
  a. opinion on b. speech about c. refusal to sign d. delay of

Number correct _____ (total 15)

Using Review Words in Context

Using context clues, determine which word from the list below best fits in each blank. Write the word in the blank. Each word will be used only once.

acquire	despite	duplicate	outlook	technological
debt	diameter	financial	survive	typical
defect	domestic	obstacle	system	volume

Sound Shopping

On a bright autumn day, Mari went to the department store at the mall, hoping to _____ a complete sound _____. She wanted one that included a compact disc player, a tape deck, and a radio.

While browsing through the showroom, she noticed a system that the label claimed could _____ the sound of a live performance. The salesperson drew her attention to the speakers which were fourteen inches in _____. He described them as a _____ wonder, representing the latest advances in scientific knowledge. Even when the _____ was turned up to the highest level, these speakers would still produce clear and exact sound. He told her that the system, made by a _____ manufacturer, came with a great money-back guarantee, protecting the customer from any _____ in workmanship or material. With the enthusiasm _____ of an adolescent, Mari decided that she could not _____ without this splendid system.

Unfortunately, Mari's _____ changed when she discovered the $1200 price tag. A quick mental calculation revealed a major _____ in her plans to buy this product. Her _____ resources were about a thousand dollars short.

Of course, Mari did not simply give up, _____ the problem presented by the price. She went home to ask her parents for a loan, which she promised she would pay back from her allowance.

Mari's parents figured out how long Mari would be in _____ if they loaned her the money. With the hint of a smile on their faces, they told her that, unfortunately, she would have to give up her entire allowance for two years in order to borrow the money.

"It better be a great system," her mother advised, "because you won't have money for anything else. There'll be no movies, no restaurants . . . and no compact discs or tape cassettes."

Though disappointed by the news, Mari was realistic. She decided to keep her money and wait for the day when her bank account was larger or her parents were in a more generous mood.

Number correct _____ (total 15)

Part B   Review Word Reinforcement

Using Language and Thinking Skills

True-False Decide whether each statement is true (**T**) or false (**F**).

_____ 1. A *refinery* is a place for storing garbage.

_____ 2. A car with no *corrosion* might have a great deal of rust.

_____ 3. When airline clerks ask customers about their *destination,* they want to know where the customers are headed.

_____ 4. An attacking army might try to *dislodge* its enemy from a protected position.

_____ 5. A book that contains an *extract* of a famous poem would include the entire poem.

_____ 6. A *trace* of rain is not enough to cause a flood.

_____ 7. A football coach would be pleased if his team *monopolized* the game.

_____ 8. A *fixture* is always changing and never stays in the same place.

_____ 9. An *application* for a job is a booklet that explains the nature of the work.

_____ 10. If you were responsible for the *maintenance* of a car, you would try to keep it running smoothly.

Number correct _____ (total 10)

Practicing for Standardized Tests

Synonyms Write the letter of the word that is closest in meaning to the capitalized word.

_____ 1. CONSIDERABLE: (A) large (B) small (C) easy (D) puzzling (E) mysterious

_____ 2. DECLINE: (A) accept (B) improve (C) refuse (D) deceive (E) push

_____ 3. DEFINITELY: (A) perhaps (B) certainly (C) quickly (D) thoughtlessly (E) kindly

_____ 4. ECONOMICAL: (A) expensive (B) generous (C) foolish (D) thrifty (E) worthless

_____ 5. FALTER: (A) resolve (B) hesitate (C) surge (D) continue (E) pursue

_____ 6. INNOVATION: (A) tradition (B) process (C) security (D) agreement (E) change

_____ 7. OBVIOUSLY: (A) early (B) slowly (C) wisely (D) clearly (E) confusingly

_____ 8. POPULATE: (A) refine (B) please (C) empty (D) assist (E) inhabit

_____ 9. REQUIREMENT: (A) similarity (B) luxury (C) necessity (D) difficulty (E) solution

_____ 10. SHEER: (A) steep (B) thick (C) risky (D) heavy (E) dull

Number correct _____ (total 10)

Antonyms Write the letter of the word that is most nearly _opposite_ in meaning to the capitalized word.

_____ 1. ABANDON: (A) force (B) keep (C) reject (D) spend (E) pay

_____ 2. ACHIEVEMENT: (A) deed (B) success (C) failure (D) conclusion (E) departure

_____ 3. CONTEND: (A) fight (B) elude (C) surrender (D) decline (E) give

_____ 4. CONSUME: (A) spend (B) eat (C) enjoy (D) work (E) preserve

_____ 5. DESPERATE: (A) annoying (B) intelligent (C) confident (D) dangerous (E) accurate

_____ 6. ELIGIBLE: (A) qualified (B) admirable (C) sensible (D) unsuitable (E) favorable

_____ 7. EFFICIENTLY: (A) skillfully   (B) quietly   (C) ineffectively
(D) powerfully   (E) actively

_____ 8. EXISTENCE: (A) life   (B) determination   (C) reality
(D) death   (E) illness

_____ 9. ISOLATE: (A) separate   (B) unite   (C) remove   (D) leave
(E) return

_____ 10. PROMINENT: (A) sullen   (B) outstanding   (C) dense
(D) certain   (E) unnoticed

Number correct _____ (total 10)

Analogies Determine the relationship between the pair of capitalized words.
Then decide which other word pair expresses a similar relationship. Write the
letter of this word pair.

_____ 1. GASOLINE : REFINERY :: (A) foot : shoe   (B) water : ice
(C) lumber : lumbermill   (D) soldier : army   (E) teacher : student

_____ 2. PORTION : WHOLE :: (A) room : house   (B) circle : square
(C) mathematics : science   (D) yard : inch   (E) length : ruler

_____ 3. DEBT : OBLIGATION :: (A) loan : banker   (B) doctor : illness
(C) departure : arrival   (D) prize : award   (E) learning : school

_____ 4. FIXTURE : METAL :: (A) wood : tree   (B) coal : energy
(C) dictionary : library   (D) window : glass
(E) stove : appliance

_____ 5. CORROSION : AUTOMOBILE :: (A) freedom : prison
(B) liquid : solid   (C) lion : animal   (D) nurse : doctor
(E) termites : wood

_____ 6. RELISH : DISLIKE :: (A) delay : stop   (B) push : press
(C) cry : scream   (D) hide : reveal   (E) damage : destroy

_____ 7. DOMESTIC : FOREIGN :: (A) large : huge   (B) foolish : wise
(C) smart : brilliant   (D) strong : unbreakable
(E) comfortable : relaxed

_____ 8. VAGABOND : HOMELESS :: (A) meal : expensive
(B) dance : musical   (C) millionaire : wealthy   (D) brick : soft
(E) skin : skinny

_____ 9. TRACE : PICTURE :: (A) duplicate : poem   (B) rake : autumn
(C) swim : swimmer   (D) walk : shoe   (E) cheer : team

_____ 10. ABANDON : DESERT :: (A) move : stop   (B) whisper : shout
(C) buy : borrow   (D) crawl : walk   (E) deny : refuse

Number correct _____ (total 10)

Spelling and Wordplay

Fill-ins Spell the target word in the blanks following its definition.

1. mental attitude; way of looking at something: _ _ _ _ o o _

2. place to which one travels: _ _ _ _ i n _ _ _ _ _

3. end of the line; depot: _ e r _ _ _ _ _

4. a main road; a vessel carrying blood from the heart: _ r _ _ r _

5. anything firmly in place: _ i x _ _ _ _

6. all over the world: _ _ _ v e _ _ _ l

7. very small amount; sign or mark: _ _ _ c e

8. something that is necessary: _ _ q u _ _ _ _ _

9. to keep something to oneself: m o _ _ _ _ _ z _

10. keeping something in good repair: _ a _ n _ _ _ _ _ _ _

Number correct _____ (total 10)

Part C   Related Word Reinforcement

Using Related Words

Sentence Completion Write the word from the list below that best completes the meaning of the sentence. Each word will be used only once.

apply   defective   efficiency   finance   maintain
contention   disassembly   exclude   inclination   project

_____ 1. According to the new regulations, the team must ? anyone whose grade point average is below C.

_____ 2. The dance instructor told her students that to reach a professional level, they must ? themselves in practice.

_____ 3. The police said the accident was caused by ? brakes.

_____ 4. It took weeks to build the set for the play, but its ? took only a few hours.

_____ 5. Computers do calculations with great ? .

_____ 6. The scout troop did not know how they would ? their trip to Montana.

_____ 7. The jury did not agree with the lawyer's ? that her client was innocent.

_____ 8. Even though Gabriela was an excellent runner, she had no __?__ to join the track team.

_____ 9. The chorus leader told Darius that he needed to __?__ his voice.

_____ 10. Ahmed hoped to __?__ his undefeated record in the video game tournament.

Number correct _____ (total 10)

Reviewing Word Structures

The Roots *ject, cline, uni,* and *mono* Complete each of the following sentences with a review word that has a *ject, cline, uni,* or *mono* root. Follow the directions in parentheses.

_____ 1. Mrs. Martinez regretted that she had to __?__ the invitation because of other commitments. (Use a word with the root *cline.*)

_____ 2. The doctor asked the patient to __?__ on the examination table. (Use a word with the root *cline.*)

_____ 3. Some astronomers believe that the __?__ is expanding. (Use a word with the root *uni.*)

_____ 4. Until recently, all phone service was handled by a single company, which operated as a __?__. (Use a word with the root *mono.*)

_____ 5. Most people have an __?__ to relax in hot weather. (Use a word with the root *cline.*)

_____ 6. The boy seemed __?__ after learning about his low test score. (Use a word with the root *ject.*)

_____ 7. The judge was expected to __?__ the prisoner's plea for a new trial. (Use a word with the root *ject.*)

_____ 8. The victory last weekend seemed to __?__ new life into the team. (Use a word with the root *ject.*)

_____ 9. The house was built on a steep __?__. (Use a word with the root *cline.*)

_____ 10. The government ruled that the corporation could not __?__ the developing industry. (Use a word with the root *mono.*)

Number correct _____ (total 10)

Number correct in unit _____ (total 100)

101

Vocab Lab 2

FOCUS ON: *Areas of Study*

For a change of pace, take a look at the following words that refer to various subjects studied by people.

anthropology (an′ thrə päl′ ə jē) n. the scientific study of the cultures and social structures of societies around the world. ● Margaret Mead made important contributions to *anthropology* when she studied family structures in several primitive societies.

archaeology (är′ kē äl′ ə jē) n. the study of the life and cultures of ancient peoples, as based on the recovery and examination of ancient objects. ● The discovery in 1748 of the buried Roman city of Pompeii caused many people to become interested in *archaeology*.

botany (bät′ ′n ē) n. the scientific study of plants. ● Gregor Mendel's experiments in plant breeding helped advance the science of *botany*.

criminology (krim′ ə näl′ ə jē) n. the study of crime, criminals, and punishment. ● One branch of *criminology* focuses on efforts to rehabilitate criminals.

entomology (en′ tə mäl′ ə jē) n. the scientific study of insects. ● Those who investigate how insects pollinate fruit crops are working in the field of *entomology*.

etymology (et′ ə mäl′ ə jē) the study of the origin and development of words. ● Experts in *etymology* have to be familiar with many different languages because they need to know how words have changed in meaning as they moved from one language to another.

geology (jē äl′ ə jē) n. the science dealing with the physical nature and history of the earth. ● Scientists in the field of *geology* have been able to estimate the age of the earth by studying its rocks.

geometry (jē äm′ ə trē) n. the branch of mathematics that deals with the measurement, properties, and relationships of points, lines, angles, surfaces, and solids. ● The principles of *geometry* make it possible to determine the exact position of a ship at sea by measuring the angles formed between two stars and the horizon.

linguistics (liŋ gwis′ tiks) n. the science of language, especially its structures and developments. ● People who study *linguistics* examine such matters as how languages change and how children learn language.

meteorology (mēt′ ē ə räl′ ə jē) n. the science of the weather and the atmosphere. ● If you want to be a weather forecaster, you need to study *meteorology*.

ornithology (ôr′ nə thäl′ ə jē) n. the scientific study of birds. ● How birds migrate is one of the questions answered by the science of *ornithology*.

paleontology (pā′ lē än täl′ ə jē) n. the branch of geology that studies fossils to learn about ancient forms of plant and animal life. ● *Paleontology* helps in locating oil deposits because oil is often found in rocks that contain fossils.

political science (pə lit′ i k'l sī′ əns) n. the study of government and political institutions. ● The low turnout of voters in recent elections has been the subject of many studies in *political science*.

theology (thē äl′ ə jē) n. the study of God and of religious beliefs and practices. ● *Theology* is concerned with questions such as whether God exists and how humans may know or experience God.

zoology (zō äl′ ə jē) n. the scientific study of animals. ● The demonstration of the circulation of blood in animals was an important development in *zoology*.

Sentence Completion Write the focus word that best applies to each situation described below.

_____ 1. how human infants learn language

_____ 2. the effect of television on voting patterns

_____ 3. how geese know when to fly south

_____ 4. ancient Greek pottery

_____ 5. the origins of the word *opera*

_____ 6. the eating habits of the African lion

_____ 7. the question of whether it is possible to know the nature of God

_____ 8. the measurement of large tracks of land

_____ 9. the living habits of a tribe of people from New Guinea

_____ 10. the development of a soybean that is more resistant to disease

_____ 11. the reasons why some nations have a higher rate of violent crime than others

_____ 12. the highest and lowest temperatures recorded during a particular year in Pittsburgh

_____ 13. the shifting of large land masses beneath the ocean

_____ 14. the life expectancy of the mayfly

_____ 15. an extinct fish whose remains have been preserved in rock

Number correct _____ (total 15)

FOCUS ON: *Word Origins*

No other language in the world is growing as rapidly as the English language. Some experts have estimated that a thousand new words enter our language every year. Where do these words come from?

Compounds, Blends, Extended Words, and Clipped Words

New words are sometimes made by joining existing words or parts of words. Compounds such as *spacewalk, rollerblades,* and *videocassette* are formed by combining entire words. Blends are formed from parts of words; the word *brunch* combines the *br* in *breakfast* with the *unch* in *lunch.* Similarly, *smog* was formed from *smoke* and *fog. Nylon* was formed from *vinyl* and *cotton.*

Often, new words are rooted in the past. The word *astronaut* is a combination of two ancient Greek words: *astron,* meaning "star," and *nautes,* meaning "sailor." Thus, an astronaut is one who sails among the stars.

Other new words are formed simply by adding or dropping part of a word. *Pollster* and *gangster,* for example, were produced by adding to a base word the suffix *-ster,* meaning "a person who does" or "a person who is associated with." On the other hand, subtraction of syllables explains the origin of the words *bus* and *cab,* which come from *omnibus* and *cabriolet,* the latter being a horsedrawn two-wheeled vehicle once used as a carriage for hire.

People and Place Names, Acronyms, and Borrowed Words

Sometimes, words originate from the names of people or places. The name of Scottish scientist James Watt was given to a unit of power, the *watt;* similarly, *volt* comes from the Italian Alessandro Volta and *ohm* comes from the German Georg Simon Ohm. The word *guillotine* comes from the name of French doctor Joseph Guillotin, who first advocated its use as a "humane" way of executing criminals. Other words are derived from geographic locations associated with a product or invention—examples include *cologne* (Cologne, Germany), *hamburger* (Hamburg, Germany), and *bayonet* (Bayonne, France).

Acronyms are occasionally a source of new words. An acronym is a word formed from the first letters of a group of words. For example, NOW is the acronym for the *N*ational *O*rganization of *W*omen, and MADD is for *M*others *A*gainst *D*runk *D*riving. Some acronyms have been so accepted into the language that they are now ordinary words. The word *radar* is the acronym for *ra*dio *d*etecting *a*nd *r*anging, while *laser* comes from *l*ight *a*mplification by *s*timulated *e*mission of *r*adiation.

Many words come into the English language directly from other languages. From Italian we have taken *carnival* and *pizza;* from Spanish we have *mosquito* and *ranch; typhoon* comes from Chinese; and *bandanna* comes from the Hindi language of India. Experts believe that borrowings such as these may explain the origins of perhaps 75 percent of the words in our language.

Finding Word Origins Briefly explain the origin of each of the following words. Use the word history, or etymology, information in your dictionary.

1. sousaphone

_____

2. sandwich

_____

3. scuba

_____

4. ragamuffin

_____

5. Esperanto

_____

6. sequoia

_____

7. Pollyanna

_____

8. spaniel

_____

9. robot

_____

10. jeep

_____

11. ritzy

_____

12. orangutan

_____

13. tuxedo

_____

14. pasteurize

_____

15. boycott

_____

Number correct _____ (total 15)

Number correct in Vocab Lab _____ (total 30)

Taking Standardized Vocabulary Tests

At various times during your years in school, you have taken standardized tests. These tests are given to large groups of students around the country. Teachers use the test scores to compare your knowledge and skills with those of other students who have completed the same number of years of school.

During the next few years you will be taking many other standardized tests. Because these tests usually contain vocabulary questions, it is to your advantage to spend time becoming familiar with the major types of vocabulary test questions. These types of questions include **synonyms, antonyms,** and **sentence completion**.

This special unit offers strategies for taking standardized tests, as well as additional practice.

Part A Synonyms

As you know, **synonyms** are words that have the same meaning. Standardized test questions covering synonyms are answered by selecting the word that is closest in meaning to the given word. A typical synonym question looks like this:

FORWARD: (A) slowly (B) soon (C) ahead (D) sideways (E) backward

To answer a synonym question, use the following guidelines:

1. Try to determine the meaning of the given word before you look at the answer choices. Pay attention to any prefix, suffix, or root that may help reveal the meaning.
2. Look carefully at the answer choices. Remember to look only for words with *similar* meanings. Do not be thrown off by *antonyms*—words that are opposite in meaning. In the example above, choice (E), *backward,* is an antonym for the given word, *forward.*
3. Keep in mind that many words have more than one meaning. For example, *forward* means both "too bold" and "toward the front." If none of the answer choices seems to fit your sense of the given word's meaning, think about other meanings.
4. If you cannot readily identify the correct answer, try to eliminate any obviously incorrect answers.
5. Remember that you are looking for the *best* answer, the word that is *closest* in meaning to the given word. In the example above, *sideways* and *slow* have meanings related to movement. However, choice (C), *ahead,* is closest in meaning to *forward.*

Exercise Write the letter of the word that is closest in meaning to the capitalized word.

_____ 1. GUARANTEE: (A) product (B) topic (C) assistance
(D) warranty (E) guardian

_____ 2. OBSERVANT: (A) unconcerned (B) visible (C) breakable
(D) alert (E) wise

_____ 3. DESPERATE: (A) hopeful (B) fast (C) stupid
(D) hopeless (E) confident

_____ 4. MOBILE: (A) fixed (B) established (C) damaged
(D) movable (E) remote

_____ 5. RECALL: (A) pursue (B) communicate (C) remember
(D) forget (E) reduce

_____ 6. HAZARDOUS: (A) stubborn (B) safe (C) wicked
(D) ridiculous (E) dangerous

_____ 7. FURIOUS: (A) human (B) angry (C) crude (D) expensive
(E) calm

_____ 8. PECULIAR: (A) amusing (B) normal (C) odd (D) serious
(E) dishonest

_____ 9. PURPOSE: (A) intention (B) origin (C) cost (D) decision
(E) weakness

_____ 10. ASTONISH: (A) surprise (B) bore (C) delay (D) collect
(E) win

Number correct _____ (total 10)

Part B Antonyms

As you know, **antonyms** are words that are opposite in meaning. Standardized test questions covering antonyms are answered by selecting the word that is most nearly opposite in meaning to a given word. A typical question looks like this:

ANXIOUS: (A) calm (B) bored (C) alone (D) angry
(E) worried

To complete an antonym question, use the following guidelines:

1. Try to determine the meaning of the given word before you look at the answer choices. Pay attention to any prefix, suffix, or root that may help reveal the meaning.

2. Look carefully at the answer choices. Remember that you must find a word that is opposite in meaning. Do not be thrown off by *synonyms*—words that are similar in meaning. In the example above, choice (E), *worried,* is a synonym for the given word, *anxious.*

3. Keep in mind that many words have more than one meaning. For example, *anxious* means both "worried" and "eager." If none of the answer choices seems to fit your sense of the opposite meaning, think about other meanings for the given word.

4. If you cannot readily identify the correct answer, try to eliminate any obviously incorrect answers.

5. Remember that you are looking for the *best* answer, the word that is *most nearly opposite* in meaning. In the example above, *bored* has a meaning related to a lack of anxiety. However, choice (A), *calm,* is the most nearly opposite in meaning to *anxious.*

Exercise Write the letter of the word that is most nearly *opposite* in meaning to the capitalized word.

_____ 1. FREQUENT: (A) happy (B) common (C) seldom (D) often (E) always

_____ 2. MAGNIFICENT: (A) damaged (B) wealthy (C) splendid (D) ordinary (E) concerned

_____ 3. MUTE: (A) silent (B) talkative (C) speechless (D) whispering (E) deaf

_____ 4. CONSTANT: (A) faithful (B) steady (C) criminal (D) fast (E) changeable

_____ 5. GRASP: (A) clasp (B) hold (C) release (D) grip (E) compliment

_____ 6. DISTRIBUTE: (A) give (B) collect (C) disable (D) desire (E) spread

_____ 7. UNAWARE: (A) conscious (B) asleep (C) ignorant (D) ambitious (E) unable

_____ 8. VIVID: (A) colorful (B) sad (C) angry (D) dull (E) bright

_____ 9. INNOCENT: (A) quiet (B) blameless (C) lively (D) careful (E) guilty

_____ 10. GIGANTIC: (A) average (B) giant (C) tiny (D) heavy (E) weak

Number correct _____ (total 10)

Part C *Sentence Completion*

Sentence Completion questions test your ability to use words and to recognize relationships among parts of a sentence. A sentence-completion question gives you a sentence in which one or two words are missing. You must then choose the word or set of words that best completes the sentence. A typical sentence completion question looks like this:

A _?_ of the class needed extra instruction on the homework assignment, but only a _?_ of the students stayed after school for help.
(A) student ... few   (B) part ... portion   (C) majority ... few
(D) teacher ... minority   (E) leader ... group

To answer sentence completion questions, use the following guidelines:

1. Read the entire sentence carefully, noting key words. Pay particular attention to words such as *but* and *however*, which indicate contrast. Note any words that might indicate similarity, such as *and, the same as,* and *another.* Also look for words that might indicate cause and effect, such as *because, as a result,* and *therefore.* In the example above, the word *but* suggests that the correct word pair may contain words that are opposite in meaning.
2. Try each of the choices in the sentence. Eliminate those choices that make no sense or those that contradict some other part of the statement. In a sentence with two blanks, the right answer must correctly fill *both* blanks. A wrong answer choice often includes one correct and one incorrect word.
3. After choosing an answer, reread the entire sentence to make sure that it makes sense. Be sure that you have not ignored an answer that would create a more logical sentence than your choice.

Exercise Write the letter of the word or words that best completes the sentence.

_____ 1. Nancy talks so softly and so quickly that her speech is often _?_ .
(A) loud   (B) unintelligible   (C) interesting   (D) intelligent
(E) silly

_____ 2. The movie was so _?_ that my heart was pounding.
(A) suspenseful   (B) funny   (C) boring   (D) foreign
(E) complicated

____ 3. My uncle is a _?_ in the field of chemistry and is considered an authority on the subject.

(A) student   (B) beginner   (C) specialist   (D) stranger
(E) failure

____ 4. Ms. Barshay is so _?_ that her boss feels _?_ to give her a raise.

(A) slow ... pressured   (B) sarcastic ... inclined
(C) happy ... guilty   (D) friendly ... silly
(E) efficient ... obliged

____ 5. The author spoke _?_ about his painful and _?_ experience as a prisoner of war.

(A) eloquently ... pure   (B) bitterly ... pleasant
(C) movingly ... degrading   (D) quickly ... enjoyable
(E) fondly ... rewarding

____ 6. The smoke from the burning hamburgers _?_ the entire house, so we had to open all the windows.

(A) burned up   (B) removed   (C) spread through
(D) avoided   (E) ignited

____ 7. Although most of Ted's dreams were _?_, he had one recurring nightmare that was _?_ .

(A) silly ... funny   (B) logical ... depressing
(C) dull ... terrifying   (D) similar ... positive
(E) scary ... boring

____ 8. Janis is a trustworthy, _?_ person who would never _?_ the law.

(A) reliable ... violate   (B) safe ... obey   (C) sly ... break
(D) friendly ... study   (E) intelligent ... like

____ 9. Gary _?_ the choice of Sunset Park for the class picnic because he believed the park was too small.

(A) supported   (B) praised   (C) opposed   (D) neglected
(E) studied

____ 10. The candidate managed to _?_ enough votes to _?_ her initial lead and win the election.

(A) lose ... upset   (B) gather ... hold   (C) require ... pass
(D) gain ... lose   (E) sell ... deny

Number correct _____ (total 10)

Number correct in unit _____ (total 30)

Part D *General Strategies*

No matter what type of question you are solving, certain strategies can be applied to any part of a standardized test. Keep the following guidelines in mind. They can help you increase your chance of success. Remember, too, that a good mental attitude, plenty of rest the night before a test, and the ability to relax will further improve your test performance.

Basic Strategies for Taking Standardized Tests

1. **Read and listen to directions carefully.** This may seem obvious, but many students do poorly on tests because they misunderstand the directions or fail to read each item completely. For each question, read all of the choices before choosing an answer.

2. **Budget your time carefully.** Most standardized tests are timed, so it is important that you not spend too much time on any single item.

3. **Complete the test items you know first.** Skip items that you do not know the answer for, but mark them so that you can return to them later. After you have answered the items that you know, go back and tackle the more difficult items.

4. **Mark the answer sheet carefully and correctly.** Most standardized tests make use of computerized answer sheets. You are required to fill in a circle corresponding to the correct answer in the test booklet, as follows:

10.   Ⓐ   Ⓑ   Ⓒ   ●   Ⓔ

When using such computerized answer sheets, follow these guidelines:

a. Always completely fill in the circle for the correct answer.

b. Periodically check your numbering on the answer sheet, especially if you skip an item. Make sure your answer matches the number of the test item.

c. Never make notes or stray marks on the answer sheet. These could be misread as wrong answers by the scoring machine. Instead, write on the test booklet itself or on scratch paper, whichever is indicated in the directions.

5. **Make guesses only if you can eliminate some of the answer choices.** Random guessing is unlikely to improve your score. In fact, on some standardized tests, points are subtracted for incorrect answers. In such cases it is a better idea to leave an item blank rather than to guess wildly. However, if you can eliminate one or more of the choices, then your chance of guessing the correct answer is increased.

UNIT 9

Part A *Target Words and Their Meanings*

1. burrow (bur′ ō, -ə) n., v.
2. colleague (käl′ ēg) n.
3. component (kəm pō′ nənt) adj., n.
4. dilution (di lōō′ shən) n.
5. effective (ə fek′ tiv, i-) adj.
6. factor (fak′ tər) n.
7. habitat (hab′ ə tat′) n.
8. immunity (i myōōn′ ə tē) n.
9. lethal (lē′ thəl) adj.
10. multiple (mul′ tə p'l) adj., n.
11. particular (pər tik′ yə lər, pär-) adj., n.
12. preliminary (pri lim′ ə ner′ ē) adj.
13. prompt (prämpt) v., adj.
14. proportion (prə pôr′ shən) n., v.
15. propose (prə pōz′) v.
16. resistance (ri zis′ təns) n.
17. rodent (rōd′ 'nt) n.
18. temperament (tem′ prə mənt, -pər ə mənt) n.
19. toxin (täk′ sin) n.
20. venom (ven′ əm) n.

Inferring Meaning from Context

For each sentence write the letter of the word or phrase that is closest in meaning to the word or words in italics. Use context clues to help you choose the correct answer. (For information about how context helps you understand vocabulary, see pages 1–6.)

_____ 1. Squirrels may live in hollow trees and bears in caves, but rabbits dig *burrows* in the ground.

a. dirt b. holes c. walls d. carrots

_____ 2. Mr. Del Rio got along very well with the other employees at the library; they were his *colleagues,* and they were also his friends.

a. enemies b. neighbors c. fellow workers d. relatives

_____ 3. The electronics store in the mall sells all the *components* of a good stereo system, including speakers and turntables.

a. brands b. tools c. parts d. instructions

_____ 4. The lemonade was so strong that Andrea added more water to it, making a *dilution* of the drink.

a. mess b. weaker version c. thickening d. medicine

_____ 5. Hammers are not designed for cracking nuts, but they can be *effective*.

a. wrong b. typical c. useful d. useless

112

_____ 6. The traffic accident was the result of several *factors,* one of which was the wet pavement.

a. causes   b. systems   c. methods   d. surprises

_____ 7. Forests and wooded areas have always been the deer's *habitat,* but deer can also be found in the suburbs, where they eat shrubs and garden plants.

a. diet   b. fear   c. natural family   d. natural environment

_____ 8. Some people have severe reactions to poison ivy, but others seem to have a natural *immunity to* it.

a. attraction to   b. enjoyment of   c. protection against
d. hatred of

_____ 9. Carbon monoxide can be *lethal,* causing death in a very short period of time.

a. deadly   b. unpleasant   c. healthful   d. useful

_____ 10. A rosebush does not produce only one flower; it has *multiple* blossoms.

a. many   b. complicated   c. beautiful   d. large

_____ 11. There were hundreds of books of all kinds on the shelves, but the *particular* one she wanted was not there.

a. typical   b. specific   c. fictional   d. duplicate

_____ 12. In *preliminary* rehearsals for a play, actors may not yet know all their lines, and the stage may be just a room with a few folding chairs.

a. quick   b. beginning   c. efficient   d. final

_____ 13. Peggy's need for extra money *prompted* her search for a job.

a. prevented   b. caused   c. delayed   d. ended

_____ 14. When he asked what *proportion* of our team had scored in the last game, I said I thought it was about half.

a. leader   b. strategy   c. member   d. fraction

_____ 15. Ms. Hernandez asked for possible solutions to the litter problem. Joel *proposed* that more trash cans be put on the school grounds.

a. suggested   b. disliked the idea   c. proved   d. complained

_____ 16. Because Verna's *resistance* was low, she quickly caught the flu from her brother.

a. eligibility   b. ability to fight illness   c. integrity   d. ability to get medication.

_____ 17. Rats, mice, squirrels, and other *rodents* all have large front teeth because they do so much chewing.

a. gnawing mammals   b. dangerous mammals   c. small animals
d. pets

____ 18. In trying to understand why Tom got so angry, you must consider his *temperament;* he's just an angry sort of person.

    a. self-control b. nature c. patience d. illness

____ 19. These two mushrooms look very much alike, but the one on the left is harmless while the one on the right contains a strong *toxin.*

    a. flavor b. aroma c. poison d. texture

____ 20. The *venom* that some spiders inject into the body quickly flows into the bloodstream, causing pain, swelling, and sometimes death.

    a. stinger b. powerful medicine c. poisonous liquid
    d. soreness

Number correct _____ total (20)

Part B *Target Words in Reading and Literature*

You should now have a general idea of the meaning of each target word. Sharpen your understanding by studying how these words are used in the following selection.

Wood Rat Laughs at Rattlesnake Venom

James Coomber

John Perez, a biological researcher, uncovered an unexpected relationship in nature. In the case of the rattlesnake and the wood rat, Perez found that "good immunity makes good neighbors."

Even in a housing shortage, few people would want to room with a poisonous rattlesnake. Nevertheless, a common southwestern **rodent,** the wood rat, finds the Western diamondback rattler an acceptable **burrow** mate. Researchers at Texas A&I University in Kingsville, Texas, have discovered that it is the wood rat's blood chemistry, not **temperament,** that   5 allows this **particular** cohabitation.

Observations that wood rats can survive **multiple** rattlesnake bites **prompted** the laboratory experiments. First, the researchers obtained **venom** from caged rattlesnakes. Then, John Perez and his **colleagues** injected rodents with various **dilutions** of rattlesnake venom, as well as   10 with the full-strength venom. They found that two milliliters of full-strength venom is required to kill half of a sample group of wood rats. This dose is 140 times larger than that needed to kill the same **proportion** of mice.

"The natural **resistance** in wood rats is not surprising," says Perez, "since wood rats and rattlesnakes live in the same **habitat**—often in the   15 same burrows."

Does that mean no wood rat ever dies from a rattler bite? Not exactly. "There is no good way to measure the amount of venom released in a rattlesnake bite," Perez says. "A large rattlesnake could release three milliliters. So a large snake could kill a wood rat, but a small snake couldn't." [20] [25]

The researchers then went on to see if they could transfer the wood rat's **immunity** to venom to another animal. Perez and coworkers removed the cells from wood rat blood and injected half a milliliter of the resulting [30] serum[1] into mice. The experiment was a success. "The mice could then withstand about three times the amount of venom," Perez says.

The scientists are now working to discover what **factor** in the wood [35] rat's blood protects against the venom. **Preliminary** experiments indicate that the substance, whatever it is, does not fight the poison head-on, like a vaccine. Mixing wood rat serum and venom does not produce the same kind of chemical activity that mixing venom and vaccine does. The anti-**lethal** factor in the blood may instead be an enzyme[2] that breaks down [40] the venom **components.**

Perez is not looking only at the wood rat these days. Snakes are typically resistant to their own venom, and Perez also finds immunity in the Mexican ground squirrel, a fierce rodent that can kill a rattlesnake. He **proposes** that factors isolated in these and other studies will be useful in [45] snakebite treatment. "Venom is a very complex **toxin.** It destroys muscle and affects blood," Perez explains. That makes it dangerous and difficult to combat. However, the answer may just lie in nature's own laboratory. The most **effective** weapons against snakebites may be substances taken from the blood of rodents and from the rattlesnakes themselves. [50]

---

[1] serum: a blood fluid used as an antitoxin, taken from an animal made immune to a specific disease by inoculation

[2] enzyme: a proteinlike substance formed in plant and animal cells that helps in starting or speeding up chemical changes in other substances.

Refining Your Understanding

For each of the following items, consider how the target word is used in the passage. Write the letter of the word or phrase that best completes the sentence.

_____ 1. *Dilutions* of rattlesnake venom (line 10) would be venom that has been a. watered down b. increased in strength c. produced artificially in the laboratory.

_____ 2. If you have *resistance* (line 14) to a poison, it means that poison is a. less harmful to you b. more harmful to you c. useful to you.

_____ 3. Of the following items the one that is most likely to be *lethal* (line 40) is a. a parade b. a nuclear explosion c. a cough syrup.

_____ 4. One useful *component* (line 41) of wood rat blood may be a. milk b. water c. an enzyme.

_____ 5. Perez *proposes* (line 45) that the things learned in his studies will be useful in snakebite treatment. By using the word *proposes,* the writer indicates that Perez is a. certain b. doubtful c. predicting.

Number correct _____ (total 5)

Part C   Ways To Make New Words Your Own

By now you are familiar with the target words and their meanings. This section presents activities that will help you make the words part of your permanent vocabulary.

Using Language and Thinking Skills

Understanding Multiple Meanings Each box in this exercise contains a boldfaced word with its definitions. Read the definitions and then the sentences that use the word. Write the letter of the definition that applies to each sentence.

> **effective**
> a. producing the desired result, useful (adj.)
> b. impressive, striking (adj.)
> c. in effect, operative, activated (adj.)

_____ 1. The new dress code is *effective* as of the beginning of the school year.

_____ 2. Penicillin is highly *effective* in combating a number of serious illnesses.

116

_____ 3. That streak of red across the bright white canvas is very *effective,* don't you think?

---

particular
a. relating to a single person or thing, specific (adj.)
b. concerned with details, picky (adj.)
c. an item of information, a detail of news (n.)

_____ 4. Oh, I'll wear anything that's in my closet. I'm not *particular.*

_____ 5. We know all about the game. Lyle gave us the *particulars* when he got home.

_____ 6. That *particular* plant seems much healthier than the others.

---

prompt
a. to move to action (v.)
b. to remind someone of forgotten words (v.)
c. quick, instant, unhesitating, without delay (adj.)
d. on time, punctual, not tardy (adj.)

_____ 7. We're leaving for the party at 7:45. Be *prompt* or be left behind!

_____ 8. What in the world *prompted* you to dye your hair pink the week before the family reunion?

_____ 9. Aisha, would you watch the script and *prompt* the actors until they learn their lines?

_____ 10. A good office worker is always *prompt* in responding to letters and memos.

Number correct _____ (total 10)

Word's Worth: temperament

Sometimes a slight change in the form of a word can lead to a big change in meaning. The word *temperament* can refer to any kind of personality. You can have a calm temperament or an excitable one, an angry or a peaceful one. However, the adjective *temperamental* is used to describe a person who is moody and likely to lose his or her temper at the drop of a hat. Interestingly, though we talk about "temper tantrums" and having a "bad temper," the Latin word *temperare* means "to have a proper balance." That's why "losing one's temper" means getting angry.

True–False Decide whether each statement is true (**T**) or false (**F**).

_____ 1. In the *preliminary* stages of a painting, the finishing touches are applied.

_____ 2. If safety is a major *factor* in your decision, you would probably decide not to become a race car driver.

_____ 3. A bone that had suffered a *multiple* fracture would have more than one crack.

_____ 4. *Toxins* make dairy products better.

_____ 5. An office picnic can be a good place to get to know *colleagues* better.

_____ 6. If there is an increasing *proportion* of homeless people in a city, it probably means the city's economy is improving.

_____ 7. Many harmless snakes produce *venom*.

_____ 8. The natural *habitat* of the mouse is an owl's nest.

_____ 9. A person's *temperament* influences his or her reactions to different situations.

_____ 10. A person with natural *immunity* to measles can get measles easily.

Number correct _____ (total 10)

Practicing for Standardized Tests

Analogies Determine the relationship between the pair of capitalized words. Then decide which other word pair expresses a similar relationship. Write the letter of this word pair.

_____ 1. RAT : RODENT : : (A) canine : dog (B) feline : cat (C) snake : reptile (D) turtle : tortoise (E) zookeeper : zoo

_____ 2. PROMPT : DISCOURAGE : : (A) invent : create (B) eat : devour (C) find : lose (D) shout : communicate (E) hop : jump

_____ 3. POISON : LETHAL : : (A) book : knowledgeable (B) medicine : healing (C) race : fast (D) car : expensive (E) news report : fictional

_____ 4. PRELIMINARY : EARLY : : (A) lifelike : unrealistic (B) central : outer (C) physical : psychological (D) final : concluding (E) friendly : mean

_____ 5. PARTICULAR : GENERAL : : (A) hot : cold (B) difficult : hard (C) exterior : outside (D) childish : childlike (E) reluctant : hesitant

Number correct _____ (total 5)

Spelling and Wordplay

Word Maze Find and circle each target word in this maze.

```
A  C  O  L  L  E  A  G  U  E  J  M  F  B
E  R  O  D  E  N  T  P  M  O  R  P  A  O
I  E  M  H  P  A  R  T  I  C  U  L  A  R
X  S  Y  R  A  N  I  M  I  L  E  R  P  B
C  I  E  T  N  B  R  W  P  V  E  N  O  M
O  S  F  O  W  V  I  M  M  U  N  I  T  Y
M  T  F  X  O  L  E  T  H  A  L  U  G  N
P  A  E  I  R  X  A  F  A  C  T  O  R  Z
O  N  C  N  R  Z  M  U  L  T  I  P  L  E
N  C  T  L  U  S  Y  T  A  T  I  B  A  H
E  E  I  H  B  D  I  L  U  T  I  O  N  K
N  N  V  P  R  O  P  O  R  T  I  O  N  C
T  E  E  T  N  E  M  A  R  E  P  M  E  T
Z  P  R  O  P  O  S  E  O  X  A  R  L  N
```

burrow
colleague
component
dilution
effective
factor
habitat
immunity
lethal
multiple
particular
preliminary
prompt
proportion
propose
resistance
rodent
temperament
toxin
venom

Turn to **The Prefix _com-_** on page 218 of the **Spelling Handbook.** Read the rule and complete the exercise provided.

Part D   Related Words

The words below are closely related to the target words. Use your knowledge of the target words and of word parts to determine the meanings of these words. (For information about word parts analysis, see pages 7–13.) Use your dictionary if necessary.

1. dilute (di lōōt′, dī-) v.
2. dispose (dis pōz′) v.
3. effectively (ə fek′ tiv lē, i-) adv.
4. immune (i myōōn′) adj.
5. impose (im pōz′) v.
6. impostor (im päs′ tər) n.
7. inhabit (in hab′ it) v.
8. inhabitant (in hab′ i tənt) n.
9. nontoxic (nän′ täk′ sik) adj.
10. opponent (ə pō′ nənt) n.
11. promptness (prämpt′ nes) n.
12. proponent (prə pō′ nənt) n.
13. proportional (prə pôr′ shən ′l) adj.
14. proposal (prə pō′ z′l) n.
15. toxic (täk′ sik) adj.

Understanding Related Words

Sentence Completion Write the word from the list below that best completes the meaning of the sentence.

dilute   immune   inhabitant   promptness   proposal
effectively inhabit   nontoxic   proportional   toxic

_____ 1. It is sometimes necessary to __?__ paint so that it will be thin enough to flow smoothly from the brush.

_____ 2. The Roosevelt elk is a(n) __?__ of Washington state's rain forests, as are deer, squirrels, and a great many woodpeckers.

_____ 3. In Scandinavia, being late is considered extremely rude; __?__ is expected of any polite person.

_____ 4. A good diet can strengthen the __?__ system of the body, making the body more effective in fighting off disease.

_____ 5. Garbage that is __?__ is dangerous and must be taken to special dumps.

_____ 6. Due to the extreme cold, few people __?__ the areas around the North and South poles.

_____ 7. A lot of us had suggestions about how to improve the school elections, but Felipe was the only one who presented his __?__ to the student council.

_____ 8. The committee members worked together __?__; in a very short period of time they came up with several great ideas.

_____ 9. In the United States Senate, each state has two senators, but representation in the House is __?__, based on the relative populations of the states.

_____ 10. All art supplies used by young children should be __?__ because children so often put things in their mouths.

Number correct _____ (total 10)

Analyzing Word Parts

The Latin Root *pon/pos* The target words *component* and *propose* come from the Latin *ponere*, meaning "to put" or "to place." *Component* literally means "something placed together" (with other things), and *propose* means "to put forth." The following related words also come from this Latin word (notice that the root can be either *pon* or *pos*).

dispose   impose   impostor   opponent   proponent

In your dictionary look up the definition of each word you do not know. Then write the word from the list that best completes the meaning of the sentence.

_____ 1. In a democracy, one party should not be able to use the law to _?_ its beliefs on another.

_____ 2. Some people thought that the woman named Anastasia was a member of the Russian royal family, but others thought she was a(n) _?_ .

_____ 3. Senator Levy was willing to debate, but her _?_ in the campaign refused.

_____ 4. Hospitals are required by law to _?_ of toxic material very carefully.

_____ 5. The main _?_ of the bill gave a powerful speech in favor of it.

Number correct _____ (total 5)

Number correct in unit _____ (total 65)

The Last Word

Writing

Write a paragraph describing the *habitat* of an animal of your choice. In what part(s) of the world does this animal live? What is the climate? Does the animal change its habitat with the seasons? How does the animal's *particular* habitat aid in the animal's survival?

Speaking

Many people are *particular* about one thing or another. For example, people may be particular about their clothes, the way their room is arranged, or how their food is cooked. Explain to your class what you are most particular about and why. Are the members of your family particular about the same things? Have you always been particular about this? Do you ever wish you were not so particular?

Group Discussion

Various situations in life have the potential of being *lethal*. In small groups, develop a list of objects or situations found in your school, home, and community that might prove to be harmful or even deadly. Then make a list of suggestions for removing or avoiding these things.

UNIT 10

Part A Target Words and Their Meanings

1. adjacent (ə jā′ s'nt) adj.
2. briskly (brisk′ lē) adv.
3. contented (kən ten′ tid) adj.
4. convey (kən vā′) v.
5. curious (kyoor′ ē əs) adj.
6. delicately (del′ i kit lē) adv.
7. gesture (jes′ cher) n., v.
8. hesitate (hez′ ə tāt′) v.
9. intently (in tent′ lē) adv.
10. materialize (mə tir′ ē ə līz′) v.
11. methodically (mə thăd′ i k'l ē) adv.
12. occasional (ə kā′ zhən 'l) adj.
13. peer (pir) v., n.
14. properly (prăp′ ər lē) adv.
15. recede (ri sēd′) v.
16. responsive (ri spăn′ siv) adj.
17. stray (strā) v., n., adj.
18. transfer (trans fur′) v. (trans′ fər) n.
19. utterly (ut′ ər lē) adv.
20. wistfully (wist′ fəl ē) adv.

Inferring Meaning from Context

For each sentence write the letter of the word or phrase that is closest in meaning to the word or words in italics. Use context clues to choose the correct answer. (For information about how context helps you understand vocabulary, see pages 1–6.)

_____ 1. The plan of the house was unusual in many ways, but the garage was in the usual place, *adjacent to* the house.
    a. next to   b. around   c. across from   d. on top of

_____ 2. Kim felt wonderfully alive that fine morning, and her movements matched her mood as she walked *briskly* through the woods.
    a. casually   b. angrily   c. energetically   d. gravely

_____ 3. After Thanksgiving dinner, the family always looked well-fed and *contented*.
    a. dismayed   b. satisfied   c. convinced   d. responsible

_____ 4. Ling told us there was nothing to worry about, but the worried expression on her face *conveyed* her real concern.
    a. hid   b. communicated   c. masked   d. abandoned

_____ 5. Jake was interested not in ordinary photographs but in *curious* old pictures of unusual people and places.
    a. ugly   b. effective   c. odd   d. typical

_____ 6. Terry moved so *delicately* through the garden that not a single flower was bruised or a leaf crushed.

a. clumsily b. quickly c. daintily d. obviously

_____ 7. Tanya's wave of the arm was an enthusiastic *gesture* of greeting.

a. avoidance b. expression c. dream d. factor

_____ 8. I knew Lila wasn't sure of her next move because she *hesitated* before she put her hand on the chess piece.

a. paused uncertainly b. gazed steadily c. stood up
d. reclined

_____ 9. Lorenzo looked *intently* into the microscope, concentration showing in every line of his face.

a. briefly b. with keen attention c. with idle curiosity d. lazily

_____ 10. "What kind of ghost is this?" said Amy after reading my ghost story. "Your ghost doesn't *materialize* out of nowhere. It opens the door and walks in."

a. suddenly shout b. suddenly appear c. suddenly run away
d. suddenly disappear

_____ 11. Inspector Vance searched the office *methodically*, dividing it into sections and finishing each one before she went on to the next.

a. hurriedly b. languidly c. in an orderly way d. oddly

_____ 12. The Lorges don't go into town often, but they do make *occasional* trips for supplies.

a. remarkable b. infrequent c. strange d. fast

_____ 13. Sherlock Holmes *peered* into the small jeweled box for a long moment and then closed it with a snap.

a. glanced b. looked closely c. disappeared d. spoke

_____ 14. If you've used the drill *properly*, there should be three clean holes in the wood.

a. quickly b. correctly c. for fun d. sloppily

_____ 15. As the wave *receded*, we chased it down the beach toward the ocean.

a. rose b. became violent c. moved forward d. moved back

_____ 16. Our principal, Mr. Esperanzo, *was responsive to* our request; he answered our questions and calmed our fears immediately.

a. ignored b. read c. reacted positively to d. scolded us for

_____ 17. Dogs are not allowed in the nature preserve because they tend to *stray* from the path, damaging plants and frightening birds.

a. hurry b. vanish c. wander d. bark

_____ 18. Tired from standing all day, Keesha *transferred* her weight from one foot to another.

a. shifted   b. lost   c. increased   d. transformed

_____ 19. There was no chance the Skyhawks would win that day; the situation was *utterly* hopeless.

a. approximately   b. relatively   c. completely   d. terrifyingly

_____ 20. Since Penny and Shirelle had no money, they could only stare *wistfully* at the shiny ten-speed bicycles in the store window.

a. with desire but without hope   b. reluctantly   c. without any real interest   d. happily

Number correct _____ (total 20)

Part B   *Target Words in Reading and Literature*

You should now have a general idea of the meaning of each target word. Sharpen your understanding by studying how these words are used in the following selection.

The Incredible Journey

Sheila Burnford

The following excerpt is the beginning of a novel about an incredible journey taken by three friends—a cat and two dogs—to find their master. Through the vivid description in this passage, the author makes the three animals seem almost human.

There was a slight mist when John Longridge rose early the following morning, having fought a losing battle for the middle of the bed with his uninvited bedfellow. He shaved and dressed quickly, watching the mist roll back over the fields and the early morning sun break through. It would be a perfect fall day, warm and mellow. Downstairs he found the animals   5
waiting patiently by the door for their early morning run. He let them out, then cooked and ate his solitary breakfast. He was out in the driveway loading up his car when the dogs and cat returned from the fields. He fetched some biscuits for them, and they lay by the wall of the house in the early sun, watching him. He threw the last item into the back of the   10
car, thankful that he had already packed the guns and hunting equipment before the Labrador had seen them, then walked over and patted the heads of his audience, one by one.

"Be good," he said. "Mrs. Oakes will be here soon. Goodbye, Luath," he said to the Labrador, "I wish I could have taken you with me, but there   15 wouldn't be room in the canoe for the three of us." He put his hand under the young dog's soft muzzle. The golden-brown eyes looked steadily into his, and then the dog did an unexpected thing: he lifted his right paw and placed it in the man's hand. Longridge had seen him do this many a time to his own master, and he was curiously touched and affected by the trust it **conveyed,** almost wishing he did not have to leave immediately just after the dog had shown his first **responsive gesture.**

He looked at his watch and realized he was already late. He had no worries about leaving the animals alone outside, as they had never attempted to **stray** beyond the large garden and the **adjacent** fields; and they could return inside the house if they wished, for the kitchen door was the kind that closed slowly on a spring. All that he had to do was shoot the inside bolt while the door was open, and after that it did not close **properly** and could be pushed open from the outside. They looked **contented** enough, too—the cat was washing **methodically** behind his ears; the old dog sat on his haunches, panting after his run, his long pink tongue lolling[1] out of his grinning mouth; and the Labrador lay quietly by his side.

Longridge started the car and waved to them out of the window as he drove slowly down the drive, feeling rather foolish as he did so. "What do I expect them to do in return?" he asked himself with a smile. "Wave back or shout 'Goodbye'? The trouble is I've lived too long alone with them, and I'm becoming far too attached to them."

---

[1] lolling: hanging loosely

The car turned around the bend at the end of the long, tree-lined drive, and the animals heard the sound of the engine **receding** in the distance. The cat **transferred** his attention to a hind leg; the old dog stopped panting and lay down; the young dog remained stretched out, only his eyes moving and an **occasional** twitch of his nose. 40

Twenty minutes passed by and no move was made; then suddenly the young dog rose, stretched himself, and stood looking **intently** down the drive. He remained like this for several minutes, while the cat watched closely, one leg still pointing upward; then slowly the Labrador walked down the driveway and stood at the curve, looking back as though inviting the others to come. The old dog rose too, somewhat stiffly, and followed. Together they turned the corner, out of sight. 45 50

The cat remained **utterly** still for a full minute, blue eyes blazing in the dark mask. Then, with a **curious hesitating** run, he set off in pursuit. The dogs were waiting by the gate when he turned the corner, the old dog **peering wistfully** back, as though he hoped to see his friend Mrs. Oakes **materialize** with a juicy bone; but when the Labrador started up the road, he followed. The cat still paused by the gate, one paw lifted **delicately** in the air—undecided, questioning, hesitant until suddenly, some inner decision reached, he followed the dogs. Presently, all three disappeared from sight down the dusty road, trotting **briskly** and with purpose. 55

Refining Your Understanding

For each of the following items, consider how the target word is used in the passage. Write the letter of the word or phrase that best completes the sentence.

_____ 1. The dog's *"responsive gesture"* (line 22) indicated that the dog was beginning to   a. like the man   b. fear the man   c. recover from its illness.

_____ 2. When the man saw that the animals looked *"contented* enough" (line 29), he concluded that they would   a. be all right alone for a while   b. be restless   c. probably follow his car for miles.

_____ 3. The cat's "washing *methodically* behind his ears" (line 30) suggests that the cat washed   a. constantly   b. occasionally   c. carefully.

_____ 4. The cat's *"hesitating* run" (line 52) suggests the cat is   a. speedy   b. uncertain   c. in pain.

_____ 5. The old dog's *"peering wistfully* back" (line 54) indicates that he   a. is eager to go on a journey   b. is afraid to go anywhere   c. wishes he could stay at home.

Number correct _____ (total 5)

Part C Ways to Make New Words Your Own

By now you are familiar with the target words and their meanings. This section presents activities that will help you make the words part of your permanent vocabulary.

Using Language and Thinking Skills

Matching Examples Write the word from the list below that is most clearly related to the situation described in each sentence.

adjacent   gesture   methodically   recede   utterly
convey   hesitate   peer   transfer   wistfully

_____ 1. Harvey and his family will move to California next year, and he will go to another school.

_____ 2. In most houses, the kitchen is next to the dining room so that serving meals is easy.

_____ 3. Maria stood at the door, unsure whether she should enter the room.

_____ 4. Petra looked at the gold medal worn by his rival, wishing he had won it.

_____ 5. The waiter cleared away the plates, forks, knives, spoons, and napkins, in that order.

_____ 6. At the finish of the marathon, Lili was completely and totally exhausted.

_____ 7. The sailor's SOS was communicated by Morse code.

_____ 8. We had to stare into the dark basement until our eyes adjusted to the lack of light.

_____ 9. As the parade's winning float passed, we gave the winners the thumbs-up sign.

_____ 10. As we drove east, the mountains seemed to move away into the distance.

Number correct _____ (total 10)

Practicing for Standardized Tests

Antonyms Write the letter of the word that is most nearly *opposite* in meaning to the capitalized word.

_____ 1. MATERIALIZE: (A) disappear (B) show (C) build (D) emerge (E) manufacture

_____ 2. CONTENTED: (A) uninterested (B) delighted (C) dissatisfied (D) peaceful (E) complicated

_____ 3. DELICATELY: (A) gracefully (B) crudely (C) weakly (D) ordinarily (E) definitely

_____ 4. INTENTLY: (A) curiously (B) earnestly (C) efficiently (D) casually (E) obviously

_____ 5. OCCASIONAL: (A) special (B) constant (C) seldom (D) usual (E) methodical

_____ 6. PROPERLY: (A) strangely (B) incorrectly (C) precisely (D) typically (E) accurately

_____ 7. CURIOUS: (A) strange (B) distant (C) aloof (D) ordinary (E) dangerous

_____ 8. RESPONSIVE: (A) silent (B) energetic (C) creative (D) open-minded (E) sympathetic

_____ 9. STRAY: (A) wander (B) lose (C) remain (D) hate (E) fall

_____ 10. BRISKLY: (A) quickly (B) oddly (C) actively (D) gracefully (E) languidly

Number correct _____ (total 10)

Word's Worth: curious

You have probably known one meaning of the word *curious* for a long time. That meaning is "inquisitive" or "wanting to know." In the selection in this unit, *curious* has a different meaning: "strange" or "unusual." This meaning is related to the first meaning. You would probably be inquisitive about something strange or unusual. In other words, you might be curious about a curious object.

Curious is a member of an interesting family of words, a family that comes from the Latin word *curare,* meaning "to take care." The result of taking care may be to *cure* someone. The result may also be a precise, *accurate* job. A *curator* is one who takes care of a museum. In a museum one may look carefully at unusual things, or *curios.*

Spelling and Wordplay

Crossword Puzzle Read the clues and print the correct answer to each in the proper squares. There are 14 target words in this puzzle.

ACROSS

2. Infrequent
11. Groups of sheep
12. Language of ancient Rome
13. Adjective form of intently
16. Abbr. envelope
17. Abbr. railroad
18. An exclamation of surprise
19. A competition
22. Ocean
23. A negative word
24. _____ shucks!
25. A word of agreement
26. A necessity
28. _____ me a story
30. To go up
32. Suffix to form plurals
33. A hen lays them
37. Short for Alfred
38. See 5 Down
39. Completely
40. Abbr. Energy, Research, and Development Administration
42. I am, you _____, he or she is
43. To pause uncertainly
49. Short for Calvin
50. With thoughtful yearning
51. That man
52. To go by car
54. Appropriately
55. To look closely

DOWN

1. Gracefully; finely
2. Frequently
3. Actor: _____ Eastwood
4. To express

5. Abbr. alternating current
6. Lower parts of dresses
7. I am, you are, he or she _____
8. A Catholic Sister
9. A falsehood
10. Systematically
14. To relocate
15. Not any
20. Is in debt
21. Abbr. southeast
22. To wander off
27. Eeee__ __ eeek!
29. Allow
31. Abbr. Illinois
34. Abbr. Georgia Tech.
35. Indicate by a signal
36. Abbr. senior
38. An advertisement
41. Retreat; become less
43. Hello
44. Abbr. street
45. In case that
46. Abbr. American League
47. Abbr. total loss or true love
48. Turk __ __, monk __ __, donk __ __
50. The two of us
51. The joint formed by the thigh bone and pelvis
53. Abbr. Electrical Engineer

Part D *Related Words*

The words below are closely related to the target words. Use your knowledge of the target words and of word parts to determine the meaning of these words. (For information about word parts analysis, see pages 7–13.) Use your dictionary if necessary.

1. briskness (brisk′ nəs) n.
2. confer (kən fur′) v.
3. defer (di fur′) v.
4. hesitation (hez′ ə tā′ shən) n.
5. infer (in fur′) v.
6. intention (in ten′ shən) n.
7. material (mə tir′ ē əl) adj., n.
8. method (meth′ əd) n.
9. methodical (mə thäd′ i k′l) adj.
10. precede (pri sēd′) v.
11. refer (ri fur′) v.
12. utter (ut′ ər) adj.
13. wistful (wist′ fəl) adj.

Understanding Related Words

Close Relatives Use one of these pairs of closely related words in each sentence below. Determine which word belongs in each blank. Use a dictionary to find the meaning of any word you do not know.

material	intention	infer	precede	method
materialize	intently	transfer	recede	methodically

_____ 1. The scientist ? followed every step of the new ? for identifying bacteria.

_____ 2. From the bus driver's expression I could ? that my ? was no longer valid.

_____ 3. The seamstress kept looking in the drawer, as though her lost ? would suddenly ? there.

_____ 4. If you are concerned about your hairline starting to ? , then a special scalp treatment should ? every haircut.

_____ 5. It is my ? to win this year's Academic Award; therefore, I plan to study as ? as I can.

Number correct _____ (total 5)

Finding the Unrelated Word Write the letter of the word that is not related in meaning to the other words in the set.

_____ 1. a. utter b. absolute c. somewhat d. complete

_____ 2. a. yearning b. confident c. longing d. wistful

____ 3. a. planned   b. methodical   c. orderly   d. unorganized

____ 4. a. hesitation   b. doubt   c. certainty   d. indecision

____ 5. a. quickness   b. briskness   c. swiftness   d. laziness

Number correct _____ (total 5)

Analyzing Word Parts

The Latin Root *fer*   The target word *transfer* comes from the Latin prefix *trans-,* meaning "across," and the Latin word *ferre,* meaning "to carry" or "to bear." The following related words also contain the root *fer: confer, defer, infer, refer.* In your dictionary look up the definition of each word you do not know. Think about how the idea of carrying is contained in each word. Then write the word from the list below that best completes the meaning of the sentence.

confer   defer   infer   refer   transfer

_____   1. Before we reach a decision, I think the people who will be most affected should _?_ with each other.

_____   2. Often, an encyclopedia entry will _?_ you to other possible sources of information.

_____   3. From the evidence, Miss Marple was able to _?_ that the crime was committed by a red-haired man with a beard.

_____   4. It is possible to _?_ information from one computer system to another.

_____   5. Joanna has more experience in journalism than the rest of the class, so they usually _?_ to her when a difficult question arises.

Number correct _____ (total 5)

Number correct in unit _____ (total 60)

Turn to **Doubling the Final Consonant** and **Words with the "Seed" Sound** on pages 226 and 230 of the **Spelling Handbook.** Read the rules and complete the exercises provided.

The Last Word

Writing

Write a short description about the things in life that you need in order to feel *contented*. Your discussion may include such categories as possessions, character traits, goals, and other people. Also answer this question: Do you think it would be good to be *utterly* contented?

Speaking

Give a speech to your class about your favorite pet. Explain why you like the pet and relate any interesting stories involving the pet's behavior. It may be your own pet or a friend's or neighbor's pet that you particularly like.

Group Discussion

Stray animals have become a major problem in our country, particularly in large cities. In small groups discuss ways to solve the problem of stray animals. What are the responsibilities of pet owners? What groups or agencies can help?

UNIT 11

Part A   Target Words and Their Meanings

1. aide (ād) n.
2. apprentice (ə pren′ tis) n., v.
3. aspiration (as′ pə rā′ shən) n.
4. attitude (at′ ə tōōd′, -tyōōd′) n.
5. benefit (ben′ ə fit) n., v.
6. condition (kən dish′ ən) n., v.
7. counsel (koun′ s'l) n., v.
8. diligence (dil′ ə jəns) n.
9. employment (im ploi′ mənt) n.
10. federal (fed′ ər əl, fed′ rəl) adj.
11. immigrate (im′ ə grāt′) v.
12. industry (in′ dəs trē) n.
13. mason (mā′ s'n) n.
14. passive (pas′ iv) adj.
15. perseverance (pʉr′ sə vir′ əns) n.
16. poverty (päv′ ər tē) n.
17. private (prī′ vit) adj., n.
18. specialist (spesh′ əl ist) n.
19. sponsor (spän′ sər) n., v.
20. technically (tek′ ni k'l lē, -klē) adv.

Inferring Meaning from Context

For each sentence write the letter of the word or phrase that is closest in meaning to the word or words in italics. Use context clues to help you choose the correct answer. (For information about how context helps you understand vocabulary, see pages 1–6.)

_____ 1. As Senator Black's *aide*, Jeremy helps the senator with the many tasks he must carry out every day.

a. critic   b. assistant   c. acquaintance   d. colleague

_____ 2. *An apprentice* seldom makes much money, but the training he or she receives is very valuable.

a. An executive   b. A foreman   c. A vagabond   d. A person who learns a trade on the job

_____ 3. One of Leroy's *aspirations* is to become a doctor, and his other goal is to learn to play the piano.

a. considerations   b. ambitions   c. fears   d. requirements

_____ 4. It's not so much what Veronica does that makes people respond positively to her; it's her *attitude toward* life.

a. fear about   b. problems in   c. accomplishments in
d. outlook on

_____ 5. Cleaning up our environment today will be a real *benefit* in the future.

a. gesture   b. advantage   c. problem   d. plan

_____ 6. The task force set up to study *conditions* in developing countries dealt with everything from housing and health to recreational opportunities.

    a. existing circumstances b. government c. basic conflicts

    d. diseases

_____ 7. If you want someone to *counsel* you about your problems, you might try an older person you like and respect.

    a. advise b. warn c. lecture d. notify

_____ 8. Many of our employees work steadily and well, but Ramon's *diligence* is remarkable even here.

    a. curiosity b. poor behavior c. hard work d. recreation

_____ 9. Lorenzo plans to find *employment* as a teacher after college.

    a. work b. education c. responsibility d. recreation

_____ 10. Sacramento is the headquarters of a state government, whereas Washington, D.C., is the headquarters of the *federal* government.

    a. legislative b. universal c. city d. national

_____ 11. Years ago, people who *immigrated to* the United States first came to Ellis Island to be questioned and given health examinations.

    a. visited b. considered c. moved out of d. moved to

_____ 12. Many people insist that filmmaking is no longer an art, but only a huge *industry,* entirely devoted to making money.

    a. craft b. talent c. business d. achievement

_____ 13. The *mason* made the exterior of the church using granite from a quarry one hundred miles away.

    a. architect b. pastor c. persons who builds with stone

    d. person who raises money

_____ 14. *A passive* person can never be a good leader. For that, you need someone with get-up-and-go.

    a. A frightened b. An inactive c. A typical d. A resistant

_____ 15. Aunt Della never gave up, and in the end, her *perseverance* paid off.

    a. integrity b. relaxation c. constant effort d. intelligence

_____ 16. The fact that ninety million people in the world live on less than seventy-five dollars a year per person shows what a huge problem *poverty* is.

    a. poor behavior b. crime c. the state of being poor

    d. failure to spend money

_____ 17. Many of the small parks in London are *private,* owned not by the city but by the people whose houses surround them.

    a. popular b. darkly sheltered c. not controlled by the public

    d. military

_____ 18. Lorraine knows a great deal about science in general, but she is a marine biology *specialist*. She often gives lectures about ocean life.

a. student   b. failure   c. doctor   d. expert

_____ 19. Every year the Music Club holds a rummage sale. Money from the sale helps the club *sponsor* one student at music camp.

a. visit regularly   b. pay for   c. teach   d. pursue

_____ 20. Coach Green allowed Roberto to join the basketball team. Although *technically* Roberto was not old enough to play, the principal agreed to make an exception to the regulations.

a. possibly   b. according to the rules   c. physically
d. according to his parents

Number correct _____ (total 20)

Part B *Target Words in Reading and Literature*

You should now have a general idea of the meaning of each target word. Sharpen your understanding by studying how these words are used in the following selection.

La Vida Nueva (The New Life)

Arnold Dobrin

Ray Garcia is a Mexican American who has tried to improve living conditions in East Los Angeles. This selection tells a little about him.

Ray has the husky build of an athlete. His eyes are clear and sparkling, his hair black and glistening. He has an easy, gentle manner. But Ray Garcia grew up in a tough neighborhood—in a barrio of East Los Angeles.

Now he is working hard to change **conditions** within those barrios, the Mexican neighborhoods that have grown up near or within large cities.   5
Recently, he recalled, "When I was very young, the **attitude** was **passive.**
People said, 'Well, we are Mexicans and most Mexicans have always lived in **poverty.** They always will, so there is no point in struggling."

Ray knows this is no longer true, and most forward-thinking young people agree that there has been a remarkable change of attitude among   10
Mexican Americans in recent years. "People are trying hard," Ray says.
"Their **aspirations** are higher . . . they have more hope."

Far more people with only a limited education are speaking out. They are working together in some of the programs for community betterment.
Ray Garcia, who works for the Pacific Telephone Company, is actively   15
involved in the new programs which have attracted many Mexican Ameri-

cans. These new programs are **sponsored** by **private industry** and state and **federal** governments. "I don't think you can put a poor person with a limited education in a very responsible position right off the bat. But he or she can come in as an **aide**—and this is being done in many instances."

Diligence and **perseverance** are qualities Ray learned from his father. When he was only twelve years old, Ray Garcia's father began working as a cowboy riding the Mexican ranges from sunup to sundown. At sixteen he **immigrated** to El Paso where he worked as a farm laborer, a **mason's apprentice,** and at many other jobs. Ray recalls, "He told me the stories of how he worked as a boy, not in a bragging way but because I wanted to know and kept asking. To me, the stories said that if you have a job to do, and you really want to do it, you can. I was fortunate also in that certain teachers and older people took an interest in me. Mrs. Green, for instance, encouraged me in my artwork in grade school days. She would put up as many as ten pictures of trees on the bulletin board at the same time. Some years later another fine teacher, Mrs. Crane, helped arrange for me to attend night school when I was still in my teens, although **technically** it was for adults only.

"Later, my years of Army experience worked to my **benefit** also. I was able to prove to myself that I had the abilities I had felt were mine—the abilities to write, to speak, to teach, to **counsel.** Duty as a public information **specialist** and an NCO[1] Academy instructor gave me these opportunities."

Now that Ray has a fine family and a good job, he has turned his attention to community needs. "Those of us who are concerned with the problems of the city will need to work hard. We'll need faith, and certainly we can use a little luck if we're to deal with the problems. In East Los Angeles, as in other cities, we face problems of **employment,** housing, and education—with education the greatest problem of them all."

---

[1] NCO: Noncommissioned Officer

Refining Your Understanding

For each of the following items, consider how the target word is used in the passage. Write the letter of the word or phrase that best completes the sentence.

_____ 1. Improving *conditions* (line 4) in a neighborhood would most likely require   a. better housing   b. a party   c. moving.

_____ 2. An *aide* (line 20) in an office would be most likely to   a. make important decisions   b. hire and fire people   c. help with research.

_____ 3. A business that *sponsors* (line 17) a softball team provides, as its main contribution,   a. money   b. fans   c. encouragement.

_____ 4. Faced with a serious problem, a person with *perseverance* (line 22) would probably   a. give up   b. have second thoughts   c. work hard to find a solution.

_____ 5. A carpentry *apprentice* (line 26) would spend most of the working day   a. in a woodworking school   b. helping experienced carpenters   c. out talking to customers.

Number correct _____ (total 5)

Part C   Ways to Make New Words Your Own

By now you are familiar with the target words and their meanings. This section presents activities that will help you make the words part of your permanent vocabulary.

Using Language and Thinking Skills

Understanding Multiple Meanings Each box in this exercise contains a bold-faced word with its definitions. Read the definitions and then the sentences that use the word. Write the letter of the definition that applies to each sentence.

> **condition**
> a. a circumstance or situation (n.)
> b. a state of health (n.)
> c. anything required before the performance or completion of something else (n.)

_____ 1. Living *conditions* in some Third World countries get worse with every passing day.

_____ 2. I'll do the dishes on one *condition:* you will have to clear the table.

_____ 3. Frank is working out every day in order to get himself into *condition*.

---

counsel
a. to give advice to (v.)
b. a lawyer; one who gives legal advice to a client (n.)

_____ 4. *Counsel* for the defense objected to that line of questioning.

_____ 5. Felix's ambition is to *counsel* young people with family problems.

Number correct _____ (total 5)

Sentence Completion Write the word from the list below that best completes the meaning of the sentence.

counsel	employment	immigrate	mason	specialist
diligence	federal	industry	private	technically

_____ 1. On April 15 every year, my parents mail their state and __?__ income tax forms.

_____ 2. All through American history, people from other countries have wanted to __?__ to the United States.

_____ 3. Much of the oil __?__ in the United States is located in Texas, Alaska, and Oklahoma because these states have large oil deposits.

_____ 4. In many countries the government owns gas and electric companies, but in the United States, there is __?__ ownership of utility companies.

_____ 5. Giorgio is lazy and easygoing, but his brother Antonio is remarkable for his __?__ .

_____ 6. Many students looking for part-time jobs find __?__ in shops and restaurants.

_____ 7. Enid's boss let her take a week's vacation even though __?__ she had earned only four days of vacation time.

_____ 8. My uncle made an appointment with a doctor who is a well-known __?__ in the treatment of heart disease.

_____ 9. The Washingtons' new house is built of imported brick and stone that the __?__ obtained for them.

_____ 10. Every high school should have someone available to __?__ students about possibilities for further education.

Number correct _____ (total 10)

Practicing for Standardized Tests

Synonyms Write the letter of the word that is closest in meaning to the capitalized word.

____ 1. ASPIRATION: (A) hopelessness (B) carefulness (C) gloom (D) ambition (E) dismay

____ 2. ATTITUDE: (A) point of view (B) height (C) life goal (D) information (E) abandonment

____ 3. BENEFIT: (A) power (B) drawback (C) harm (D) interest (E) advantage

____ 4. CONDITION: (A) assembly (B) inquiry (C) situation (D) prominence (E) veto

____ 5. COUNSEL: (A) guide (B) consume (C) threaten (D) contend (E) legislate

____ 6. PASSIVE: (A) lifeless (B) aloof (C) active (D) brisk (E) busy

____ 7. PERSEVERANCE: (A) languor (B) mistreatment (C) defense (D) persistence (E) hesitation

____ 8. POVERTY: (A) riches (B) neediness (C) work (D) economics (E) problem

____ 9. SPECIALIST: (A) assistant (B) employer (C) entertainer (D) bookkeeper (E) expert

____ 10. SPONSOR: (A) answer (B) confront (C) support (D) oppose (E) express

Number correct _____ (total 10)

Word's Worth: aide

Aide-de-camp is a French word for an officer in the armed forces who acts as an assistant to a superior officer. That term was brought into the English language with the same spelling and meaning. *Aide,* a shortened form of the word, denotes not only a military assistant but anyone who assists someone. It is now often used to refer to the assistants of politicians and government officials as well as business leaders.

Spelling and Wordplay

Word Maze Find and circle each target word in this maze.

```
P A S S I V E B F U I Y N
O E D U T I T T A Q M R O
M C R O S N O P S A M T I
E N L S P E C I A L I S T
R E S A E T Y O J I G U A
A G Z E R V J H F Y R D R
L I A D F E E X V T A N I
E L Q I Z K D R C U T I P
S I M A S O N E A V E K S
N D E C E N L U F N I P A
U X Y L L A C I N H C E T
O M A P P R E N T I C E G
C O N D I T I O N W O L C
Z Y X T N E M Y O L P M E
Y T R E V O P R I V A T E
```

aide
apprentice
aspiration
attitude
condition
counsel
diligence
employment
federal
immigrate
industry
mason
passive
perseverance
poverty
private
specialist
sponsor
technically

Part D Related Words

The words below are closely related to the target words. Use your knowledge of the target words and of word parts to determine the meanings of these words. (For information about word parts analysis, see pages 7–13.) Use your dictionary if necessary.

1. aid (ād) n., v.
2. apprenticeship (ə pren′ tis ship′) n.
3. aspire (ə spīr′) v.
4. conditional (kən dish′ ən ’l) adj.
5. conspire (kən spīr′) v.
6. council (koun′ s’l) n.
7. diligent (dil′ ə jənt) adj.
8. expire (ik spīr′) v.
9. federation (fed′ ə rā′ shən) n.
10. immigrant (im′ ə grənt) adj., n.
11. inspire (in spīr′) v.
12. masonry (mā′ s’n rē) n.
13. migrate (mī′ grāt) v.
14. technique (tek nēk′) n.

Understanding Related Words

Context Definitions Define the italicized word in each of the following sentences by examining the word's context, or how it is used in the sentence. Write your definition in the blank. Check your definitions with those in the dictionary.

1. Josh's grandparents are European *immigrants,* having come to the United States from Europe in the 1930's.

   _____

2. Many birds *migrate* south for the winter.

   _____

3. As a Girl Scout, Sonia learned the proper *technique* for building a fire.

   _____

4. Before his half-time talk, Coach Brown thought of a way to *inspire* his football players to play harder in the second half of the game.

   _____

5. Mario had to fulfill a one-year *apprenticeship* at the print shop before he could work on his own.

   _____

6. Leslie *aspires* to be a great actress, and she will not settle for less.

   _____

7. The *federation* of Central American nations signed a trade agreement.

   _____

8. Lorraine is a *diligent* student whose assignments are always done carefully.

   _____

9. Until Milton has fulfilled the last two requirements for the loan, the approval of his application will be *conditional.*

   _____

10. The outside of the bank building is constructed of *masonry.*

    _____

Number correct _____ (total 10)

Turn to **The Prefix *ad-*** on page 217 of the **Spelling Handbook.** Read the rule and complete the exercise provided.

Homonyms Words with the same pronunciation but different meanings and different spellings are homonyms. Pairs of homonyms are listed in the boxes. The definitions of each word are given. In the sentences that follow, choose the correct word to fill each blank. (Note that for one sentence there are two correct choices.)

aid	**aide**
a. help; assistance (n.)	a. an assistant (n.)
b. a helper or assistant (n.)	b. an officer in the armed forces serving as an assistant to a superior (n.)

_____ 1. My grandfather was recently fitted for a hearing __?__ .

_____ 2. In the general's absence, his __?__ attended the meeting.

_____ 3. Ms. Landon is the new teacher's __?__ for the kindergarten class.

_____ 4. John and Maria came to my __?__ yesterday when I fell off my bicycle.

_____ 5. The onlookers tried to __?__ us in our attempt to coax the kitten down from the tree.

counsel	**council**
a. advice (n.)	a. a group of people called together to make rules or give advice, as a town or church council (n.)
b. to give advice (v.)	

_____ 6. Many homeroom teachers also __?__ students about their problems.

_____ 7. Harry is president of the student __?__ .

_____ 8. The lawyer gave my parents good __?__ regarding the purchase of our new house.

_____ 9. The city __?__ voted against the proposed law.

_____ 10. Dr. Kim felt he should __?__ Al about his health.

Number correct _____ (total 10)

143

Analyzing Word Parts

The Latin Root *spir* The target word *aspiration* comes from the Latin word *spirare,* meaning "to breathe." The following words also come from this same Latin word.

aspire   conspire   inspire   expire   perspire

In your dictionary look up the definition of each word you do not know. Then use each word in one of the following sentences.

_____ 1. My mother's driver's license was about to ? , so she went to the Department of Motor Vehicles to renew it.

_____ 2. If you want a good workout, you can't be afraid to ? .

_____ 3. I will never be satisfied with less than my best; I will always ? to great heights.

_____ 4. My father's talks always ? me to work harder.

_____ 5. I wish I had been alive over two centuries ago to hear Paul Revere, Samuel Adams, and other American revolutionaries ? to overthrow the British government.

Number correct _____ (total 5)

Number correct in unit _____ (total 75)

The Last Word

Writing

Staying in good physical *condition* is beneficial to a person's health. Write a paragraph about what you might do to stay in good shape. Include information on nutrition, exercise, sleeping habits, and any other factors that might affect your physical condition.

Speaking

Do you know someone who is a *specialist*? Perhaps someone in your family has special knowledge in one particular field. Or someone working in your school may be an expert in an area such as food preparation, counseling, or maintenance. Interview a specialist and present your findings in the form of a speech to your class. Tell what training the specialist received and how the person uses the special knowledge today.

Group Discussion

In the reading selection you learned about how Ray Garcia became a success—in school, at home, on the job, and in the community. In small groups, make a list of the traits you think are important for achieving success. Each group should present its list to the class, giving reasons why each trait was chosen. Finally, make a list of those traits mentioned by more than one of the groups.

UNIT 12: Review of Units 9–11

Part A Review Word List

Unit 9 Target Words

1. burrow
2. colleague
3. component
4. dilution
5. effective
6. factor
7. habitat
8. immunity
9. lethal
10. multiple
11. particular
12. preliminary
13. prompt
14. proportion
15. propose
16. resistance
17. rodent
18. temperament
19. toxin
20. venom

Unit 9 Related Words

1. dilute
2. dispose
3. effectively
4. immune
5. impose
6. impostor
7. inhabit
8. inhabitant
9. nontoxic
10. opponent
11. promptness
12. proponent
13. proportional
14. proposal
15. toxic

Unit 10 Target Words

1. adjacent
2. briskly
3. contented
4. convey
5. curious
6. delicately
7. gesture
8. hesitate
9. intently
10. materialize
11. methodically
12. occasional
13. peer
14. properly
15. recede
16. responsive
17. stray
18. transfer
19. utterly
20. wistfully

Unit 10 Related Words

1. briskness
2. confer
3. defer
4. hesitation
5. infer
6. intention
7. material
8. method
9. methodical
10. precede
11. refer
12. utter
13. wistful

Unit 11 Target Words

1. aide
2. apprentice
3. aspiration
4. attitude
5. benefit
6. condition
7. counsel
8. diligence
9. employment
10. federal
11. immigrate
12. industry
13. mason
14. passive
15. perseverance
16. poverty
17. private
18. specialist
19. sponsor
20. technically

Unit 11 Related Words

1. aid
2. apprenticeship
3. aspire
4. conditional
5. conspire
6. council
7. diligent
8. expire
9. federation
10. immigrant
11. inspire
12. masonry
13. migrate
14. technique

Inferring Meaning from Context

For each sentence write the letter of the word or phrase that is closest in meaning to the word or words in italics.

____ 1. Instead of getting all her knowledge from school, Andi is hoping to work as an electrician's *apprentice* after she graduates.
a. secretary   b. trainee   c. conductor   d. colleague

____ 2. In order to warm up for the game, Chad walked *briskly* around the park.
a. slowly   b. delicately   c. energetically   d. sadly

____ 3. The rabbit peeked out of its *burrow* to look for food.
a. tree   b. hole   c. lodge   d. bough

____ 4. The way Bette stood at the starting line *conveyed* her determination to win the race.
a. communicated   b. denied   c. hid   d. ruined

____ 5. The major *factor in* Ms. Blackwell's decision to change jobs was the long distance she had to travel to work.
a. problem in   b. benefit of   c. result of   d. cause of

____ 6. Because he was unsure of the answer, Craig *hesitated* before responding to the question.
a. explained   b. smiled   c. paused   d. gestured

____ 7. Colleen's grandparents *immigrated to* this country from Ireland.
a. escaped to   b. vacationed in   c. went out of   d. came into

____ 8. Because of his *immunity to* the disease, Kelly was able to help care for his sisters when they had the measles.
a. protection against   b. bad case of   c. interest in
d. accord with

____ 9. Some of the money for the retraining program came from the government, but most of the money came from the computer *industry*, which would profit in the long run.
a. building   b. business   c. school   d. machinery

____ 10. Mr. Franklin is *an occasional* dinner guest at my house.
a. an infrequent   b. a methodical   c. a frequent   d. a rude

____ 11. Margaret writes with one *particular* pen; she will not use any others.
a. private   b. specific   c. adjacent   d. remarkable

____ 12. If you are *passive* about things in which you are involved, you will have little control of your life.
a. intent   b. careful   c. inactive   d. secretive

_____ 13. It takes a great deal of *perseverance* to become a doctor.
a. intelligence   b. determination   c. luck   d. study

_____ 14. The campers became lost when they *strayed* off the trail.
a. hiked   b. burrowed   c. wandered   d. fell

_____ 15. Because of Violet's nasty *temperament,* I do not like to be with her.
a. friends   b. gesture   c. family   d. personality

Number correct _____ (total 15)

Using Review Words in Context

Using context clues, determine which word from the list below best fits in each blank. Write the word in the blank. Each word may be used only once.

adjacent	conditions	intently	prompted	technically
aide	contented	methodically	propose	utterly
component	diligence	preliminary	specialist	wistfully

Planning Ahead

As spring approached, the eighth graders at Elm School began to plan for their class picnic. A small committee got together to make some _____ plans. Luann spoke up at once.

"Picnics are great if it doesn't rain. But I want to know what's going to happen if _____ don't allow us to be outside."

"Oh, don't worry," said Darnell. "We'll have the picnic in the gym. The main _____ of a good picnic is food, not dirt and ants."

"Hold on!" said Bill. "We're getting ahead of ourselves. If I may make a suggestion, I _____ that we elect committee officers, make an agenda, set a date for the next meeting—"

"Oh, do you have to do everything so _____?" Luann interrupted. "The rest of us arc perfectly _____ just to talk about things."

"Let's not argue about how to do it," said Willie. "Let's just do it. Darnell, you're a food expert, so you're in charge of food. Luann's our sports and games _____, so she can take care of activities. I'll find the location. Randy, will you work on transportation? And Bill, you can write up the minutes of the meeting."

Most of the committee members wanted to get the meeting over with, and their eagerness _____ them to agree to their assignments.

148

At the next meeting, it turned out that they had all worked hard and their _____ had paid off in a well-planned picnic. "I have arranged for us to use the forest preserve that is _____ to Lake Meadow," said Willie.

"I thought that preserve closed at 4:00," said Bill.

"_____ it does, but I talked to the ranger's _____. He helps the ranger with special arrangements, and he gave us permission to stay until 5:30 P.M."

Next Darnell passed out a list of foods, which the group studied _____ enough to make it clear Darnell was not the only one who thought food was important. "This menu is _____ wonderful!" said Willie. It was approved unanimously.

The rest of the meeting went just as quickly, and, in no time, most of the members were on their way to the movies. Only Bill remained, looking _____ at *Robert's Rules of Order,* a book about how to run a meeting.

Number correct _____ (total 15)

Part B   *Review Word Reinforcement*

Using Language and Thinking Skills

True–False Decide whether each statement is true (T) or false (F).

____ 1. The *components* of a necklace might include beads and string.

____ 2. A hot day might make you want to walk more *briskly*.

____ 3. A baseball player with very high *aspirations* probably won't be happy playing anywhere except the Major Leagues.

____ 4. *Gestures* are made with the voice.

____ 5. *Private* support for a project would come from the government.

____ 6. The *venom* from a snake is usually toxic.

____ 7. A mayor's office is likely to be in the *federal* government building.

____ 8. A squirrel is considered a *rodent* because it gnaws.

____ 9. A *mason* would be a good person to hire to build a wooden bookcase.

____ 10. A *dilution* contains more water than a full-strength liquid.

Number correct _____ (total 10)

Practicing for Standardized Tests

Antonyms Write the letter of the word that is most nearly *opposite* in meaning to the capitalized word.

____ 1. CONTENTED: (A) happy (B) full (C) tired (D) dissatisfied (E) lucky

____ 2. DELICATE: (A) graceful (B) clumsy (C) weak (D) dreamy (E) emotional

____ 3. EFFECTIVE: (A) useless (B) drastic (C) unique (D) energetic (E) practical

____ 4. MULTIPLE: (A) many (B) divided (C) single (D) additional (E) accurate

____ 5. OCCASIONAL: (A) unusual (B) fancy (C) rural (D) frequent (E) clear

____ 6. PARTICULAR: (A) specific (B) picky (C) tiny (D) strange (E) general

____ 7. PASSIVE: (A) active (B) idle (C) quiet (D) strange (E) tragic

____ 8. POVERTY: (A) neediness (B) wealth (C) hardship (D) suffering (E) health

____ 9. PRELIMINARY: (A) beginning (B) early (C) grave (D) final (E) diverse

____ 10. PROPERLY: (A) accurately (B) incorrectly (C) willingly (D) casually (E) obviously

Number correct _____ (total 10)

Synonyms Write the letter of the word that is closest in meaning to the capitalized word.

____ 1. ASPIRATION: (A) ambition (B) defeat (C) devotion (D) expression (E) fear

____ 2. ATTITUDE: (A) work (B) height (C) outlook (D) ability (E) association

____ 3. BENEFIT: (A) economy (B) advantage (C) charity (D) reluctance (E) drawback

____ 4. COLLEAGUE: (A) co-worker (B) friend (C) husband (D) cooperation (E) group

_____ 5. CONVEY: (A) lead (B) memorize (C) argue (D) consume
(E) express

_____ 6. CURIOUS: (A) ordinary (B) dangerous (C) odd (D) specific
(E) tragic

_____ 7. LETHAL: (A) unfair (B) offensive (C) defective (D) deadly
(E) wishful

_____ 8. SPONSOR: (A) applaud (B) support (C) discourage (D) create
(E) resist

_____ 9. TOXIN: (A) veto (B) factor (C) poison (D) snake
(E) immunity

_____ 10. UTTERLY: (A) completely (B) properly (C) casually
(D) willingly (E) sadly

Number correct _____ (total 10)

Analogies Determine the relationship between the pair of capitalized words.
Then decide which other word pair expresses a similar relationship. Write the
letter of this word pair.

_____ 1. ADVISOR : COUNSEL :: (A) student : teach (B) track : run
(C) salesperson : buy (D) writer : write (E) book : read

_____ 2. HABITAT : FOREST :: (A) animal : cat (B) light : darkness
(C) dream : sleep (D) chair : table (E) burrow : hole

_____ 3. PROPOSE : SUGGEST :: (A) surge : fall (B) plan : build
(C) hear : see (D) work : walk (E) toss : throw

_____ 4. MATERIALIZE : DISAPPEAR :: (A) pursue : follow
(B) build : construct (C) love : hate (D) admire : imitate
(E) draw : paint

_____ 5. MASON : STONE :: (A) book : paper (B) carpenter : wood
(C) rodent : rat (D) pedestrian : sidewalk (E) seamstress : tailor

Number correct _____ (total 5)

Spelling and Wordplay

Proofreading Find the misspelled word in each of the headlines below. Spell the
word correctly in the blank.

_____ 1. TAILOR'S TEMPARMANT TIPS

_____ 2. CLOUDY SKIES WITH OCCASSIONAL SPRINKLES

_____ 3. ADJASENT HOUSES FALL TO WRECKER

_____ 4. COBRA'S VENOM IS LETHEL

151

_____ 5. RIVER'S FLOOD WATERS RECEED

_____ 6. TOP TALKS ARE PRIVITE

_____ 7. VACCINE CREATES IMUNITY

_____ 8. AIDE CALLS CHARGES UTERRLY RIDICULOUS

_____ 9. PERSEVERENCE KNOCKS OUT POVERTY

_____ 10. MAYOR RISPONSIVE TO CRITICS

Number correct _____ (total 10)

Part C   *Related Word Reinforcement*

Using Related Words

Matching Idioms An idiom is an accepted expression with a meaning different from the normal meanings of the words it contains. For example, "face the music" is an idiom meaning "accept the consequences." Match each idiom with the related word that has the same meaning. Write the letter of the matching idiom in the blank.

Related Word	**Idiom**
____ 1. impostor	a. figure out
____ 2. be diligent	b. what you have in mind
____ 3. hesitation	c. lend a hand
____ 4. confer	d. keep your nose to the grindstone
____ 5. methodical	e. run its course
____ 6. dilute	f. water down
____ 7. infer	g. by the book
____ 8. expire	h. thinking twice
____ 9. intention	i. compare notes
____ 10. aid	j. a wolf in sheep's clothing

Number correct _____ (total 10)

Reviewing Word Structures

Double Word Pyramid The suffix *-tion* is used to create an abstract noun from another part of speech. The prefix *pro-* means "in favor of" or "forward." Build a double word pyramid using the code at the base of the pyramid.

tion   pro

__ __ __ tion pro __ __ __
12 11 13   6 8 15

__ __ __ __ tion pro __ __ __ __
4 8 9 16   12 11 14 5

__ __ __ __ __ tion pro __ __ __ __ __
8 10 15 5 10   12 11 14 1 9

__ __ __ __ __ __ tion pro __ __ __ __ __
6 5 4 5 13 1   12 5 13 9 18

__ __ __ __ __ __ tion pro __ __ __ __ __ __
7 5 14 8 15 1   12 11 10 5 10 15

A B C D E F H I L N O P R S T U V Y
1 2 3 4 5 6 7 8 9 10 11 12 13 14 15 16 17 18

Match the pyramid words with their correct definitions below. Write the matching word in the blank.

_____ 1. a thinned-out mixture

_____ 2. a union of smaller powers

_____ 3. to suggest

_____ 4. money made by a business

_____ 5. purpose

_____ 6. a suggested course of action

_____ 7. uncertainty

_____ 8. correctly

_____ 9. one who is for a cause or candidate

_____ 10. a part or a serving

Number correct _____ (total 10)

Number correct in unit _____ (total 95)

Vocab Lab 3

FOCUS ON: **Geography**

The following words are used in the field of geography. Study these words and complete the exercise that follows.

butte (byo͞ot) n. a steep hill standing alone on a plain. ● While traveling across Montana, our family saw many *buttes* rising abruptly on the horizon.

canal (kə nal´) n. a channel dug for irrigation or transportation. ● The Suez *Canal* in Egypt provides a water route between the Mediterranean and Red seas.

chaparral (chap´ ə ral´, shap´-) n. a group of shrubs, thorny bushes, etc. ● In the Southwestern United States, *chaparrals* cover certain areas of the landscape.

delta (del´ tə) n. land built up by soil deposits at the mouth of a river. ● The Mississippi River *Delta* forms where the Mississippi River meets the Atlantic Ocean in the Gulf of Mexico.

estuary (es´ cho͞o wer´ ē) n. an inlet or arm of a body of water; especially, the wide mouth of a river, where the ocean tide meets the river current. ● *Estuaries* usually contain a mixture of fresh water and salt water.

fjord (fyôrd) n. a narrow inlet of the sea between steep banks or cliffs. ● The *fjords* along the mountainous coast of Norway were formed millions of years ago by glaciers.

isthmus (is´ məs) n. a narrow strip of land having water on each side and connecting two larger bodies of land. ● The *Isthmus* of Panama connects North America and South America.

marsh (märsh) n. a tract of low, wet land where grasses grow. ● Crocodiles live in the *marshes* of Florida.

oasis (ō ā´ sis) n. a place in the desert where water is found in a spring or well. ● The presence of an *oasis* in the desert makes possible the growth of crops.

peninsula (pə nin´ sə lə, -syo͞o-) n. land that is almost entirely surrounded by water, connected to a mainland on one side. ● The state of Florida is an example of a *peninsula*.

prairie (prer´ ē) n. a large region of level or slightly rolling land with tall grasses and without many trees. ● Over one hundred years ago, pioneers crossed the *prairies* of what is known today as the Midwestern United States.

savanna (se van´ ə) n. a level grassland with scattered trees, usually located in or near the Tropics. ● During the rainy season, the grass on a *savanna* grows quickly.

steppe (step) n. a large area of short, dry grass, usually located near deserts. ● In most *steppes* there is not enough rainfall to support tree growth.

tributary (trib´ yo͞o ter´ ē) n. a river or stream that flows into a larger river or stream. ● The *tributary* of the Colorado River near our house empties into the river ten miles south.

tundra (tun´ drə, toon´-) n. a large, flat, treeless plain near the polar regions of the earth. • Many flowering plants grow in the top layer of *tundra,* which thaws in spring and summer.

True–False Decide whether each statement is true **(T)** or false **(F).**

_____ 1. One would most likely find an *estuary* at the top of a mountain.

_____ 2. *Marshes* are formed where the land is low and wet.

_____ 3. *Tundra* is located in tropical regions of the world.

_____ 4. A *butte* would be easy to recognize.

_____ 5. An *oasis* is one of the few sources of water available in the desert.

_____ 6. Most *savannas* are located near the polar ice caps.

_____ 7. The state of Florida is an example of an *isthmus.*

_____ 8. *Prairies* are located in mountainous regions of the United States.

_____ 9. A *delta* connects two large bodies of land.

_____ 10. *Tributaries* always lead to similar but larger bodies of water.

_____ 11. *Steppes* are located near deserts.

_____ 12. The word *chaparral* refers to a special kind of river.

_____ 13. A *peninsula* differs from an island in that it is attached to a larger body of land.

_____ 14. Jagged cliffs often surround *fjords.*

_____ 15. *Canals* are built for the purpose of irrigation or transportation.

Number correct _____ (total 15)

FOCUS ON: *Choosing the Correct Word*

In order to communicate ideas effectively in both your writing and speaking, it is important to be precise. As you have learned in the various exercises in this book, many words in our language have similar meanings. However, even two words with similar meanings do not have *exactly* the same meaning. Knowing the differences in the meanings of words and choosing the right word is a key to successful communication.

The words *tell, relate, narrate,* and *report* all mean "to give information." However, each of these words has a slightly different meaning from the rest. One dictionary distinguishes the differences in meaning in the following way:

1. The word *tell* is a general term that means "to give the facts about some situation or occurrence."

   Example: Elizabeth would like to *tell* you what happened.

2. The word *relate* suggests the telling of some occurrence that has been personally experienced, seen, or heard.

   Example: The police officer asked Tony to *relate* the events he had witnessed.

3. The word *narrate* applies to the telling of an occurrence, as in a story or novel. Narration usually includes the development of a plot that leads toward a climax.

   Example: The storyteller will *narrate* the legend of Robin Hood for the children.

4. The word *report* suggests the giving to others of information that one has observed or studied.

   Example: The inspector was required to *report* her findings immediately.

Note that each of the above sentences presents a situation that requires the use of a specific word. If you were to replace one of the words with another, the meaning of the sentence would be less precise. Example 4 can be used to illustrate this.

The inspector was required to *tell* her findings immediately.

Although the use of the word *tell* still conveys the same general idea—that the inspector gave information to someone—the absence of the word *report* makes the sentence less descriptive. The word *report* paints a more precise picture of the way in which the inspector gave the information.

Whether speaking or writing, choose your words carefully. Precision in language is essential to effective communication.

Matching Situations Match each situation with the one synonym from the pair that best describes it. Use your dictionary if necessary.

____	1. trying to catch the bus	a. jog
____	2. getting your daily exercise	b. run
____	3. an angry skunk	a. scent
____	4. a hint of fresh flowers	b. aroma
____	5. a three-room house	a. small
____	6. a half-pound puppy	b. tiny
____	7. meeting an angry toy terrier	a. terror
____	8. meeting an angry bear	b. fright
____	9. a friend's face	a. familiar
____	10. a fact	b. known

Number correct _____ (total 10)

Using Synonyms Correctly Look up the words below in your dictionary. On the first line underneath each word, write a sentence using that word correctly. On the second line underneath each word, write a sentence using a *synonym* of that word. Your pair of sentences should correctly suggest the different shade of meaning between the original word and its synonym.

amuse

1. _____

2. _____

naive

3. _____

4. _____

poor

5. _____

6. _____

ask

7. _____

8. _____

complex

9. _____

10. _____

Number correct _____ (total 10)

Number correct in Vocab Lab _____ (total 35)

UNIT 13

Part A *Target Words and Their Meanings*

1. belated (bi lāt′id) adj.
2. belligerent (bə lij′ər ənt) adj., n.
3. bounteous (boun′tē əs) adj.
4. contemptuous (kən temp′choo wəs) adj.
5. deport (di pôrt′) v.
6. endear (in dir′) v.
7. flounder (floun′dər) v., n.
8. jubilant (joo′b'l ənt) adj.
9. memento (mi men′tō, mə-) n.
10. nucleus (noo′klē əs, nyoo′-) n.
11. operative (äp′ə rā′tiv, -er ə-) adj., n.
12. profitable (präf′it ə b'l) adj.
13. prosper (präs′pər) v.
14. quip (kwip) n., v.
15. random (ran′dəm) adj.
16. revert (ri vurt′) v.
17. sympathize (sim′pə thīz′) v.
18. tariff (tar′if) n., v.
19. unpretentious (un pri ten′shəs) adj.
20. warrant (wôr′ənt, wär′-) v., n.

Inferring Meaning from Context

For each sentence write the letter of the word or phrase that is closest in meaning to the word or words in italics. Use context clues to help you choose the correct answer. (For information about how context helps you understand vocabulary, see pages 1–6.)

_____ 1. Since Shirley's birthday was last week, the birthday party we are having for her this evening is *belated*.

a. preliminary b. surprising c. exclusive d. late

_____ 2. With someone as *belligerent* as Tom around, arguments break out all the time.

a. quarrelsome b. delicate c. friendly d. diligent

_____ 3. A *bounteous* meal filled the tables to overflowing at Thanksgiving.

a. more than sufficient b. plain and healthful c. thrifty d. grave

_____ 4. Catherine insisted she was not *contemptuous* of the television show we chose, but she sneered and made fun of it all the time we were watching.

a. proud b. scornful c. fearful d. respectful

_____ 5. A person who is *deported from* the United States usually returns to the country from which he or she came.

a. sent out of b. brought into c. imprisoned in d. accused in

_____ 6. Mary's appealing ways *endear her to* everyone who meets her.
   a. make her different from   b. make her liked by
   c. make her devoted to   d. make her more energetic than

_____ 7. Trying to get out of the swamp, Ben *floundered,* almost falling, and eventually had to call for help.
   a. swam   b. hesitated   c. struggled   d. proposed

_____ 8. The whole school was *jubilant* when our team won the tournament.
   a. passive   b. effective   c. tired   d. joyful

_____ 9. When we moved, I kept a rock from the back yard as a *memento* of our first house.
   a. reminder   b. vagabond   c. picture   d. description

_____ 10. The *nucleus* of our city is the downtown area; everything else surrounds it.
   a. exterior   b. habitat   c. diameter   d. central part

_____ 11. The new student code of behavior will be *operative* November 15. From that day on, all students will be expected to obey the new rules.
   a. wrong   b. in effect   c. realistic   d. eligible

_____ 12. Babysitting every weekend must be *profitable* for Suzanne; I just saw her in a new leather jacket.
   a. tiring   b. offensive   c. moneymaking   d. difficult

_____ 13. It is the immigrant's dream to come to the United States and *prosper.*
   a. do well   b. get by   c. leave soon   d. wander

_____ 14. People on television are always trading *quips,* but I can never think of anything funny to say until it's too late.
   a. expressions   b. gestures   c. clever remarks
   d. strange responses

_____ 15. Instead of calling on students in alphabetical order, the teacher chose students *at random.*
   a. in an unplanned way   b. carefully   c. hurriedly
   d. in a confusing way

_____ 16. As oil becomes more scarce, we may have to *revert to* sources of energy used more commonly years ago, such as coal and wood.
   a. give up   b. invent   c. go back to   d. waste

_____ 17. Fred *sympathized with* the Johnsons' problems, so he offered to help.
   a. was annoyed with   b. understood   c. sponsored   d. envied

_____ 18. The *tariffs* that a government places on goods that come into a country increase the prices of the goods.
   a. seals   b. taxes   c. discounts   d. guards

_____ 19. Although her family is one of the richest and most powerful in our town, Isabel is really a very *unpretentious* person.

a. conceited   b. proud   c. modest   d. responsive

_____ 20. Danny knew he was wrong, but he didn't think his mistake *warranted* the harsh punishment he received.

a. prevented   b. erased   c. affected   d. justified

Number correct _____ (total 20)

Part B **Target Words in Reading and Literature**

You should now have a general idea of the meaning of each target word. Sharpen your understanding by studying how these words are used in the following selection.

The Cajuns

Howard Peet

The Cajuns are a group of people who live mainly in southern Louisiana. They are descendants of the Acadians, French settlers who, in the 1600's and early 1700's, lived in southeastern Canada. This selection relates the unusual history of this group.

This is the forest primeval[1]; but where are the hearts that beneath it
Leaped like the roe,[2] when he hears in the woodland the voice of the huntsman?
Where is the thatch-roofed village, the home of Acadian farmers,—

—Henry Wadsworth Longfellow

In Henry Wadsworth Longfellow's poem *Evangeline,* the history of the Cajun culture unfolds in a moving tale of love and loyalty. Cajun history begins in the region that now includes Nova Scotia, New Brunswick, Prince Edward Island, parts of Quebec, and parts of Maine. The French settlers of this area called it Acadia. At first, they lived happily and well.   5
The land produced a **bounteous** harvest, and the farms were **profitable.** The sea, the forests, and the mountains were breathtaking in their beauty. There were no taxes or government **tariffs** to drain the wealth of the people. The Acadians, an **unpretentious** folk who enjoyed a simple existence, **prospered.**   10

However, both France and Great Britain claimed this region as their own. In 1713, the Treaty of Utrecht gave Acadia to Britain. The British were **jubilant,** of course, but the Acadians were not. They were not a

---

[1] primeval: belonging to the first ages of the world
[2] roe: a small deer

British soldiers
deporting
the Acadians

belligerent or warlike people; they did not openly rebel when British rule
became **operative.** They did, however, **sympathize** with France, their   15
native country. Their attitude, expressed in **contemptuous quips** about
the new British king and his rule, did not **endear** the Acadians to their
British neighbors—or to King George I.

In the years that followed, war between Britain and France in North
America seemed more and more likely. The British were afraid that the   20
Acadians would **revert** to their French loyalties in wartime. So, in 1755,
all Acadians who refused to take an oath of allegiance to the King of
Great Britain were **deported.** People sympathetic to the Acadians have
always argued that nothing the Acadians had done **warranted** such
severe treatment. Nonetheless, they were forced to leave behind their   25
land, homes, and most of their possessions. They were allowed to carry
only a few personal **mementos** with them.

It was a tragic time for the Acadians. They were scattered in a **random**
pattern among British colonies to the south. Many of them drifted into the
deep southern United States. For some time they **floundered** in their   30
efforts to keep their identity, but they held onto their close feelings toward
one another. Finally, a community of Acadians began to form again. Its
nucleus was near the Mississippi River Delta.

Longfellow's poem tells the story of two Acadians, Evangeline and
Gabriel, who were separated during this forced move. Evangeline's life-   35
long search for Gabriel represents the Acadians' search for their lost
home. In fact, Evangeline's kind of loyalty became one of the highest val-
ues in the culture.

The Acadians, now called the Cajuns, keep the memory of Evangeline
and the tradition of the old days alive. Under the big Evangeline Oak in   40
St. Martinville, Louisiana, is a plaque. The plaque, which bears the
names of the real-life Evangeline and Gabriel, stands as a **belated**
recognition of their devotion.

Refining Your Understanding

For each of the following items, consider how the target word is used in the passage. Write the letter of the word or phrase that best completes the sentence.

_____ 1. *Unpretentious* people such as the Acadians (line 9) would be unlikely to own   a. farms   b. warm clothes   c. expensive jewelry.

_____ 2. When the author says the Acadians *prospered* (line 10), he suggests they had   a. little to call their own   b. just enough to get by   c. all they needed and more.

_____ 3. The British people who were *jubilant* after the Treaty of Utrecht (line 13) might have   a. talked about their worries   b. had a party   c. smiled quietly.

_____ 4. The Acadians' deeds might have *warranted* the English actions against them (line 24) if the Acadians had   a. gone on with their farming   b. organized an army   c. grumbled about the situation.

_____ 5. When the author says that the Acadians "*floundered* in their efforts to keep their identity" (lines 30–31), he suggests that their attempts were   a. effective   b. ridiculous   c. not immediately successful.

Number correct _____ (total 5)

Part C Ways to Make New Words Your Own

By now you are familiar with the target words and their meanings. This section presents activities that will help you make the words part of your permanent vocabulary.

Using Language and Thinking Skills

Matching Ideas Write the letter of the word from the list below that is most clearly related to the situation described in the sentence or group of sentences.

a. deport   b. flounder   c. memento   d. prosper   e. random

_____ 1. Walking across a field, Hector suddenly stepped into a muddy area. Caught by surprise, he kicked and stumbled, trying to get to the other side.

_____ 2. The young child was told to select one gift from the pile. She could not decide which one to choose, so she closed her eyes and took the first one she touched.

_____ 3. The detectives caught the foreign criminal. He was arrested and was soon sent back to his native country.

_____ 4. The business was successful from the start. The advertising campaign attracted many customers, and sales increased every week.

_____ 5. Aiko kept a box on the shelf of her closet and into it she put old letters, special photographs, party invitations, and other souvenirs.

Number correct _____ (total 5)

True–False Decide whether each statement is true (**T**) or false (**F**).

_____ 1. If your business is _profitable_, you will probably be forced to close it soon.

_____ 2. An _unpretentious_ person usually brags a lot.

_____ 3. A _belated_ award is given some time after the achievement.

_____ 4. A _contemptuous_ person shows respect for others.

_____ 5. A person who _reverts_ to the behavior of childhood might throw food.

_____ 6. If a harvest is _bounteous,_ the farmer will probably make a great deal of money that year.

_____ 7. If your furnace is _operative,_ it can keep your house warm.

_____ 8. A grandmother would not want to spend the afternoon with a grandson who has _endeared_ himself to her.

_____ 9. If you are _deported,_ you do not go to another country.

_____ 10. Warmhearted people _sympathize_ easily with others.

Number correct _____ (total 10)

Practicing for Standardized Tests

Synonyms Write the letter of the word that is closest in meaning to the capitalized word.

_____ 1. BELLIGERENT: (A) peaceful   (B) diligent   (C) warlike   (D) impolite   (E) joyous

_____ 2. JUBILANT: (A) curious   (B) joyous   (C) sullen   (D) wistful   (E) brisk

_____ 3. MEMENTO: (A) item   (B) memo   (C) veto   (D) particle   (E) souvenir

_____ 4. NUCLEUS: (A) center   (B) rim   (C) bomb   (D) exterior   (E) factor

_____ 5. PROSPER: (A) peer (B) propose (C) succeed
(D) proceed (E) recede

_____ 6. QUIP: (A) wisecrack (B) dream (C) ending (D) strike
(E) comedian

_____ 7. SYMPATHIZE: (A) understand (B) dislike (C) sponsor
(D) oppose (E) neglect

_____ 8. TARIFF: (A) fight (B) emotion (C) tax (D) attitude
(E) port

_____ 9. UNPRETENTIOUS: (A) humble (B) barbaric (C) imaginary
(D) powerful (E) worried

_____ 10. WARRANT: (A) offend (B) compliment (C) refine
(D) arrest (E) justify

Number correct _____ (total 10)

Word's Worth: memento

In Latin, the word _memento_ means "Remember!" It is the imperative, or command, form of the verb _meminisse,_ meaning "to remember." Because of this sense of command, the English word _memento_ referred for many years not just to a reminder but to a warning. The skull-and-crossbones symbol on a bottle of lethal chemicals would have been a memento. A letter threatening a lawsuit unless a bill was paid would have been a memento. A note on a midterm report card indicating the student had better work harder if he or she wanted to pass would also have been a memento.

Over the years, however, the word _memento_ came to refer to a reminder of things past. Today it is used to refer to snapshots, dried flowers, and souvenir postcards—and not to the Surgeon General's warning on a package of cigarettes.

Spelling and Wordplay

Crossword Puzzle Read the clues and print the correct answer to each in the proper squares. There are twelve target words in this puzzle.

ACROSS

2. What a baby wears while eating
5. A clever comment
8. Not on time
11. Not odd
12. To make dear
16. The opposite of borrow
17. Small round, green vegetables
18. To make a bow or knot
19. Abbr. lane
20. With up, it means adult.
22. What you row with
24. It comes before two.
25. It can cause an illness.
28. A tax
32. To help
34. Base_ _ _ _, foot_ _ _ _, basket_ _ _ _
35. Chance; unplanned
36. Another word for Hark!
37. Abbr. dozen
38. To request
39. Abbr. Union of Soviet Socialist Republics
42. Center
45. You use it to catch butterflies.
46. An inside-out bump
47. Thoughts
50. A reminder
51. To be successful

DOWN

1. One more than six
2. Two guitars, a keyboard, and drums

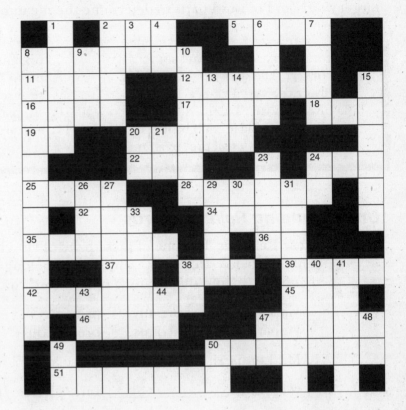

3. That thing
4. To exist
6. Employs
7. A component
8. Liking to fight
9. Short for Leonard
10. To send out of a country
13. Not old
14. Short for Daniel
15. To go back to an old way
20. Opposite of stay
21. Abbr. radium
23. To make full
24. Joan _ _ Arc

26. Past tense of run
27. Between the beginning and the end
29. Belonging to Lincoln
30. Egyptian sun god
31. To struggle awkwardly
33. Twelve
38. Abbr. Anglo-Saxon
40. A homonym for scene
41. Alaska or Iowa or Ohio
43. Abbr. compact disc
44. Abbr. of Utah
47. Contraction for I am
48. Therefore
49. Opposite of down
50. Abbr. Mister

Part D Related Words

The words below are closely related to the target words. Use your knowledge of the target words and of word parts to determine the meanings of these words.

1. controversy (kän′trə vʉr′sē) n.
2. convert (kən vʉrt′) v. (kän′vʉrt) n.
3. divert (də vʉrt′) v.
4. invert (in vʉrt′) v. (in′vʉrt) n.
5. jubilee (jōō′bə lē′, jōō bə lē′) n.
6. pretense (pri tens′, prē′ tens) n.
7. pretentious (pri ten′ shəs) adj.
8. profit (präf′it) n., v.
9. reverse (ri vʉrs′) v., adj., n.
10. sympathy (sim′pə thē) n.
11. warranty (wôr′ən tē, wär′-) n.

Understanding Related Words

Close Relatives Use one of these pairs of closely related words in each sentence below. Determine which word belongs in each blank. Use a dictionary to find the meaning of any word you do not know.

sympathy	warranty	pretense	profit	jubilant
sympathized	warrants	pretentious	profitable	jubilee

1. Mr. Lonnigan sells his merchandise at the lowest price in town. He makes

   very little _____ on each sale, but because he sells so much,

   his business is _____.

2. Alicia is _____ about performing in the _____,
   which celebrates the fiftieth anniversary of the town's founding.

3. Donald is a very _____ person. His brother, on the other hand,

   shows no _____, even though he comes from a wealthy family.

4. I _____ with Larry when his grandfather died recently, so I

   sent him a _____ card.

5. This car will be very expensive to repair, and I think that

   _____ paying the extra fee to extend the _____.

Number correct _____ (total 10)

Turn to **The Suffix -ion** on page 228 of the **Spelling Handbook.** Read the rule and complete the exercises provided.

Analyzing Word Parts

The Latin Root *vert* The target word *revert* comes from the Latin word *vertere*, meaning "to turn." The following words all come from this same Latin word:

convert   divert   invert   reverse   controversy

Review the meanings of the prefixes used in these words by looking at pages 7–8. Then, keeping in mind the meaning of *vertere*, match each related word with its correct definition. Use your dictionary if necessary.

_____ 1. to turn upside down

_____ 2. to change from one form or belief to another; exchange for something equal in value

_____ 3. to turn backward

_____ 4. a discussion in which people oppose each other

_____ 5. to turn aside

Number correct _____ (total 5)

Number correct in unit _____ (total 65)

The Last Word

Writing

The reading selection in this unit talks about the loyalty of the Cajuns. Write a paragraph telling what you think loyalty is and why it is important. Is it *profitable*? Does it help people to *prosper*? Does it *endear* people to each other? You might give an example of a loyal act you have witnessed or heard about.

Speaking

Choose a *memento* that you have kept to remind yourself of some person or event in your life. Bring the memento to class and give a short speech telling why you kept it and what it reminds you of.

Group Discussion

What do you need to make a business *profitable*? Divide into small groups. Each group should pick a type of business and prepare a list of conditions needed to make the business *prosper*. Consider the kind of product or service the business should offer, where the business might be located, and how it should be advertised. Talk about what you would look for in an employee and what kind of work atmosphere you would like to create.

UNIT 14

Part A Target Words and Their Meanings

1. abruptly (ə brupt′ lē) adv.
2. aridity (ə rid′ ə tē) n.
3. arrest (ə rest′) v., n.
4. austerely (ô stir′ lē) adv.
5. cease (sēs) v., n.
6. chaos (kā′ äs) n.
7. intangible (in tan′ jə b′l) adj., n.
8. jostle (jäs′ ′l) v., n.
9. poise (poiz) v., n.
10. quietude (kwī′ ə tōōd′, -tyōōd′) n.
11. remote (ri mōt′) adj.
12. repose (ri pōz′) n., v.
13. resilient (ri zil′ yənt, -ē ənt) adj.
14. rigid (rij′ id) adj.
15. somnolent (säm′ nə lənt) adj.
16. spirit (spir′ it) n., v.
17. travail (trav′ āl, trə vāl′) n., v.
18. turbulent (tʉr′ byə lənt) adj.
19. verge (vʉrj) n., v.
20. vertical (vʉr′ ti k′l) adj., n.

Inferring Meaning from Context

For each sentence write the letter of the word or phrase that is closest in meaning to the word or words in italics. Use context clues to help you choose the correct answer. (For information about how context helps you understand vocabulary, see pages 1–6.)

_____ 1. The car bounced when the road changed *abruptly* from blacktop to gravel.

a. gradually b. smoothly c. suddenly d. carefully

_____ 2. Rain forests are dense and damp, while deserts are known for their emptiness and *aridity*.

a. size b. toxin c. condition d. dryness

_____ 3. The statue of the running horse was so realistic that it looked as though a real animal had been *arrested* in mid-gallop.

a. tripped b. ticketed c. brushed d. stopped

_____ 4. With little time or money for luxuries, most pioneers lived *austerely* in sod houses or log cabins.

a. wastefully b. comfortably c. plainly d. joyfully

_____ 5. The moment after the music *ceased*, it seemed as though we could still hear it.

a. stopped b. became quieter c. increased d. began

_____ 6. Aisha's room was as neat as a pin, but in Tamika's room there was total *chaos*.

a. lack of order b. noise c. happiness d. calm

_____ 7. Besides food, shelter, and other objects, human beings seem to need such *intangible* things as love to really be happy.

a. physical b. painful c. cheerful d. nonmaterial

_____ 8. The people in the crowd were basically happy and well-behaved, only *jostling* each other a little and kidding the ticket takers.

a. helping b. slugging c. pursuing d. bumping

_____ 9. The huge boulder was *poised* at the edge of the cliff as if at any moment it might topple off.

a. buried b. balanced c. shoved d. unloaded

_____ 10. Having escaped the noise of the busy city, we enjoyed the *quietude* of our uncle's farm.

a. activity b. peace c. richness d. luxuriousness

_____ 11. Many people would be unhappy at the ranger station because it is so far away from civilization. Dakota, on the other hand, loves it because it is so *remote*.

a. high b. distant c. busy d. beautiful

_____ 12. David, sitting against a tree and holding a fishing pole, enjoyed his *repose* on the sunny side of the river bank.

a. exercise b. rest c. burrow d. job

_____ 13. After the storm the grass sprang back tall and straight, *resilient* as the string of an archer's bow.

a. recovering its shape quickly b. long c. droopy d. lovely

_____ 14. When spaghetti is boiled, it becomes limp. However, when it is dry, spaghetti is completely *rigid*.

a. tasteless b. bad-tasting c. slimy d. stiff

_____ 15. Even though I was sitting up, the motion of the train made me so *somnolent* I had trouble staying awake.

a. sleepy b. pretentious c. nervous d. uncomfortable

_____ 16. Because of the people who work there, that office has such a *spirit* of fun and friendliness that few employees leave for other jobs.

a. habitat b. responsibility c. mood d. ghost

_____ 17. Though many of today's job situations are difficult, few people can imagine the *travail* of those who, a hundred years ago, had to work sixteen to eighteen hours a day.

a. scars b. profit c. hard labor d. debts

_____ 18. As the storm clouds gathered and then unleashed rain while thunder roared, many old-timers said they had never seen weather more *turbulent*.

a. brisk   b. rough   c. mild   d. sudden

_____ 19. As he felt the anger rising inside him, Kevin realized he was *on the verge of* losing his temper.

a. very close to   b. far from   c. afraid of   d. deliberately

_____ 20. The supports the carpenter put up were *vertical*, reaching from the floor to the ceiling.

a. upright   b. crooked   c. metal   d. sideways

Number correct _____ (total 20)

Part B   *Target Words in Reading and Literature*

You should now have a general idea of the meaning of each target word. Sharpen your understanding by studying how these words are used in the following selection.

All Gold Canyon

Jack London

In the following selection Jack London uses colorful descriptive language to paint an appealing picture. He describes a place of great peace and beauty.

It was the green heart of the canyon, where the walls swerved back from the **rigid** plain and relieved their harshness of line by making a little sheltered nook and filling it to the brim with sweetness and roundness and softness. Here all things rested. Even the narrow stream **ceased** its **turbulent** down-rush long enough to form a quiet pool. Knee-deep in the water, with drooping head and half-shut eyes, drowsed a red-coated, many-antlered buck.   5

On one side, beginning at the very lip of the pool, was a tiny meadow, a cool, **resilient** surface of green that extended to the base of the frowning wall. Beyond the pool a gentle slope of earth ran up and up to meet the opposing wall. Fine grass covered the slope—grass that was spangled with flowers, with here and there patches of color, orange and purple and golden. Below, the canyon was shut in. There was no view. The walls leaned together **abruptly,** and the canyon ended in a **chaos** of rocks, moss-covered and hidden by a green screen of vines and creepers and boughs of trees. Up the canyon rose far hills and peaks, the big foothills,   10   15

170

pine-covered and **remote.** And far beyond, like clouds upon the border of the sky, towered minarets[1] of white, where the Sierra's eternal snows flashed **austerely** the blazes of the sun.

There was no dust in the canyon. The leaves and flowers were clean and virginal.[2] The grass was young velvet. Over the pool three cottonwoods sent their snowy fluffs fluttering down the quiet air. On the slope the blossoms of the wine-wooded manzanita[3] filled the air with springtime odors, while the leaves, wise with experience, were already beginning their **vertical** twist against the coming **aridity** of summer. In the open spaces on the slope, beyond the farthest shadow-reach of the manzanita, **poised** the mariposa lilies, like so many flights of jeweled moths suddenly **arrested** and on the **verge** of trembling into flight again. Here and there that woods harlequin,[4] the madrone,[5] permitting itself to be caught in the act of changing its pea-green trunk to madder-red,[6] breathed its fragrance into the air from great clusters of waxen bells. Creamy white were these bells, shaped like lilies of the valley, with the sweetness of perfume that is of the springtime.

There was not a sigh of wind. The air was drowsy with its weight of perfume. It was a sweetness that would have been cloying[7] had the air been heavy and humid. But the air was sharp and thin. It was as starlight transmuted[8] into atmosphere, shot through and warmed by sunshine, and flower-drenched with sweetness.

20
25
30
35
40
45

[1] minarets: towers on mosques, Moslem places of worship
[2] virginal: pure; fresh
[3] manzanita: shrub or small tree found in the western United States
[4] harlequin: a playful clown from Italian drama
[5] madrone: evergreen tree of western North America
[6] madder-red: a bright, orangy red
[7] cloying: too sweet or rich
[8] transmuted: changed from one form to another

An occasional butterfly drifted in and out through the patches of light and shade. And from all about rose the low and sleepy hum of mountain bees—feasting Sybarites[9] that **jostled** one another good-naturedly at the board, nor found time for rough discourtesy. So quietly did the little stream drip and ripple its way through the canyon that it spoke only in faint and occasional gurgles. The voice of the stream was as a drowsy whisper, ever interrupted by dozings and silences, ever lifted again in the awakenings. 50

The motion of all things was a drifting in the heart of the canyon. Sunshine and butterflies drifted in and out among the trees. The hum of the bees and the whisper of the stream were a drifting of sound. And the drifting sound and drifting color seemed to weave together in the making of a delicate and **intangible** fabric which was the **spirit** of the place. It was a spirit of peace that was not of death, but of smooth-pulsing life, of **quietude** that was not silence, of movement that was not action, of **repose** that was quick with existence without being violent with struggle and **travail.** The spirit of the place was the spirit of the peace of the living, **somnolent** with the easement[10] and content of prosperity, and undisturbed by rumors of far wars. 55 60

---

[9] Sybarites: citizens of an ancient Greek city who prized luxury
[10] easement: comfort; relief

Refining Your Understanding

For each of the following items, consider how the target word is used in the passage. Write the letter of the word or phrase that best completes the sentence.

_____ 1. By using the word *resilient* to describe the meadow (line 9), the author might be suggesting that the meadow is   a. soft and healthy   b. cool and damp   c. new and fragile.

_____ 2. The "*chaos* of rocks" (line 14) in which the canyon ends is most likely   a. a stone wall   b. a heap of boulders   c. a pit.

_____ 3. Within the context of the selection, *arrested* (line 34) suggests moths that are   a. flying quickly   b. hurt   c. frozen in mid-flight.

_____ 4. The word *travail* (line 62) suggests work that is   a. rewarding   b. painfully difficult   c. challenging.

_____ 5. By saying that the spirit of the place is *somnolent* (line 63), the author suggests   a. brightness   b. laziness   c. hopelessness.

Number correct _____ (total 5)

Part C Ways to Make New Words Your Own

By now you are familiar with the target words and their meanings. This section presents activities that will help you make the words part of your permanent vocabulary.

Using Language and Thinking Skills

Understanding Multiple Meanings Each box in this exercise contains a bold-faced word with its definitions. Read the definitions and then the sentences that use the word. Write the letter of the definition that applies to each sentence.

---

arrest
a. legal custody (n.)
b. to seize or take into custody by authority of the law (v.)
c. to stop or bring to a halt (v.)

_____ 1. Last night, Officer Brandt *arrested* two suspects in the burglary case.

_____ 2. After placing the suspects under *arrest*, Officer Brandt took them to the police station.

_____ 3. A lack of water and sunlight *arrested* the plant's growth.

---

rigid
a. not bending or flexible; stiff (adj.)
b. severe, strict; not willing to change (adj.)

_____ 4. As the extra-strength glue dries, it becomes *rigid*.

_____ 5. The rule against smoking seems *rigid*, but the reason for it is clear.

_____ 6. Perhaps it is because Mr. Greenfield is so *rigid* in his discipline that we were shocked by his laughter.

---

poise
a. ease and dignity of manner; confidence (n.)
b. to balance; keep steady; place in air without support (v.)

_____ 7. Being a member of the debate team can give a person *poise*.

_____ 8. The eagle was *poised* on the edge of the cliff, ready to attack.

_____ 9. The earth is *poised* in space.

> **spirit**
> a. a supernatural being, such as a ghost (n.)
> b. the main principle or quality (n.)
> c. enthusiasm and loyalty (n.)
> d. to carry off secretly and swiftly (v.)

_____ 10. Our team showed a lot of *spirit* in winning last week's game.

_____ 11. The fox *spirited* away two chickens before the farmer even noticed the henhouse door was open.

_____ 12. The most frightening *spirit* in Charles Dickens's book, *A Christmas Carol*, is the Ghost of Christmas Future.

_____ 13. The American Revolution is long past, but its *spirit* lives on in the minds of those who value freedom.

> **resilient**
> a. springing back into shape after being stretched, bent, or squeezed (adj.)
> b. recovering strength or a good mood quickly (adj.)

_____ 14. Karen has been through a difficult experience, but she is *resilient* and will soon be herself again.

_____ 15. In some ways, willows are stronger than oaks because they are more *resilient*.

Number correct _____ (total 15)

True–False Decide whether each statement is true **(T)** or false **(F)**.

_____ 1. A song that ends *abruptly* fades slowly into silence.

_____ 2. A prison cell would probably be furnished *austerely*.

_____ 3. If you had a bad headache, you would want it to *cease*.

_____ 4. In the middle of *chaos*, it should be easy to find some specific thing you're looking for.

_____ 5. Love, hate, envy, and courage are all *intangible*.

_____ 6. People in a crowded place tend to *jostle* each other.

_____ 7. If a place is really *remote*, people can get to it easily.

_____ 8. If people are feeling *somnolent* after Thanksgiving dinner, they probably would like to go outside and play a game.

_____ 9. A person who is on the *verge* of speech is about to say something.

_____ 10. Flagpoles, pine trees, and silos are usually *vertical*.

Number correct _____ (total 10)

Practicing for Standardized Tests

Analogies Determine the relationship between the pair of capitalized words. Then decide which other word pair expresses a similar relationship. Write the letter of this word pair.

_____ 1. QUIETUDE : PEACE ::   (A) cake : pie   (B) pages : book
(C) truth : lies   (D) respect : admiration   (E) chaos : order

_____ 2. ARIDITY : DESERT ::   (A) flatness: plains   (B) habitat : woods
(C) courage : danger   (D) snow : rain   (E) flowers : summer

_____ 3. TRAVAIL : REPOSE ::   (A) labor : work   (B) fun : games
(C) relaxation : rest   (D) night : day   (E) sleep : dream

_____ 4. STORM : TURBULENT ::   (A) rain : windy   (B) breeze : mild
(C) sun : chilly   (D) sky : near   (E) ocean : small

_____ 5. RUBBER BAND : RESILIENT ::   (A) building : rigid   (B) pillow :
warm   (C) board : unique   (D) town : silly   (E) rope : elastic

Number correct _____ (total 5)

Spelling and Wordplay

Word Maze Find and circle each target word in this maze.

A	R	I	D	I	T	Y	Y	D	I	G	I	R
R	C	E	A	S	E	S	O	A	H	C	N	S
R	D	N	B	V	T	T	D	E	A	I	T	O
E	L	Y	K	E	E	R	E	G	B	E	A	M
S	Q	B	S	R	S	A	T	R	R	S	N	N
T	U	J	P	T	O	V	O	E	U	I	G	O
D	I	E	I	I	P	A	M	V	P	O	I	L
E	E	L	R	C	E	I	E	W	T	P	B	E
I	T	T	I	A	R	L	R	D	L	R	L	N
X	U	S	T	L	R	V	L	Y	Y	B	E	T
H	D	O	T	N	E	I	L	I	S	E	R	R
C	E	J	X	T	N	E	L	U	B	R	U	T
W	A	U	S	T	E	R	E	L	Y	V	W	C

abruptly
aridity
arrest
austerely
cease
chaos
intangible
jostle
poise
quietude
remote
repose
resilient
rigid
somnolent
spirit
travail
turbulent
verge
vertical

175

Part D Related Words

The words below are closely related to the target words. Use your knowledge of the target words and of word parts to help you determine the meaning of these words. (For information about word parts analysis, see pages 7–13.) Use your dictionary if necessary.

1. abrupt (ə brupt′) adj.
2. arid (ar′ id, er′-) adj.
3. arresting (ə rest′ iŋ) adj.
4. austere (ô stir′) adj.
5. austerity (ô ster′ ə tē) n.
6. ceaseless (sēs′ lis) adj.
7. chaotic (kā ät′ ik) adj.
8. remoteness (ri mōt′ nis, -nəs) n.
9. resilience (ri zil′ yəns, -ē əns) n.
10. rigidity (ri jid′ ə tē) n.
11. spiritual (spir′ i choo wəl, -chool) adj., n.
12. tangible (tan′ jə b'l) adj.
13. turbulence (tur′ byə ləns) n.

Understanding Related Words

Matching Definitions Match each word in the list with its definition below. Write the letter of the matching word in the blank.

abrupt   austere   chaotic   resilience   tangible
arresting   ceaseless   remoteness   rigidity   turbulence

_____ 1. going on and on and on

_____ 2. the ability to spring back into shape or to recover strength or good spirits quickly

_____ 3. so striking that it makes a person stop and take notice

_____ 4. violence of motion; uproar

_____ 5. having actual form or substance; able to be touched

_____ 6. sudden

_____ 7. the quality of being distant or secluded

_____ 8. in a completely confused condition

_____ 9. the quality of being inflexible

_____ 10. very plain; without luxury

Number correct _____ (total 10)

Turn to **The Letter c** and **The Letter g** on pages 232 and 233 of the **Spelling Handbook**. Read the rules and complete the exercises provided.

Questions About Words Based on your understanding of the target words, answer the following questions about related words.

____ 1. Imagine you are on an airplane that is experiencing a great deal of *turbulence*. What would the flight attendant suggest that you do?
   a. stand up and stretch   b. eat a sandwich
   c. use your oxygen mask   d. fasten your seat belt

____ 2. Which of the following would you be most likely to find growing in an *arid* climate?
   a. fresh flowers   b. cactuses   c. oak trees   d. vegetables

____ 3. If the President of the United States suggested that citizens follow an *austerity* program, what would he be suggesting that they do?
   a. vote   b. spend money only on needed things   c. buy new cars
   d. contribute money to charity

____ 4. If you entered a day care center and it was in a *chaotic* state, what would the children there most likely be doing?
   a. yelling and running about   b. rehearsing a play   c. singing a song   d. taking a test

____ 5. What would a book on *spiritual* matters be about?
   a. mechanics   b. sports   c. religion   d. vocabulary

Number correct _____ (total 5)

Analyzing Word Parts

The Prefixes *in-* and *im-* The prefix *in-*, which is used in the target word *intangible,* has two meanings: (1) in or into, and (2) no, not, or without. The prefix *im-* has the same two meanings. The words below use *in-*.

inappropriate   inefficiently   inhabit   inject   inoperative

Write the word that best completes the meaning of each sentence.

_____ 1. Coyotes and armadillos _?_ the American Southwest.

_____ 2. Until the mechanic gets here to repair the vending machine in the hall, it will be _?_ .

_____ 3. Most people think that jeans and a sweat shirt are _?_ clothing for a wedding.

_____ 4. The researchers had to _?_ the rats with medicine.

_____ 5. Harold wasted a great deal of time and materials; he did the job very _?_ .

Number correct _____ (total 5)

Number correct in unit _____ (total 75)

Word's Worth: chaos

According to Greek myths, before the world was created, there was *Chaos*—a limitless, formless emptiness. Out of that emptiness the goddess Gaea appeared and became the great mother of all things. Eventually the word *chaos* came to be used to describe anything that was without order. This word usually does not mean something that is empty, but something that is full of things, confusion, and messiness. What are some things you might describe as *chaotic*?

The Last Word

Writing

In the reading selection for this unit, Jack London uses colorful language to describe a favorite place. Write a paragraph about one of your favorite places, using descriptive language that will help your readers picture the place in their minds. Words such as *remote, quietude,* and *aridity* may help, as well as words that describe colors and sounds.

Speaking

Think about the *intangible* things that seem to be important in life. Choose one of these things and prepare a short speech explaining why you think it is important. You might choose, for example, love, respect, dignity, or loyalty. Then give your speech in front of your class. You might want to use an example from your own experience or knowledge to illustrate the importance of the intangible quality you have chosen.

Group Discussion

In small groups, discuss the kind of *spirit* you would like to have in your school or your community. Think of ways to create that kind of spirit. Then, in a large group, compare the ideas of each small group. Discuss their differences and similarities. Choose the best suggestions and talk about whether you could actually accomplish them.

UNIT 15

Part A Target Words and Their Meanings

1. attest (ə test′) v.
2. carburetor (kär′ bə rāt′ ər) n.
3. combustion (kəm bus′ chən) n.
4. distinct (dis tiŋkt′) adj.
5. distributor (dis trib′ yoo tər) n.
6. elite (i lēt′) adj., n.
7. emission (i mish′ ən) n.
8. encounter (in koun′ tər) n., v.
9. exotic (ig zät′ ik) adj., n.
10. external (ik stʉr′ n'l) adj.
11. generation (jen′ ə rā′ shən) n.
12. internal (in tʉr′ n'l) adj.
13. merit (mer′ it) v., n.
14. metropolitan (met′ rə päl′ ə t'n) adj.
15. propel (prə pel′) v.
16. revolutionize (rev′ ə loo′ shən īz) v.
17. supremacy (sə prem′ ə sē, soo-) n.
18. thesis (thē′ sis) n.
19. trend (trend) n.
20. virtually (vʉr′ choo wəl ē) adv.

Inferring Meaning from Context

For each sentence write the letter of the word or phrase that is closest in meaning to the word or words in italics. Use context clues to help you choose the correct answer. (For information about how context helps you understand vocabulary, see pages 1–6.)

_____ 1. We bought that particular television because the research of the leading consumer magazine *attested* that it was the best on the market.
a. proved   b. denied   c. questioned   d. proposed

_____ 2. In the *carburetor* of a car's engine, air is combined with gasoline to form an explosive combination.
a. device that mixes   b. device that cleans   c. device that dilutes
d. device that cools

_____ 3. The fireman said the *combustion* was caused by a cigarette.
a. mixing   b. burning   c. alarm   d. chaos

_____ 4. As we walked by the garden, there was a *distinct* fragrance of roses.
a. mysterious   b. pretentious   c. clearly recognizable
d. pleasant

_____ 5. Electricity comes into the *distributor* and then goes out to each of the four, six, or eight spark plugs.
a. device that stops   b. device that opens   c. device that saves
d. device that divides and gives out

_____ 6. Because so few people manage to get to the summit, those who have climbed Mount Everest form an *elite* group.

a. boring   b. small and special   c. pretentious   d. diverse

_____ 7. The *emission* from the old car's exhaust pipe was thick black smoke.

a. gasoline   b. discharge   c. intake   d. corrosion

_____ 8. Each year, hundreds of people claim to *encounter* creatures from other planets.

a. fear   b. avoid   c. meet   d. photograph

_____ 9. To Americans, the idea of riding on a camel seems *exotic,* though uncomfortable.

a. courteous   b. interestingly strange   c. utterly irresponsible
d. foolish

_____ 10. The *external* parts of our house, such as the roof, gutters, shutters, and siding, suffered serious damage from the storm.

a. expensive   b. outside   c. defective   d. broken

_____ 11. With my great-grandmother, my grandmother, my mother, and me in the room, four *generations* were represented.

a. species   b. relationships   c. political parties   d. stages in a
family's history

_____ 12. The *internal* parts of your body include your heart, lungs, bones, and veins, but not your skin or hair.

a. inner   b. working   c. unique   d. fragile

_____ 13. Because Rick left his project for someone else to finish, I don't think he *merits* our highest award.

a. understands   b. needs   c. maintains   d. deserves

_____ 14. The Cincinnati *metropolitan* area includes the city and surrounding suburbs.

a. connected with a state   b. connected with a city   c. connected
with a country   d. downtown

_____ 15. A large cargo ship is powered by a mighty engine, but a small pleasure craft is more likely to be *propelled* by an outboard motor.

a. moved   b. sunk   c. pursued   d. dislodged

_____ 16. Because they enable us to work much faster, computers have *revolutionized* the way we do business today.

a. confused   b. complicated   c. slowed   d. completely changed

_____ 17. England had so many colonies that her *supremacy* among the European countries was almost unchallenged.

a. highest position   b. cruelty   c. weakness   d. belligerence

_____ 18. The professor defended the *thesis* that changes in global climate caused the extinction of the dinosaurs.

    a. concern b. proof c. fantasy d. theory

_____ 19. The *trend* in women's fashions for a while was that skirts got shorter every year.

    a. resistance b. fabric c. designer d. tendency

_____ 20. There were a few exceptions, but *virtually* everyone agreed that the carnival was a big success.

    a. not b. almost c. positively d. absolutely

Number correct _____ (total 20)

Part B *Target Words in Reading and Literature*

You should now have a general idea of the meaning of each target word. Sharpen your understanding by studying how these words are used in the following selection.

Everything Old Is New Again

Hannah Tracy

Some discoveries, inventions, and ideas catch on while others fall by the wayside. But sometimes an old idea turns out to be the solution to a new problem.

In today's world, the automobile is everywhere. Almost everyone living in a **metropolitan** area rides in a car, truck, or bus at some time every day. And the same can be said of most people who live on farms or in small towns. But there was a time, only about a hundred years ago, when a car was an **exotic** sight on the streets of even the largest cities. Only   5 an **elite** group of people could afford cars. Few of them wanted to test the **thesis** that these strange machines could get them from point A to point B. And an **encounter** between a horseless carriage and a horse usually left the horse in possession of the roadway.

And yet, the first automobile was built in 1769, several years before the   10 United States became a country. It had three wheels and was **propelled** by a steam engine. This first car, invented in France by Nicolas-Joseph Cugnot, held four people and went at the amazing speed of two miles per hour! Those who saw it had a good laugh and never imagined they were watching something that would **revolutionize** transportation and affect   15 **virtually** every area of human life.

The German inventors Gottlieb Daimler and Carl Benz, working independently of each other, are given credit for using the **internal-combustion** engine in a practical automobile in 1885. Instead of steam, this sort of car uses gasoline. The gasoline is mixed with air in the **carburetor.** 20 Then the plugs, using current from the **distributor,** give out tiny sparks, causing a series of controlled explosions. These, in turn, cause motion in the engine.

With this development the **trend** shifted toward gasoline-powered automobiles. And yet, the first automobile race ever held was won by a 25 steam-driven car. The race took place in France in 1894. The winning car went eighty miles in less than five hours—a spectacular seventeen miles per hour. A steam-driven car was also the first to go faster than two miles a minute, in Daytona Beach in 1906.

Still, the gasoline-powered car quickly gained **supremacy.** By 1898, no 30 fewer than fifty companies were manufacturing cars in the United States. Almost all of them were gasoline-powered. The American automobile industry has always shown a **distinct** indifference to the possibilities of steam.

Recent **generations,** however, are becoming more concerned about 35 saving fossil fuels and about air quality. Oil is getting scarce, and **emissions** from automobiles are now the main source of air pollution. Clearly, the steam-driven car **merits** our attention; it uses fuel more efficiently, and research reports **attest** that its **external-**combustion engine produces very little pollution. 40

A steam-powered car of the mid-1800s.

Refining Your Understanding

For each of the following items, consider how the target word is used in the passage. Write the letter of the word or phrase that best completes the sentence.

_____ 1. *Exotic* (line 5) is used here to mean   a. metallic   b. strangely beautiful   c. unfamiliar.

_____ 2. To say that an automobile is "*propelled* (line 11) by steam" means that the steam   a. moves it forward   b. heats it   c. cleans it.

_____ 3. By saying that the automobile "*revolutionized* transportation" (line 15), the author suggests that transportation was   a. thrown into confusion   b. taken out of the control of the government   c. changed completely.

_____ 4. When the gasoline-powered car "gained *supremacy*" (line 30) in the automobile industry, it achieved the   a. most efficient operation   b. most stylish car body   c. greatest acceptance in the field.

_____ 5. *Emissions* (lines 36-37) from an automobile come out of   a. the trunk   b. the exhaust pipe   c. the door.

Number correct _____ (total 5)

Part C Ways to Make New Words Your Own

By now you are familiar with the target words and their meanings. This section presents activities that will help you make the words part of your permanent vocabulary.

Using Language and Thinking Skills

Understanding Multiple Meanings Each box in this exercise contains a bold-faced word with its definitions. Read the definitions and then the sentences that use the word. Write the letter of the definition that applies to each sentence.

> **distinct**
> a. not alike; different (adj.)
> b. easily seen or heard; clear in shape or outline (adj.)
> c. so strong as to be immediately apparent (adj.)

_____ 1. Gerda has a *distinct* liking for bright colors and interesting fabrics.

_____ 2. The background of the photograph was out of focus, but the image of the horse was quite *distinct*.

_____ 3. There were four *distinct* kinds of marigolds in the garden.

> **distributor**
> a. a device for dividing and conducting electric current toward the spark plugs of a gasoline engine (n.)
> b. a business firm that sends goods from a variety of manufacturers to customers or dealers (n.)
> c. any person or institution that divides something and gives it out in shares (n.)

____ 4. The bookstore can't get that book directly from the publisher. It will have to be ordered from a *distributor*.

____ 5. In our city, the People's Kitchen is the largest *distributor* of food to the homeless.

____ 6. The problem with this car doesn't seem to be in the battery. It must be in the *distributor*.

> **encounter**
> a. a direct or unexpected meeting (n.)
> b. to meet, usually unexpectedly (v.)
> c. to face difficulties, troubles, etc. (v.)

____ 7. While we were hiking in the forest, we *encountered* a family of bears drinking at a stream.

____ 8. We did succeed in climbing the mountain, but we certainly *encountered* a lot of problems on the way.

____ 9. My first *encounter* with Joe was the time he helped me pick up all the groceries I had spilled on the sidewalk.

> **generation**
> a. the act of creation or production (n.)
> b. a single stage in the history of a family (n.)
> c. all the people born at about the same time (n.)

____ 10. The baby-boom *generation,* born in the late forties and in the fifties, has had an important influence on this country for many years.

____ 11. In our family, my aunt and I think most alike, even though we are of different *generations*.

____ 12. As a copywriter, Janet's responsibility is the *generation* of twenty pages of written material for advertisements per week.

> **merit**
> a. worth, value, or excellence (n.)
> b. to deserve or be worthy of (v.)
> c. a mark or point awarded for excellence (n.)

_____ 13. At camp today, Kevin received three *merits* for cleaning his cabin and five for passing the swimming test.

_____ 14. I think the plan *merits* our serious consideration.

_____ 15. I don't agree with everything that group says, but I think there is great *merit* in their work.

Number correct _____ (total 15)

Finding the Unrelated Word Write the letter of the word that is not related in meaning to the other words in the set.

_____ 1. a. nearly   b. entirely   c. almost   d. virtually

_____ 2. a. flame   b. combustion   c. cool   d. burning

_____ 3. a. destruction   b. creation   c. generation   d. production

_____ 4. a. merit   b. virtue   c. excellence   d. fault

_____ 5. a. swear   b. attest   c. examine   d. declare

_____ 6. a. proposal   b. thesis   c. feeling   d. idea

_____ 7. a. encounter   b. meeting   c. expression   d. appointment

_____ 8. a. trend   b. style   c. tendency   d. life

_____ 9. a. external   b. internal   c. outside   d. outer

_____ 10. a. change   b. transform   c. revolutionize   d. explain

Number correct _____ (total 10)

True–False Decide whether each statement is true (T) or false (F).

_____ 1. If an expert *attested* that a painting was an original work and not just a clever imitation, a museum would probably remove it from display.

_____ 2. An *elite* group would probably have a great many people in it.

_____ 3. If you *encountered* a group of tourists at the Washington Monument, you would probably feel surprised.

_____ 4. A fender is an *external* part of a car.

_____ 5. An employee who *merits* a raise has done the job well.

_____ 6. A *metropolitan* area has a great many more cars than cows.

_____ 7. Someone who belongs to your *generation* would be the same age as your grandfather.

_____ 8. A *thesis* is a proven piece of information.

_____ 9. A *trend* toward going barefoot would be bad news for the shoe industry.

_____ 10. If *virtually* everyone ate a balanced diet, the world would be a healthier place.

Number correct _____ (total 10)

Practicing for Standardized Tests

Analogies Determine the relationship between the capitalized pair of words. Then decide which other word pair expresses a similar relationship. Write the letter of this word pair.

_____ 1. ATTEST : DENY :: (A) realize : notice (B) work : labor (C) rise : fall (D) run : skip (E) write : draw

_____ 2. CARBURETOR : MIX :: (A) dreamer : eat (B) dishwasher : wash (C) tree : chop (D) picture : paint (E) ceiling : paint

_____ 3. SUPREMACY : SUPERIORITY :: (A) light : brightness (B) statue : painting (C) game : victory (D) forest : tree (E) wall : floor

_____ 4. PEEL : EXTERNAL :: (A) juice : thick (B) diamonds : cheap (C) floor : vertical (D) ocean : arid (E) core : internal

_____ 5. ENGINE : PROPEL :: (A) quip : laugh (B) brakes : stop (C) memento : keep (D) dream : sleep (E) pot : scrub

Number correct _____ (total 5)

Spelling and Wordplay

Fill-ins Spell the target word correctly in the blanks to the right of its definition.

1. the act or process of burning: <u>c</u> __ <u>m</u> <u>b</u> __ __ __ __ __ __

2. confirm: <u>a</u> __ __ __ __ __

3. inner: <u>i</u> __ __ __ __ __ __ __

4. fuel exhaust: __ <u>m</u> __ __ __ __ __ __

5. to change completely: _ _ v _ _ _ _ i _ _ _ _ _

6. device that mixes: c _ _ b _ _ _ _ _ _

7. outside: _ _ _ _ r _ _ _ _

8. almost: v _ _ _ u _ _ _ _

9. special; high-class: _ _ _ _ e _

10. tendency: _ _ _ n _

11. of or pertaining to a city: m _ _ _ _ p _ _ _ _ _ _

12. well-defined: d _ _ _ _ _ _ _

13. dominance: s _ p _ _ _ _ c _

14. to meet: e _ _ _ u _ _ _ _

15. group of people born in the same time period:

_ _ n _ _ a _ _ o _

16. to cause to move forward: _ _ _ p _ _

17. device that spreads electrical current; a business that allots goods to

consumers: d _ _ _ _ i _ _ _ _ _

18. theory; idea: _ _ _ s _ _

19. strange and fascinating: e _ _ _ _ _

20. to be worthy of: m _ _ _ _ _

Number correct _____ (total 20)

Word's Worth: *trend*

The Middle English word *trenden* was a geographic term used to describe the way rivers run. Specifically, it dealt with how the course of a river changes, or "turns about," in response to the contour of hills, plains, and other features of the land. A little more than a century ago, the word began to mean "direction" or "tendency." For example, it might refer to current ideas in a given field, such as literature, science, or history. In the early 1960's, the word *trendy* appeared. In referring to a current or popular style that is unlikely to last, *trendy* keeps part of the original sense of *trend*, which referred to abrupt changes in a river's course.

Part D Related Words

The words below are closely related to the target words. Use your knowledge of the target words and of word parts to help you determine the meaning of these words.

1. combustible (kəm bus′ tə b′l) adj.
2. distinction (dis tiŋk′ shən) n.
3. distinctive (dis tiŋk′ tiv) adj.
4. distribute (dis trib′ yoot) v.
5. distribution (dis′ trə byoo′ shən) n.
6. elitist (i lēt′ ist) adj., n.
7. emit (i mit′) v.
8. exotically (ig zät′ i kəl lē) adv.
9. generate (jen′ ə rāt′) v.
10. meritorious (mer′ ə tôr′ ē əs) adj.
11. propeller (prə pel′ ər) n.
12. revolt (ri vōlt′) v., n.
13. revolution (rev′ ə loo′ shēn) n.
14. supreme (sə prēm′, soo-) adj.
15. supremely (sə prēm′ lē, soo-) adv.
16. virtual (vʉr′ choo wəl) adj.

Understanding Related Words

Finding Examples Write the letter of the situation that best shows the meaning of the boldfaced word.

_____ 1. **distribute**

a. to look into the causes of air pollution
b. to get paid for baby-sitting
c. to divide money and give it to five different charities

_____ 2. **elitist**

a. making a list of chores to be done
b. inviting only a select few to a party
c. exploring an unknown area

_____ 3. **emit**

a. to leave a word out of a sentence
b. to release steam from a kettle
c. to take a breath of fresh air

_____ 4. **revolution**

a. making a great deal of noise
b. overthrowing a government in order to set up a new one
c. doing sit-ups

_____ 5. **supreme**

a. the commander in chief of the armed forces
b. the vice-president of the United States
c. a silver medal in the Olympics

Number correct _____ (total 5)

Sentence Completion Write the word from the list below that best completes the meaning of the sentence.

combustible   elitist   generate   propeller   supremely
distinctive   exotically   meritorious revolted   virtual

_____ 1. The hothouse flowers with their brilliant otherwordly colors were _?_ beautiful.

_____ 2. It is dangerous to store _?_ liquids near a furnace.

_____ 3. George was _?_ honored to be named valedictorian.

_____ 4. Many people believe that fraternities and sororities are _?_ because their memberships are made up of only a chosen few.

_____ 5. Mr. Jones is trying to _?_ new business by advertising.

_____ 6. In the past all airplanes were _?_ driven.

_____ 7. Raoul was given an award for _?_ service.

_____ 8. A zebra's coat has a _?_ pattern of black and white stripes.

_____ 9. The early colonists _?_ against the British government.

_____ 10. Although Sam and Les met once, they are _?_ strangers.

Number correct _____ (total 10)

Analyzing Word Parts

Nouns Made from Verbs Several of the verbs below are the *base words* for the boldfaced nouns in the sentences that follow. Read the verb definitions. Then, in the blank next to each sentence, write the verb from which you think the noun was made. You will not use all of the verbs, and you will use one verb more than once.

distinguish   to see or show the difference in
distribute   to divide and give out in shares
emit   to send out or give forth
employ   to make use of
revive   to bring back to life
revolve   to move in a circle or orbit; rotate

_____ 1. It takes the earth one year to make a complete **revolution** around the sun.

_____ 2. It is important to make a **distinction** between the two kinds of roses, because they need to be cut differently.

_____ 3. The treasurer will take care of the **distribution** of money to the different committees.

_____ 4. That machine is very effective, but it does give out dangerous **emissions.**

_____ 5. Our company is the **distributor** for the best brands of sportswear in this area.

Number correct _____ (total 5)

Number correct in unit _____ (total 105)

Turn to **The Prefix ex-** on pages 220 of the **Spelling Handbook.** Read the rule and complete the exercises provided.

The Last Word

Writing

Our society is very dependent on the _internal-combustion_ automobile. Write a paragraph or two describing any problems you think this dependence causes and any possible solutions to the problem. Briefly consider changes in public transportation, lifestyles, technology, and any other areas you think might be important.

Speaking

Give a brief speech to the class about a current _trend_. You may select a trend in fashion, society, politics, economics, or any other area. Your trend might be one that is popular within your community or in the nation as a whole. Be sure to discuss why you think the trend has occurred or whether you think it will last.

Group Discussion

As a class, describe your _generation_. What interests are typical of people your age? How do these interests differ from those of your parents' generation? Why do you think each new generation appears so different from the previous one?

UNIT 16: Review of Units 13–15

Part A Review Word List

Unit 13 Target Words

1. belated
2. belligerent
3. bounteous
4. contemptuous
5. deport
6. endear
7. flounder
8. jubilant
9. memento
10. nucleus
11. operative
12. profitable
13. prosper
14. quip
15. random
16. revert
17. sympathize
18. tariff
19. unpretentious
20. warrant

Unit 13 Related Words

1. controversy
2. convert
3. divert
4. invert
5. jubilee
6. pretense
7. pretentious
8. profit
9. reverse
10. sympathy
11. warranty

Unit 14 Target Words

1. abruptly
2. aridity
3. arrest
4. austerely
5. cease
6. chaos
7. intangible
8. jostle
9. poise
10. quietude
11. remote
12. repose
13. resilient
14. rigid
15. somnolent
16. spirit
17. travail
18. turbulent
19. verge
20. vertical

Unit 14 Related Words

1. abrupt
2. arid
3. arresting
4. austere
5. austerity
6. ceaseless
7. chaotic
8. remoteness
9. resilience
10. rigidity
11. spiritual
12. tangible
13. turbulence

Unit 15 Target Words

1. attest
2. carburetor
3. combustion
4. distinct
5. distributor
6. elite
7. emission
8. encounter
9. exotic
10. external
11. generation
12. internal
13. merit
14. metropolitan
15. propel
16. revolutionize
17. supremacy
18. thesis
19. trend
20. virtually

Unit 15 Related Words

1. combustible
2. distinction
3. distinctive
4. distribute
5. distribution
6. elitist
7. emit
8. exotically
9. generate
10. meritorious
11. propeller
12. revolt
13. revolution
14. supreme
15. supremely
16. virtual

Inferring Meaning from Context

For each sentence write the letter of the word or phrase that is closest in meaning to the word or words in italics.

_____ 1. An expert witness was called to *attest to* the truth of the claim that a left-handed person could not have committed the crime.
a. confirm   b. deny   c. explain   d. contend

_____ 2. Ruth decorated her bedroom *austerely,* with the simplest furniture.
a. flashily   b. unattractively   c. obviously   d. plainly

_____ 3. The highway was *in complete chaos* following the accident.
a. blocked   b. in total disorder   c. damaged   d. utterly free of traffic

_____ 4. Kenneth was *contemptuous* of anyone who couldn't climb ropes, do push-ups, and run ten laps around the gym.
a. scornful   b. afraid   c. tired   d. aware

_____ 5. Foreign criminals are sometimes *deported to* their native countries.
a. sent back to   b. kept out of   c. wanted in   d. arrested in

_____ 6. Members of the *elite* club were the only people allowed at the dance.
a. dance   b. bounteous   c. special   d. country

_____ 7. Healy's smile *endeared her to* people.
a. made her angry with   b. made her liked by
c. made her aloof to   d. made her worried about

_____ 8. Though Beth was usually a good swimmer, she *floundered* when she first jumped into the lake.
a. swam   b. drowned   c. walked   d. struggled

_____ 9. The helicopter *poised* above the pool for a moment.
a. flew   b. landed   c. hovered   d. materialized

_____ 10. Selling homemade cookies and lemonade during the baseball game was *profitable* for Greg and Jane.
a. difficult   b. economic   c. money-making   d. financial

_____ 11. That locomotive is *propelled* by a steam generator.
a. conditioned   b. moved forward   c. stopped
d. pursued upward

_____ 12. Because she was feeling tired, Helga spent the afternoon *in repose*.
a. resting   b. working   c. reading   d. waiting

_____ 13. The sophomore class showed a great deal of *spirit* at the pep rally.

      a. worries b. people c. enthusiasm d. anger

_____ 14. It is *virtually* impossible for anyone except family members to tell the Cook twins apart.

      a. particularly b. uniquely c. rarely d. almost

_____ 15. The crime did not *warrant* such a serious punishment.

      a. cause b. deserve c. involve d. lose

Number correct _____ (total 15)

Using Review Words in Context

Using context clues, determine which word fits best in each blank.

ceased	elite	floundering	merited	spirit
chaos	endear	intangible	revert	sympathize
contemptuous	exotic	jostled	revolutionize	trend

What An Idea!

"This is an amazing idea!" cried Del, waving a batch of papers in the air. "It will _____ the entire advertising industry! Nothing will ever be the same. Everybody will be doing it. It will start a major _____. No one will ever _____ to the old ways again."

"What on earth are you talking about?" grumbled Allie, not bothering to look up from her desk.

"Oh, come on, Allie. Get into the _____ of things. Wipe that look of scorn off your face. You don't have to be _____ of every idea that comes along."

"I'm not," said Allie. "Just every idea of yours. You're a good writer, but you should let someone else come up with the ideas. None of yours has ever _____ a second thought. There was the time, for example, that you tried to send our clients messages taped to the legs of turkeys, instead of using a messenger service."

"I thought turkeys would be more interesting, more unusual, more _____. Besides, they were cheap," said Del.

"But they can't fly," said Allie. "And it's a long walk across town. Not to mention the traffic. Just think about two hundred turkeys _____ through the lunch hour crowd. The police are still talking about the _____ that caused!"

"So a few streets were blocked, a few cars were dented, and a handful of people were _____ a little in the crowds. Big deal."

"That little project didn't exactly _____ you to the powers that be. Look, Del, I _____ with your desire to come up with original ideas. I mean, I can really understand your feelings. But there's a certain _____ something you need if you're going to be a successful idea person, and you don't have it."

"This time I do. This idea will put me among the chosen few, the _____ group of advertising greats."

"Well," said Allie. "I suppose it's possible. Things _____ to amaze me a long time ago. Nothing can surprise me now. What's the idea?"

"I can't tell you yet. It's going to be a surprise at the staff meeting. But I'll give you a hint. It involves turtles, zucchini, and hot air balloons."

Number correct _____ (total 15)

Part B *Review Word Reinforcement*

Using Language and Thinking Skills

True–False Decide whether each statement is true (**T**) or false (**F**).

_____ 1. When a law becomes *operative,* no one needs to worry about getting arrested for breaking it.

_____ 2. If you are on the *verge* of making an omelet, you're probably just about to break some eggs.

_____ 3. If your *carburetor* is broken, you cannot cook your hamburgers outdoors.

_____ 4. The *nucleus* of a city is likely to be its downtown area.

_____ 5. Flagpoles are usually *vertical.*

_____ 6. When a harvest is *bounteous,* there should be enough food both to eat and to sell.

_____ 7. *Emissions* go into a car when it is tuned up.

_____ 8. You and your mother belong to different *generations.*

_____ 9. A *thesis* needs to be tested and proved before it becomes fact.

_____ 10. Food, shelter, and clothing are all *intangible.*

Number correct _____ (total 10)

Practicing for Standardized Tests

Synonyms Write the letter of the word that is closest in meaning to the capitalized word.

_____ 1. ABRUPTLY: (A) suddenly (B) eagerly (C) accurately (D) emotionally (E) dishonestly

_____ 2. ARREST: (A) relax (B) try (C) criticize (D) begin (E) stop

_____ 3. BELATED: (A) happy (B) angry (C) tardy (D) early (E) devoted

_____ 4. COMBUSTION: (A) fire (B) hatred (C) confusion (D) argument (E) communion

_____ 5. DISTINCT: (A) tragic (B) blurry (C) toxic (D) smelly (E) clear

_____ 6. ENCOUNTER: (A) computer (B) expression (C) economy (D) meeting (E) escape

_____ 7. EXOTIC: (A) strange (B) nontoxic (C) ordinary (D) hateful (E) devoted

_____ 8. INTERNAL: (A) emotional (B) furious (C) required (D) inside (E) huge

_____ 9. JOSTLE: (A) shove (B) hurt (C) joke (D) pull (E) isolate

_____ 10. MEMENTO: (A) purchase (B) reminder (C) toy (D) note (E) injection

_____ 11. MERIT: (A) overcome (B) work (C) wish (D) remember (E) deserve

_____ 12. SOMNOLENT: (A) sleepy (B) grave (C) alert (D) hesitant (E) partial

_____ 13. TARIFF: (A) tax (B) veto (C) toxin (D) gift (E) technique

_____ 14. TURBULENT: (A) content (B) quiet (C) private (D) stormy (E) pure

_____ 15. UNPRETENTIOUS: (A) foolish (B) simple (C) intelligent (D) inactive (E) drastic

Number correct _____ (total 15)

Antonyms Write the letter of the word that is most nearly *opposite* in meaning to the capitalized word in each set.

_____ 1. ARIDITY: (A) dryness (B) wetness (C) economy
(D) lightness (E) stiffness

_____ 2. BELLIGERENT: (A) beautiful (B) argumentative
(C) dreamy (D) friendly (E) wasteful

_____ 3. CONTEMPTUOUS: (A) diligent (B) respectful
(C) expressive (D) confident (E) proud

_____ 4. CEASE: (A) stray (B) start (C) stop (D) consume
(E) aspire

_____ 5. ELITE: (A) common (B) snobbish (C) wistful (D) aloof
(E) strange

_____ 6. EXTERNAL: (A) outer (B) universal (C) internal
(D) conditional (E) brief

_____ 7. JUBILANT: (A) unhappy (B) curious (C) typical
(D) happy (E) elated

_____ 8. METROPOLITAN: (A) rural (B) future (C) friendly
(D) harsh (E) urban

_____ 9. PROSPER: (A) succeed (B) aspire (C) explore (D) fail
(E) recede

_____ 10. QUIETUDE: (A) clarity (B) peace (C) obstacle (D) noise
(E) efficiency

_____ 11. RANDOM: (A) planned (B) chance (C) local
(D) animated (E) threatening

_____ 12. REMOTE: (A) distant (B) wet (C) near (D) controlled
(E) removed

_____ 13. RESILIENT: (A) worried (B) fearful (C) flexible
(D) unique (E) stiff

_____ 14. RIGID: (A) poised (B) stiff (C) warm (D) spiritual
(E) flexible

_____ 15. SUPREMACY: (A) prominence (B) authority (C) immunity
(D) inferiority (E) pretentiousness

Number correct _____ (total 15)

Analogies Determine the relationship between the pair of capitalized words. Then decide which other pair expresses a similar relationship. Write the letter of this word pair.

_____ 1. COMEDIAN : QUIP ::   (A) singer : song   (B) joke : laugh   (C) book : writer   (D) block : building   (E) lamp : light

_____ 2. ARIDITY : SAHARA ::   (A) desert : storm   (B) tent : sand   (C) cold : Antarctica   (D) forest : rain   (E) animal : camel

_____ 3. MEMENTO : SNAPSHOT ::   (A) flower : seed (B) drawing : photograph   (C) paper : pen   (D) memory : dream   (E) athlete : runner

_____ 4. WORK : TRAVAIL ::   (A) light : darkness   (B) confusion : chaos (C) headache : cramp   (D) labor : union   (E) sorrow : joy

_____ 5. DISTRIBUTOR : CAR ::   (A) telephone : telegraph (B) typewriter : pencil   (C) stair : elevator   (D) chain : bicycle (E) driver : rider

Number correct _____ (total 5)

Spelling and Wordplay

Fill-ins Spell the review word correctly in the blanks to the right of its definition.

1. to stop: <u>c</u> __ __ __ __

2. confusion: __ <u>h</u> __ __ __

3. to understand the feelings of: <u>s</u> __ __ __ __ __ __ __ <u>z</u> __

4. tardy: <u>b</u> __ <u>l</u> __ <u>t</u> __ __

5. to shove: <u>j</u> __ __ __ __ __

6. to change completely: <u>r</u> __ <u>v</u> __ __ __ __ __ __ __ <u>i</u> __ __

7. rest: __ __ <u>p</u> __ __ __

8. a guarantee: __ __ __ <u>r</u> __ __ __ <u>y</u>

9. tendency: __ __ __ __ <u>d</u>

10. witty remark: <u>q</u> __ __ __

Number correct _____ (total 10)

197

Part C Related Word Reinforcement

Using Related Words

Matching Ideas Choose the word that best describes the situation and write it in the blank.

arid   inhabit   propeller   resilience supreme
ceaseless   jubilee   remoteness revolution turbulence

_____ 1. The driest desert in the world is the Atacama in Chile. The driest major city is Cairo, Egypt, which averages a little more than an inch of rain a year.

_____ 2. More than three billion people live on the continent of Asia.

_____ 3. In 1837, John Ericsson, a Swedish-American inventor, was the first to put blades on a shaft in order to move ships through water.

_____ 4. The judges on the United States' highest court are the final authority on the Constitution.

_____ 5. Point Barrow, Alaska, is the northernmost place in the United States. It lies hundreds of miles from any large city.

_____ 6. Among the projects described by scientists as being impossible is the invention of a machine that will keep moving forever without using energy.

_____ 7. A rubber band can stretch out to many times its original length and then return to that starting length.

_____ 8. This word comes from the ancient Hebrew word _yobel,_ the horn used to announce a year of celebration every fiftieth year. Now we use this word for any big celebration.

_____ 9. The war that won freedom from Great Britain for America's original thirteen colonies began on April 19, 1775.

_____ 10. Although a tornado travels at a speed of only 25 to 40 miles an hour, the whirling winds in its funnel can blow around at more than 300 miles an hour.

Number correct _____ (total 10)

Reviewing Word Structures

The Word Parts *ex-, in-, re-, mot-* **or** *mov-,* **and** *vert-* Review the following definitions:

> *ex-* means "away from" or "out"
> *in-* means "no" or "not" or "into"
> *re-* means "back" or "over again"
> *mot-* or *mov-* means "to remove"
> *vert-* means "to turn"

In the blank write the word part or parts used in each word. Keeping in mind the word-part definitions write out the definition of each word. Use your dictionary if necessary.

Word Part	Word	Definition
1. _____	convert	_____
2. _____	divert	_____
3. _____	exotically	_____
4. _____	external	_____
5. _____	inject	_____
6. _____	inoperative	_____
7. _____	invert	_____
8. _____	resilience	_____
9. _____	reverse	_____
10. _____	revert	_____

Number correct _____ (total 10)

Number correct in unit _____ (total 105)

Vocab Lab 4

FOCUS ON: *Emotions*

Emotion is that butterflies-in-the-stomach feeling. You experience it when something stirs up a response in you of joy, fear, anger, grief, or love. Because these basic feelings can be very strong, we have many words to describe the varying degrees of positive and negative reactions that we can have. Some of these words are listed below.

acquiesce (ak′ wē es′) v. to give in or reluctantly agree. ● John decided to *acquiesce* quietly when the committee voted against his proposal.

ambivalent (am biv′ ə lənt) adj. undecided because of conflicting feelings of liking and disliking something or someone. ● Heidi was *ambivalent* about football because she liked the excitement but disliked the violence.

animosity (an ə mäs′ ə tē) n. a strong feeling of hostility and hatred. ● The *animosity* between the two neighbors resulted in a lawsuit over the location of the property line.

benevolent (bə nev′ ə lənt) adj. charitable and wanting to do good. ● Most people experience a *benevolent* feeling toward others during the Christmas holiday season.

blithe (blī*th*) adj. carefree and showing a cheerful disposition. ● Verna was *blithe* and relieved as she handed in her final test.

candid (kan′ did) adj. very honest; straightforward. ● Coach Burns was *candid* in his criticism of Ramon's passing technique.

ecstasy (ek′ stə sē) n. an overpowering joy. ● Jenny was in *ecstasy* when she won the figure skating championship.

effervescent (ef′ ər ves′ ′nt) adj. high-spirited and lively. ● The carnival's colorful lights and lively music created an *effervescent* mood among the children.

empathy (em′ pə thē) n. the ability to understand another person's feelings. ● One's past experience with pain encourages *empathy* for another's suffering.

enchantment (in chant′ mənt) n. great delight. ● Terry finds himself in a state of *enchantment* every time he sees a vintage sports car.

irritable (ir′ i tə b′l) adj. impatient; easily annoyed; quick-tempered. ● The constant yapping of the little dog made Betty *irritable*.

jubilant (jo͞o′ b′l ənt) adj. triumphantly joyful; rejoicing. ● Everyone was *jubilant* over the birth of the child, and grandpa led them all in a triumphant march around the dining room table.

nonchalant (nän shə länt′) adj. lacking warmth or enthusiasm; indifferent ● Brian tried to act *nonchalant* as we showered him with compliments on his new suit.

pathos (pā′ thäs) n. a quality that arouses pity and compassion. ● As we watched the mother deer trying to help her wounded fawn, the *pathos* of the scene was almost unbearable.

vengeance (ven′ jəns) n. revenge; punishment. • After the embarrassing loss
to the Tigers, our team vowed that we
would gain *vengeance* next year.

Finding Examples Match each word from the list above with the appropriate
example below. Write the word in the blank.

_____ 1. We were all feeling bubbly and lively as we boarded
the bus.

_____ 2. The unexpected joy of being crowned Home-
coming Queen almost put Ellen in a trance.

_____ 3. We felt compassion and pity as we watched the television documentary about the homeless.

_____ 4. Ken tried to act indifferent and cool as he went up to
accept his award.

_____ 5. Liz reluctantly consented to go along on the Christmas carol walk.

_____ 6. David felt cheerful and carefree when he finished his
Saturday chores.

_____ 7. The hatred between George and Ryan flared up as
they began arguing loudly.

_____ 8. Robert couldn't make up his mind about taking the
job because he liked the work but felt the salary was
inadequate.

_____ 9. Romeo killed Tybalt for revenge because Tybalt had
killed Romeo's friend Mercutio.

_____ 10. There is an old Native American saying about not crit-
icizing someone until you have walked a mile in that
person's moccasins.

_____ 11. When my mother has a headache, she is annoyed by
the slightest disturbance.

_____ 12. The salesperson gave such a charming and delightful
description of how I would look in the dress that I
bought it without even trying it on.

_____ 13. Dad is the one person I can count on to tell the truth.

_____ 14. The annual fundraiser for the children's hospital
brings out the charitable feeling in almost everyone.

_____ 15. All of the children jumped up and down when they
heard the news that they would not have to move.

Number correct _____ (total 15)

FOCUS ON: *Clear Communication*

Clear communication is the most important function of language. Using the wrong wording may cloud your communication or offend your audience.

In order to better understand right and wrong wording, you need to be familiar with jargon, gobbledygook, clichés, and euphemisms. Although jargon and euphemisms can be effective if used properly, clichés and gobbledygook should be avoided.

Jargon

Jargon is the distinctive vocabulary used by those who work in a specialized profession. Such a vocabulary can be effective and meaningful to those in a particular field of work, but it often sounds like a foreign language to an outsider.

Nevertheless, jargon has a way of seeping into our everyday language. Therefore, it is to your advantage to make yourself familiar with some of the words in these specialized vocabularies if you want to know what is going on around you.

Here are some examples of words used in specialized areas:

Sports	end run, down, diamond, curveball, tack, rookie
Theater	act, scene, role, east, star, cue
Banking	principal, prime rate, interest, assets, trust, savings
Real Estate	mortgage, abstract, title, deed, property, appraisal

Gobbledygook

Gobbledygook is composed of difficult words and complicated sentences and is often used to try to impress someone. Instead of impressing people, however, gobbledygook usually confuses them and makes them angry. Read the following example.

Gobbledygook	Each participant in this examination is expected to remain in complete compliance with the regulations governing deception and fraud throughout the entire time period. Any infractions of this policy will be dealt with severely.
Translation	Cheaters will be punished.

Clichés

Expressions that have been so overused that they have lost their impact are called *clichés*. "Cold as ice" and "bored to death" are clichés. Excessive use of clichés can make it seem as though you don't have anything original to say.

Euphemisms

Euphemisms are expressions or synonyms that are not as embarrassing, blunt, or hurtful as the words they stand for. Common examples are the use of "senior citizen" for old person, or "plain" for unattractive.

Understanding Jargon As explained in the Jargon section, words can be used in different professions. For each of the words listed below, use a dictionary to find the meanings in both of the fields given. Then write two sentences for each word, one sentence with the word as it is used in the first field, and the second sentence with the word as it is used in the other field.

1. diamond (jewelry, sports)
2. cast (medicine, theater)
3. principal (education, banking)

4. title (literature, real estate)
5. down (emotions, football)

Number correct _____ (total 10)

Gobbledygook or Cliché Label the following sentences as either gobbledygook or cliché.

_____ 1. Henry has become slower than molasses; he is clearly over the hill.

_____ 2. The perpetrator of the infraction of the law will be properly censured.

_____ 3. That meal certainly filled the bill.

_____ 4. I believe that the prices asked are highway robbery.

_____ 5. Whereas it is presently pertinent that we all participate in ingesting our midday refreshments, we will commence.

Number correct _____ (total 5)

Translating Euphemisms Match each word or phrase on the left with its euphemism on the right.

____ 1. dead   a. memorial park

____ 2. lied   b. maintenance engineer

____ 3. old age   c. bent the truth

____ 4. janitor   d. golden years

____ 5. cemetery   e. passed away

Number correct _____ (total 5)

Number correct in Vocab Lab _____ (total 35)

Units 1–8 *Standardized Vocabulary Test*

The following items test your comprehension of words studied in the first half of the book. Test questions have been written in a way that will familiarize you with the typical standardized test format. The questions are divided into the following categories: **synonyms, sentence completion, antonyms,** and **analogies.**

Synonyms

Each question below consists of a capitalized word followed by five lettered words. In the blank, write the letter of the word that is closest in meaning to the capitalized word. Because some of the questions require you to distinguish fine shades of meaning, consider all the choices before deciding which is best.

_____ 1. DIVERSE: (A) identical (B) same (C) remarkable (D) backward (E) different

_____ 2. INSTINCTIVE: (A) private (B) natural (C) sheer (D) reluctant (E) reasoned

_____ 3. PURSUE: (A) lead (B) introduce (C) follow (D) arrest (E) survive

_____ 4. CONTEND: (A) compete (B) surrender (C) satisfy (D) yield (E) collapse

_____ 5. DISLODGE: (A) bury (B) animate (C) rent (D) remove (E) scour

_____ 6. EXCLUSIVE: (A) common (B) popular (C) selective (D) open (E) realistic

_____ 7. ACHIEVEMENT: (A) appearance (B) meaning (C) style (D) accomplishment (E) illustration

_____ 8. HUMANITARIAN: (A) grave (B) evil (C) demanding (D) charitable (E) medical

_____ 9. SUFFICIENT: (A) enough (B) scattered (C) memorable (D) courteous (E) elusive

_____ 10. RELUCTANT: (A) eager (B) impatient (C) unwilling (D) careless (E) excited

_____ 11. EXTRACT: (A) lodge (B) remove (C) inject (D) chase (E) enter

____ 12. RELISH: (A) enjoy (B) dislike (C) hate (D) season (E) surge

____ 13. COURTEOUS: (A) private (B) simple (C) polite (D) rude (E) serious

____ 14. ACCURATE: (A) imitation (B) energetic (C) mistaken (D) exact (E) agreeable

____ 15. OBSTACLE: (A) rock (B) support (C) course (D) solution (E) barrier

____ 16. ACQUIRE: (A) get (B) pardon (C) behave (D) lose (E) appear

____ 17. UNIVERSAL: (A) exclusive (B) automatic (C) patriotic (D) limited (E) widespread

____ 18. MEMORABLE: (A) pedestrian (B) unforgettable (C) distinct (D) obvious (E) commonplace

____ 19. ABANDON: (A) leave (B) defend (C) lose (D) possess (E) follow

____ 20. DEFECT: (A) perfection (B) surge (C) election (D) strength (E) fault

Number correct _____ (total 20)

Sentence Completion

Each sentence below contains one or two blanks. Each blank indicates that a word has been omitted. Beneath the sentence are five lettered words or pairs of words. In the blank to the left of each sentence, write the letter of the word or pair of words that *best* fits the meaning of the sentence as a whole.

____ 1. Catherine's grandparents were rugged _?_ who _?_ help from anyone.
   (A) humorists . . . abandoned (B) individualists . . . declined
   (C) vagabonds . . . survived (D) pedestrians . . . vetoed
   (E) humanitarians . . . duplicated

____ 2. The firm's profits went up when sales _?_ .
   (A) surged (B) required (C) declined (D) transformed
   (E) patronized

____ 3. Corinne's wise _?_ planning prevented the company from becoming _?_ .
   (A) economical . . . interior (B) fictional . . . inanimate
   (C) prominent . . . typical (D) domestic . . . prosperous
   (E) financial . . . bankrupt

_____ 4. Jeffrey __?__ the idea of competing in the marathon and began running long distances in preparation for race.

(A) relished   (B) dismissed   (C) contended   (D) excluded
(E) consumed

_____ 5. Lena's __?__ of being ahead in the search were shattered when the __?__ treasure was discovered by another explorer.

(A) superstitions . . . appropriate   (B) associates . . . obvious
(C) achievements . . . isolated   (D) illusions . . . elusive
(E) requirements . . . fictional

_____ 6. Although a(n) __?__ dresser, Charles was actually quiet and reserved.

(A) responsible   (B) flamboyant   (C) arterial   (D) inquisitive
(E) reluctant

_____ 7. The gas from the leaking chemical tank filled the building and caused much __?__.

(A) corrosion   (B) output   (C) purity   (D) habitation
(E) innovation

_____ 8. It is difficult to __?__ the __?__ that the dinosaurs disappeared because the earth's climate grew colder.

(A) monopolize . . . outlook   (B) falter . . . inclination
(C) contradict . . . theory   (D) possess . . . emotion
(E) foresee . . . defect

_____ 9. The carpenter did a(n) __?__ amount of work on the outside of the house but left the __?__ alone.

(A) realistic . . . assembly   (B) unique . . . exterior
(C) considerable . . . interior   (D) definite . . . existence
(E) offensive . . . position

_____ 10. Relatives and friends from all over the country __?__ to celebrate Hannah's 100th birthday.

(A) converged   (B) survived   (C) destined   (D) applied
(E) populated

_____ 11. The __?__ on Jane's face gave away her __?__ at coming in second.

(A) gratitude . . . integrity   (B) sullenness . . . delight
(C) communion . . . accord   (D) expression . . . dismay
(E) humor . . . tragedy

_____ 12. The book's description of life in India was __?__; the author had __?__ lived there for some time.

(A) inappropriate . . . systematically   (B) realistic . . . obviously
(C) technical . . . partially   (D) defective . . . efficiently
(E) insufficient . . . efficiently

____ 13. Many __?__ in the way people work are due to __?__ breakthroughs in the computer industry.
   (A) tragedies . . . inanimate   (B) innovations . . . technological
   (C) fixtures . . . employment   (D) applications . . . communion
   (E) requirements . . . desperate

____ 14. Steve's __?__ for acting made him a(n) __?__ choice for the leading role in the class play.
   (A) integrity . . . fictional   (B) quality . . . patronizing
   (C) devotion . . . grave   (D) efficiency . . . systematic
   (E) flair . . . obvious

____ 15. Despite Ellen's efforts to befriend the __?__ man, she managed to __?__ him by forgetting his name.
   (A) aloof . . . offend   (B) memorable . . . abandon
   (C) barbaric . . . trace   (D) emotional . . . resist
   (E) languid . . . isolate

Number correct _____ (total 15)

Antonyms

Each question below consists of a capitalized word followed by five lettered words. In the blank, write the letter of the word that is most nearly *opposite* in meaning to the capitalized word. Because some of the questions require you to distinguish fine shades of meaning, consider all the choices before deciding which is best.

____ 1. DRASTIC: (A) extreme   (B) emotional   (C) mild
   (D) worried   (E) carefree

____ 2. ECONOMICAL: (A) modest   (B) educational   (C) thrifty
   (D) dishonest   (E) wasteful

____ 3. SULLENNESS: (A) simplicity   (B) cheerfulness   (C) flair
   (D) innovation   (E) gratitude

____ 4. FLAMBOYANT: (A) colorful   (B) simple   (C) warm
   (D) showy   (E) odd

____ 5. UNIQUE: (A) aloof   (B) strange   (C) grave   (D) common
   (E) energetic

____ 6. INTEGRITY: (A) strength   (B) dishonesty   (C) cruelty
   (D) responsibility   (E) work

____ 7. BARBARIC: (A) rough   (B) interesting   (C) realistic
   (D) offensive   (E) civilized

____ 8. INANIMATE: (A) alive   (B) quiet   (C) flat   (D) likely
   (E) friendly

_____ 9. MONOPOLIZE: (A) control (B) befriend (C) share
(D) overpower (E) own

_____ 10. TYPICAL: (A) ordinary (B) written (C) unusual
(D) regular (E) specific

Number correct _____ (total 10)

Analogies

Determine the relationship between the pair of capitalized words. Then decide which other word pair expresses a similar relationship. Write the letter of the word pair.

_____ 1. NOVEL : FICTIONAL :: (A) story : funny (B) newscast : factual
(C) book : illustrated (D) play : musical (E) test : typed

_____ 2. HUMORIST : JOKE :: (A) boss : job (B) writer : computer
(C) doctor : bandage (D) storyteller : tale (E) essay : inquiry

_____ 3. BOUGH : TREE :: (A) acquaintance : family (B) diameter : area
(C) wing : bird (D) terminal : end (E) application : job

_____ 4. ARTERY : BLOOD :: (A) hand : finger (B) road : traffic
(C) arm : back (D) refinery : oil (E) outlook : view

_____ 5. COPIER : DUPLICATE :: (A) debt : decline (B) pen : erase
(C) mirror : reflect (D) responsibility : corrode
(E) pedestrian : ride

Number correct _____ (total 5)

Number correct in Units 1–8 Test _____ (total 50)

208

Units 9–16 *Standardized Vocabulary Test*

The following items test your comprehension of words studied in the second half of the book. Test items are divided into the following categories: **synonyms, sentence completion, antonyms,** and **analogies.**

Synonyms

Each test item below consists of a capitalized word followed by five lettered words. In the blank, write the letter of the word that is closest in meaning to the capitalized word. Because some of the questions require you to distinguish fine shades of meaning, consider all the choices before deciding which is best.

_____ 1. HESITATE: (A) imitate (B) appear (C) pause (D) behave (E) operate

_____ 2. BRISKLY: (A) energetically (B) lazily (C) sweetly (D) dangerously (E) warmly

_____ 3. ASPIRATION: (A) ability (B) destination (C) influence (D) goal (E) expression

_____ 4. CONTEMPTUOUS: (A) gracious (B) thoughtful (C) scornful (D) rude (E) admiring

_____ 5. JOSTLE: (A) joke (B) soothe (C) enjoy (D) surge (E) shove

_____ 6. ATTITUDE: (A) height (B) outlook (C) method (D) habit (E) fashion

_____ 7. TEMPERAMENT: (A) personality (B) intelligence (C) opposition (D) anger (E) temperature

_____ 8. PROPERLY: (A) forcefully (B) wittily (C) happily (D) abruptly (E) correctly

_____ 9. PERSEVERANCE: (A) surrender (B) mistreatment (C) determination (D) achievement (E) integrity

_____ 10. REVERT: (A) progress (B) remind (C) proceed (D) return (E) remain

_____ 11. INTANGIBLE: (A) obvious (B) untouchable (C) pale (D) physical (E) noticeable

_____ 12. VIRTUALLY: (A) practically (B) honestly (C) obviously (D) truly (E) probably

_____ 13. COUNSEL: (A) bargain (B) order (C) command
(D) advise (E) consider

_____ 14. ABRUPTLY: (A) crudely (B) warmly (C) suddenly
(D) anxiously (E) worriedly

_____ 15. COMPONENT: (A) competitor (B) whole (C) system
(D) ability (E) part

_____ 16. CEASE: (A) possess (B) stop (C) exist (D) refine
(E) begin

_____ 17. BENEFIT: (A) fashion (B) condition (C) advantage
(D) loss (E) clarity

_____ 18. MEMENTO: (A) moment (B) wish (C) application
(D) souvenir (E) spice

_____ 19. PROSPER: (A) propose (B) succeed (C) possess (D) fail
(E) promise

_____ 20. TURBULENT: (A) inanimate (B) methodical (C) drastic
(D) tame (E) stormy

Number correct _____ (total 20)

Sentence Completion

Each sentence below contains one or two blanks. Each blank indicates that
a word has been omitted. Beneath the sentence are five lettered words or
pairs of words. In the blank to the left of each sentence, write the letter of the
word or pair of words that _best_ fits the meaning of the sentence as a whole.

_____ 1. The animal behavior __?__ studied the __?__ of the zebra to
determine the effects of water supply on the animal's eating habits.
(A) sponsor . . . spirit (B) aide . . . generation
(C) specialist . . . habitat (D) colleague . . . nucleus
(E) apprentice . . . supremacy

_____ 2. The Nelsons lived __?__ and sounded __?__ when they said others
surround themselves with unnecessary luxuries.
(A) methodically . . . bounteous (B) austerely . . . contemptuous
(C) unpretentiously . . . passive (D) virtually . . . belligerent
(E) wistfully . . . jubilant

_____ 3. The pedestrians looked nervously up at the kitten, which was __?__
unsteadily on the ledge of a third floor window.
(A) warranted (B) receding (C) jostled (D) deported
(E) poised

210

_____ 4. Gwen looked _?_ at the sailboat and wished that the lake were less _?_ so that she could sail safely.

    (A) wistfully . . . turbulent   (B) utterly . . . lethal
    (C) intently . . . particular   (D) abruptly . . . metropolitan
    (E) ceaselessly . . . operative

_____ 5. Many _?_ have been required to reduce the _?_ of harmful gases.

    (A) federations . . . dilution   (B) rodents . . . generation
    (C) masons . . . toxins   (D) industries . . . emission
    (E) factors . . . multiplication

_____ 6. Jason was embarrassed by the question and _?_ awkwardly for an answer.

    (A) propelled   (B) sympathized   (C) reverted   (D) verged
    (E) floundered

_____ 7. Although Sarah had no _?_ to chicken pox, she was a(n) _?_ child who quickly recovered from the disease.

    (A) perseverance . . . diligent   (B) trend . . . prompt
    (C) immunity . . . resilient   (D) venom . . . temperamental
    (E) aspiration . . . intangible

_____ 8. The mechanic discovered that the problem with the car involved a missing _?_ in the _?_ .

    (A) portion . . . vertical   (B) condition . . . propeller
    (C) license . . . distributor   (D) technique . . . combustion
    (E) component . . . carburetor

_____ 9. Kate became highly skilled in design while she worked as a(n) _?_ at the architectural firm.

    (A) sponsor   (B) tariff   (C) counsel   (D) apprentice
    (E) memento

_____ 10. Bret _?_ the child ahead of him in line; his behavior _?_ a scolding from the teacher.

    (A) jostled . . . warranted   (B) quipped . . . arrested
    (C) counseled . . . materialized   (D) revolutionized . . . preceded
    (E) endeared . . . prompted

_____ 11. The committee members made _?_ plans to study the _?_ opportunities in their town.

    (A) exotic . . . wistful   (B) belated . . . poverty
    (C) preliminary . . . employment   (D) passive . . . supremacy
    (E) spiritual . . . industry

_____ 12. Martha held __?__ political __?__ that had not changed in twenty years and probably never would.

    (A) multiple . . . conditions   (B) rigid . . . attitudes

    (C) curious . . . temperaments   (D) virtual . . . transformations

    (E) prosperous . . . trends

_____ 13. Joe had a __?__ feeling when he left the turbulence of the city for the __?__ of the country.

    (A) careful . . . fame   (B) prompt . . . immunity

    (C) sponsored . . . isolation   (D) burrowing . . . aspirations

    (E) contented . . . quietude

_____ 14. Rosa responded to the naughty child with a sudden __?__ of disapproval.

    (A) resistance   (B) travail   (C) gesture   (D) trend

    (E) condition

_____ 15. The candidate waged a(n) __?__ campaign in which he declared his __?__ for his opponent.

    (A) endearing . . . belligerence   (B) belated . . . briskness

    (C) methodical . . . resilience   (D) venomous . . . contempt

    (E) remote . . . combustion

Number correct _____ (total 15)

Antonyms

Each question below consists of a capitalized word followed by five lettered words. In the blank, write the letter of the word that is most nearly *opposite* in meaning to the capitalized word. Because some of the questions require you to distinguish fine shades of meaning, consider all the choices before deciding which is best.

_____ 1. PARTICULAR: (A) universal (B) specific (C) profitable
    (D) private (E) individual

_____ 2. RECEDE: (A) decline (B) withdraw (C) advance
    (D) reveal (E) concede

_____ 3. REMOTE: (A) distant (B) pointless (C) unrelated
    (D) useless (E) nearby

_____ 4. UNPRETENTIOUS: (A) modest (B) flamboyant (C) brisk
    (D) natural (E) annoying

_____ 5. EXTERNAL: (A) shallow (B) outer (C) medical
    (D) terminal (E) internal

_____ 6. ELITE: (A) special (B) common (C) occasional (D) royal
    (E) bright

_____ 7. JUBILANT: (A) careless (B) sorrowful (C) dishonest
(D) joyful (E) patient

_____ 8. BELLIGERENT: (A) unfriendly (B) intelligent (C) peaceful
(D) beautiful (E) quarrelsome

_____ 9. AUSTERELY: (A) simply (B) strictly (C) reasonably
(D) luxuriously (E) helpfully

_____ 10. OCCASIONAL: (A) remarkable (B) random
(C) uncommon (D) frequent (E) unclear

Number correct _____ (total 10)

Analogies

Determine the relationship between the pair of capitalized words. Then decide which other word pair expresses a similar relationship. Write the letter of the word pair.

_____ 1. PRIVATE : PUBLIC :: (A) warm : hot (B) exotic : exciting
(C) lethal : harmless (D) personal : individual
(E) desperate : worried

_____ 2. HABITAT : FOREST :: (A) book : novel (B) apple : core
(C) poem : play (D) song : singer (E) ocean : sea

_____ 3. MASON : STONE :: (A) builder : house (B) sculptor : statue
(C) carpenter : wood (D) tariff : tax (E) doctor : hospital

_____ 4. ADJACENT : NEIGHBORING :: (A) foggy : clear
(B) somnolent : sleepy (C) shiny : smooth
(D) operative : wrong (E) passive : private

_____ 5. ARIDITY : DESERT :: (A) nucleus : bomb
(B) belligerence : poverty (C) endearment : profit
(D) chaos : employment (E) turbulence : tornado

Number correct _____ (total 5)

Number correct in Units 9–16 Test _____ (total 50)

SPELLING HANDBOOK

Knowing the meanings of words is essential to using language correctly. However, another important skill is knowing how to spell the words you use.

Almost everyone has at least some problems with spelling. If you have trouble spelling, you might be encouraged to know that many others like you have learned to avoid spelling errors by following these suggestions:

1. **Proofread everything you write.** Everyone occasionally makes errors through carelessness or haste. By carefully reading through what you have written, you will catch many of your errors.

2. **Look up difficult words in a dictionary.** If you are not sure about the spelling of a word, don't guess at it. Take the time to look up the word.

3. **Learn to look at the letters in a word.** Learn to spell a word by examining various letter combinations contained in the word. Note the prefix, suffix, or double letters. Close your eyes and visualize the word. Then write the word from memory. Look at the word again to check your spelling.

4. **Pronounce words carefully.** It may be that you misspell certain words because you do not pronounce them correctly. For example, if you write *probly* instead of *probably,* it is likely that you are mispronouncing the word. Learning how to pronounce words and memorizing the letter combinations that create the sounds will improve your spelling.

5. **Keep a list of your "spelling demons."** Although you may not think about it, you *do* correctly spell most of the words you use. It is usually a few specific words that give you the most trouble. Keep a list of the words you have trouble spelling, and concentrate on learning them. Also, look for patterns in the words you misspell and learn those patterns.

6. **Use memory helps, called mnemonic devices, for words that give you trouble.** *Stationery* has *er* as in *letter;* there is *a rat* in *separate; Wednesday* contains *wed.*

7. **Learn and apply the rules given in this section.** Make sure you understand these rules. Then practice using them until they become automatic.

Words with Prefixes

The Addition of Prefixes

A prefix is a group of letters added to the beginning of a word to change its meaning. When a prefix is added to a base word, the spelling of the base word remains the same. (For further information about word parts, see pages 7–13.)

in- + dependent = independent   *un-* + interesting = uninteresting
de- + value = devalue   *re-* + cycle = recycle
fore- + fathers = forefathers   *trans-* + form = transform

A prefix can be added to a root as well as to a base word. A root is a word part that cannot stand alone; it must be joined to other parts to form a word. A root can be joined with many different prefixes to form words with different meanings. **However, the spelling of the prefix and the root remains the same.**

in- + quire = inquire   *in-* + terior = interior
re- + quire = require   *ex-* + terior = exterior

Exercise A Add the prefixes as indicated, and write the new word.

1. *dis-* + lodge = _____

2. *de-* + generate = _____

3. *un-* + pretentious = _____

4. *re-* + call = _____

5. *a-* + typical = _____

6. *in-* + habit = _____

7. *ex-* + change = _____

8. *mis-* + represent = _____

9. *pre-* + serve = _____

10. *fore-* + warn = _____

Number correct _____ (total 10)

Exercise B Using words from the following list, complete each sentence with two words that have the same root.

assumed	decline	external	injection	offended
conferred	defended	imported	inquire	reject
consume	excluded	inclined	internal	required
contained	exported	included	maintain	transferring

1. After watching Wally _____ great quantities of

   watermelon at the picnic, everyone _____ he would have
   a stomachache.

2. Barbara _____ her close friends when making a guest list

   but _____ those classmates she did not know well.

3. Bananas are usually _____ into this country, while

   produce grown in this country is _____ to other places in
   the world.

4. The pamphlet _____ in the glove compartment gave

   valuable information on how to _____ the car.

5. Luis not only _____ people with his frankness but

   _____ his right to do so.

6. After a busy day of hard work, we were _____ to

   _____ the invitation for dinner.

7. Please _____ at the hotel desk to see if you are

   _____ to check in every day.

8. Danielle's constant _____ of humor into even the most

   serious situation caused many people to _____ her as a
   friend.

9. Before _____ into a more difficult math class, Marguerite

   _____ with her teacher.

10. Although there were no _____, visible signs of Ms.

    Mansfield's illness, doctors detected _____ problems with
    the aid of X-rays.

Number correct _____ (total 20)

The Prefix *ad-*

When some prefixes are added to certain roots and words, the spelling of the prefix changes. The prefix *ad-* changes only in the following cases to create a double consonant:

ac- before *c*   *ag-* before *g*   *an-* before *n*   *ar-* before *r*   *at-* before *t*
af- before *f*   *al-* before *l*   *ap-* before *p*   *as-* before *s*

Examples:

ad- + claim = acclaim   ad- + prentice = apprentice
ad- + fect = affect   ad- + range = arrange
ad- + gravate = aggravate   ad- + sign = assign
ad- + low = allow   ad- + tend = attend
ad- + noy = annoy

Exercise Add the prefix *ad-* to each of the roots or base words below. Change the spelling of the prefix as appropriate, and write the word.

1. *ad-* + jacent = _____

2. *ad-* + commodation = _____

3. *ad-* + rest = _____

4. *ad-* + sociate = _____

5. *ad-* + propriate = _____

6. *ad-* + locate = _____

7. *ad-* + nounce = _____

8. *ad-* + gression = _____

9. *ad-* + here = _____

10. *ad-* + opt = _____

11. *ad-* + ply = _____

12. *ad-* + firm = _____

13. *ad-* + semble = _____

14. *ad-* + mit = _____

15. *ad-* + count = _____

Number correct _____ (total 15)

The Prefix *com-*

The spelling of the prefix *com-* does not change when it is added to roots or words that begin with the letter *m*, *p*, or *b*.

com- + mon = common   com- + ponent = component

com- + mit = commit   com- + bine = combine

The prefix *com-* changes to *con-* when added to roots or words that begin with the letter *c*, *d*, *g*, *j*, *n*, *q*, *s*, *t*, or *v*.

com- + centrate = concentrate   com- + sist = consist

com- + nect = connect   com- + tinue = continue

The prefix *com-* changes to *col-* when added to roots or words that begin with the letter *l*, to create a double consonant.

com- + league = colleague   com- + lide = collide

The prefix *com-* changes to *cor-* when added to roots or words that begin with the letter *r*, to create a double consonant.

com- + rect = correct   com- + rupt = corrupt

Exercise Add the prefix *com-* to each of the roots or base words below. Change the spelling of the prefix as appropriate, and write the word.

1. *com-* + fer = _____

2. *com-* + vert = _____

3. *com-* + rode = _____

4. *com-* + tempt = _____

5. *com-* + mercial = _____

6. *com-* + vince = _____

7. *com-* + cept = _____

8. *com-* + dition = _____

9. *com-* + lect = _____

10. *com-* + tend = _____

11. *com-* + bustion = _____

12. *com-* + tent = _____

13. *com-* + gregation = _____

14. *com-* + prehension = _____

15. *com-* + sider = _____

Number correct _____ (total 15)

The Prefix *in-*

The spelling of the prefix *in-* does not change, except in the following cases:

(a) The prefix *in-* changes to *im-* when added to roots or words beginning with *m, p,* or *b.*

in- + mediate = immediate	*in-* + port = import
in- + partial = impartial	*in-* + balance = imbalance

(b) The prefix *in-* changes to *il-* when added to roots or words beginning with *l,* to create a double consonant.

in- + legal = illegal   *in-* + lusion = illusion

(c) The prefix *in-* changes to *ir-* when added to roots or words beginning with *r,* to create a double consonant.

in- + regular = irregular   *in-* + resistible = irresistible

Exercise Find the misspelled word in each group. Write the word correctly.

_____	1. inappropriate imhabit increase impossible	_____	6. intend inresponsible intact insulate
_____	2. imdividual immature immodest imperceptible	_____	7. imsult involve ineligible inhabit
_____	3. illustrate ilvest illiterate illuminate	_____	8. insure irrational inconsistent imscription
_____	4. irrigate instinct impede inbecile	_____	9. inject inspire incline imdebted
_____	5. infer inmune inquire imperfect	_____	10. inept inexperienced inmigrate innocent

Number correct _____ (total 10)

The Prefix *ex-*

The spelling of the prefix *ex-* does not change when it is added to roots or words beginning with vowels or with the consonant *p, t, h,* or *c.*

ex- + pert = expert	*ex-* + cuse = excuse
ex- + tinct = extinct	*ex-* + it = exit
ex- + haust = exhaust	*ex-* + ample = example

Exception: *Ex-* becomes *ec-* before *c* in the word *eccentric.*

The prefix *ex-* changes to *ef-* when added to roots or words beginning with *f.*

ex- + fort = effort	*ex-* + fect = effect

The prefix *ex-* changes to *e-* before most other consonants.

ex- + migrate = emigrate	*ex-* + mit = emit
ex- + lapse = elapse	*ex-* + rase = erase

No common English words begin with the letters *exs.* When the prefix *ex-* is joined to roots that begin with the letter *s,* the *s* is dropped.

ex- + sert = exert	*ex-* + sist = exist

Exercise Find the misspelled word in each group. Write the word correctly.

_____ 1. exterior
    export
    exminent
    examine

_____ 2. explore
    excel
    exlongate
    extend

_____ 3. efface
    efficiently
    efclusive
    effective

_____ 4. erode
    elate
    exale
    exile

_____ 5. emotion
    edit
    exlect
    explain

_____ 6. exhibit
    exclaim
    experiment
    exvolve

_____ 7. eloquent
    elevate
    elrupt
    elope

_____ 8. execute
    exligible
    expand
    extreme

_____ 9. expel
    eliminate
    exite
    exuberant

_____ 10. except
    effervesce
    elude
    elmancipate

Number correct _____ (total 10)

Words with Suffixes

Words Ending in *y*

A suffix is a letter or group of letters added to the end of a word that changes the word's meaning.

When a suffix is added to a word ending in *y* preceded by a consonant, the *y* is usually changed to *i*.

apply + *-ed* = applied   refinery + *-es* = refineries

artery + *al* = arterial   plenty + *-ful* = plentiful

Exceptions:

(a) **When *-ing* is added, the *y* does not change.**

apply + *-ing* = applying   carry + *-ing* = carrying

try + *-ing* = trying   rely + *-ing* = relying

(b) **In some one-syllable words, the *y* does not change.**

dry + *-ness* = dryness   shy + *-ness* = shyness

When a suffix is added to a word ending in *y* preceded by a vowel, the *y* usually does not change.

annoy + *-ed* = annoyed   play + *-er* = player

enjoy + *-able* = enjoyable   joy + *-ful* = joyful

Exceptions: day + *-ly* = daily   gay + *-ly* = gaily

Exercise A In these sentences, find each misspelled word, and write the correct spelling on the line following the sentence. There may be more than one misspelled word in a sentence.

1. "Your destinys lie in your abilitys and goals," the speaker declared at the assembly.

_____

2. Gene multiplyed the number of people by two and arrived at an estimate of how many sandwiches to make.

_____

3. The corner store was known for its delicacyes, including imported honey, smoked oysters, and caviar.

_____

4. The corn crop was unusually bountyful this year.

_____

5. The friendlyness between our families increased through the years, and we tryed to do many activities together.

_____

6. The sales clerk showed us the fancyest and most expensive model, but we could only afford the most economycal one.

_____

7. The cat straied into unfamiliar territory and was missing for days.

_____

Number correct _____ (total 10)

Exercise B Add the suffixes as indicated, and write the word in the blank.

1. curiosity + *-es* = _____

2. pray + *-ing* = _____

3. crafty + *-ness* = _____

4. defy + *-ed* = _____

5. deny + *-able* = _____

6. cry + *-ing* = _____

7. tragedy + *-es* = _____

8. laboratory + *-es* = _____

9. drowsy + *-ly* = _____

10. multiplicity + *-es* = _____

11. fray + *-ed* = _____

12. sly + *-ness* = _____

13. warranty + *-es* = _____

14. gray + *-ish* = _____

15. rectify + *-ed* = _____

16. immunity + *-es* = _____

17. obey + *-ing* = _____

18. array + *-ed* = _____

19. comply + *-ing* = _____

20. witty + *-er* = _____

21. buy + *-er* = _____

22. crazy + *-ness* = _____

23. envy + -able = _____

24. lazy + -ly = _____

25. dry + -er = _____

26. preliminary + -ly = _____

27. costly + -ness = _____

28. lucky + -est = _____

29. contradictory + -ly = _____

30. mystery + -ous = _____

Number correct _____ (total 30)

The Final Silent *e*

When a suffix beginning with a vowel is added to a word ending in a silent *e*, the *e* is usually dropped.

assemble + -ed = assembled   survive + -al = survival

fame + -ous = famous   lodge + -ing = lodging

recline + -er = recliner   considerate + -ion = consideration

When a suffix beginning with a consonant is added to a word ending in a silent *e*, the *e* is usually retained.

definite + -ly = definitely   name + -less = nameless

spite + -ful = spiteful   simple + -ness = simpleness

entire + -ty = entirety   amaze + -ment = amazement

Exceptions:

true + -ly = truly   whole + -ly = wholly

argue + -ment = argument   awe + -ful = awful

Exercise A In these sentences, find each misspelled word, and write the correct spelling on the line following the sentence. There may be more than one misspelled word in a sentence.

1. Various consumeer groups inquired into the inflated prices of canned goods.

   _____

2. A feeling of desperateion swept over the boy as he realized he had taken the wrong bus.

   _____

3. The Department of Agriculture is concerned about the possibility of people bringing diseaseed plants into the country.

_____

4. Professor Pratt sent a belatd note of congratulation.

_____

5. Peter found it difficult to resist the ceasless attempts by club members to make him president.

_____

6. The tightrope walker needed persevereance to remain poised on the thin wire.

_____

7. The new owners felt that the remotness of the cottage was one of its most desireable features.

_____

8. Arnold deviseed a scheme that requird the utmost caution.

_____

9. Nan's strong resembleance to her aunt was amazeing.

_____

10. The committee offered a diverseity of ideas for the graduation party.

_____

11. Sonia's immigrant grandparents never truely felt at home in the United States.

_____

12. The cost of makeing the copies was ninteen dollars.

_____

13. The appropriatness of Lisa's observeations surprised everyone.

_____

14. The school bus hesitated at the corner, then acceleratd.

_____

15. Jerry delicately lifted the expenseive vase from the mantle.

_____   _____

Number correct _____ (total 20)

Exercise B Add the suffixes indicated, and write the new word in the blank.

1. bribe + *-ed* = _____

2. emote + *-ion* = _____

3. isolate + -ed = _____

4. consume + -able = _____

5. universe + -al = _____

6. apprentice + -ship = _____

7. refine + -ment = _____

8. active + -ate = _____

9. supreme + -ly = _____

10. exercise + -ing = _____

11. achieve + -ment = _____

12. time + -ly = _____

13. hope + -less = _____

14. precede + -ed = _____

15. operate + -ion = _____

16. converge + -ed = _____

17. exclude + -ing = _____

18. jostle + -ed = _____

19. recede + -ing = _____

20. pore + -ous = _____

21. expanse + -ive = _____

22. aspire + -ing = _____

23. announce + -ed = _____

24. offense + -ive = _____

25. passive + -ity = _____

26. entire + -ly = _____

27. elite + -ist = _____

28. nine + -ty = _____

29. specialize + -ed = _____

30. generate + -ion = _____

Number correct _____ (total 30)

Doubling the Final Consonant

In one-syllable words that end with a single consonant preceded by a single vowel, double the final consonant before adding a suffix beginning with a vowel.

pin + *-ing* = pinning   fat + *-er* = fatter

Before adding a suffix beginning with a vowel to a word of two or more syllables, double the final consonant only if both of the following conditions exist:
1. The word ends with a single consonant preceded by a single vowel.
2. The word is accented on the last syllable.

con fer′ + *-ed* = con ferred′   re fer′ + *-al* = re fer′ ral

pro pel′ + *-er* = pro pel′ ler   per mit′ + *-ing* = per mit′ ting

com mit′ + *-ed* = com mit′ ted   de ter′ + *-ence* = de ter′ rence

Note in the examples above that the syllable accented in the new word is the same syllable that was accented before adding the suffix.

If the newly formed word is accented on a different syllable, the final consonant is not doubled.

con fer′ + *-ence* = con′ fer ence   in fer′ + *-ence* = in′ fer ence

Exercise Each word below is divided into syllables. Determine which syllable in each word is accented, and insert the accent mark. Then add the suffix indicated, writing the new word in the blank. Repeat this procedure with the second suffix indicated.

Example: e mit′ + *-ed* = emitted + *-ing* = emitting

1. pro fit + *-ed* = _____ + *-ing* = _____

2. gov ern + *-ed* = _____ + *-ing* = _____

3. re pel + *-ing* = _____ + *-ent* = _____

4. ut ter + *-ed* = _____ + *-ing* = _____

5. vis it + *-ed* = _____ + *-or* = _____

6. dis pel + *-ed* = _____ + *-ing* = _____

7. oc cur + *-ed* = _____ + *-ence* = _____

8. o mit + *-ed* = _____ + *-ing* = _____

9. ed it + *-ed* = _____ + *-or* = _____

10. pre fer + *-ed* = _____ + *-ence* = _____

11. e quip + -ed   = _____ + -ing = _____
12. in hib it + -ed = _____ + -ing = _____
13. re fer + -ed   = _____ + -ence = _____
14. la bor + -ed   = _____ + -er = _____
15. ben e fit + -ed = _____ + -ing = _____
16. bick er + -ed   = _____ + -ing = _____
17. con sid er + -ed = _____ + -able = _____
18. dif fer + -ed   = _____ + -ent = _____
19. de liv er + -ed = _____ + -able = _____
20. prof it + -ed   = _____ + -able = _____

Number correct _____ (total 40)

Words Ending in *-ize* or *-ise*

The suffix *-ize* is usually added to base words to form verbs meaning "to make" or "to become."

public + *-ize* = publicize (to make public)
general + *-ize* = generalize (to make general)

The *-ise* ending is less common. It is usually part of the base word itself rather than a suffix.

advertise   surprise   televise   devise

Exercise Decide whether *-ize* or *-ise* should be added to each word or letter group. Then write the complete word in the blank.

1. real _____	11. author _____
2. comprom _____	12. custom _____
3. internal _____	13. enterpr _____
4. special _____	14. rational _____
5. dev _____	15. rev _____
6. exerc _____	16. critic _____
7. superv _____	17. telev _____
8. revolution _____	18. compr _____
9. idol _____	19. merchand _____
10. hospital _____	20. final _____

Number correct _____ (total 20)

The Suffix -ion

The -ion suffix can change verbs to nouns.

operate + -ion = operation   emote + -ion = emotion

locate + -ion = location   express + -ion = expression

In the examples above, -ion is either added directly to the verb form, or the final e is dropped before -ion is added.

Some verbs when made into nouns have irregular spellings.

compose + -ion = composition   persuade + -ion = persuasion

assume + -ion = assumption   proclaim + -ion = proclamation

In the case of words that do not follow regular spelling patterns, you must memorize their spellings.

Exercise A Add -ion to each of the following words. Then write the new word.

1. isolate _____
2. elevate _____
3. reject _____
4. appropriate _____
5. correct _____
6. associate _____
7. impress _____
8. decorate _____
9. duplicate _____
10. contradict _____
11. detect _____
12. congregate _____
13. object _____
14. situate _____
15. regulate _____
16. donate _____
17. hesitate _____
18. appreciate _____
19. extract _____
20. navigate _____

Number correct _____ (total 20)

Exercise B Each of the following nouns was formed by adding the -ion suffix to a verb. In each case, the verb has been modified before -ion was added. Write the verb from which the word was formed. Use a dictionary when needed.

1. revolution _____
2. inclusion _____
3. subscription _____
4. seclusion _____
5. production _____
6. transmission _____
7. presentation _____
8. exclamation _____
9. diminution _____
10. provision _____
11. transformation _____
12. contention _____
13. continuation _____
14. division _____
15. recommendation _____

Number correct _____ (total 15)

Other Spelling Problems

Words with ie and ei

When the sound is long *e* (ē), it is spelled *ie* except after *c*. If the vowel combination sounds like a long *a* (ā), spell it *ei*.

i before e

thief	yield	believe	niece	fierce
chief	grief	brief	relieve	

except after c

ceiling	deceive	perceive	receive	deceit	receipt

or when sounded as a

neighbor	weigh	reign

Exceptions: either, weird, seize, financier, neither, species, leisure

You can remember these words by combining them into the following sentence: *Neither financier seized either weird species of leisure.*

Exercise A In these sentences, find each misspelled word, and write the correct spelling on the line following the sentence.

1. Frank decieved others into thinking he was full of grief.

   _____

2. Mr. Atkins tried to retreive his neighbor's newspaper from the tree.

   _____

3. Carmen siezed the sack of potatoes, which weighed nineteen pounds.

   _____

4. The theif had conceived a plan for stealing the yacht from the pier.

   _____

5. The financeir did not believe the pessimistic predictions about the stock market.

   _____

6. The ceiling was so cracked that niether the plasterer nor the painter could achieve the desired results.

   _____

7. The firefighter's chief concern was to contain the fierce blaze before it spread to the nearby feild.

   _____

8. The weird species of insect had transparent wings that were difficult to percieve with the naked eye.

_____

9. A brief consultation with the doctor relieved my niece of her worries.

_____

10. The freight train yeilded the right of way to the passenger train.

_____

Number correct _____ (total 10)

Exercise B Fill in the blanks with *ie* or *ei*.

1. w __ __ rd

2. bel __ __ ve

3. conc __ __ ted

4. s __ __ ge

5. sh __ __ ld

6. p __ __ ce

7. rel __ __ f

8. sl __ __ gh

9. handkerch __ __ f

10. __ __ ther

11. shr __ __ k

12. rec __ __ pt

13. __ __ ght

14. dec __ __ t

15. l __ __ sure

Number correct _____ (total 15)

Words with the "Seed" Sound

One English word ends in *sede*:
supersede

Three words end in *ceed*:
exceed   proceed   succeed

All other words ending in the sound of *seed* are spelled with *cede*:
accede   concede   precede   recede   secede

Exercise A In these sentences, find each misspelled word, and write the correct spelling on the line following the sentence.

1. Proceed with your plans to seceed from the federation.

_____

2. The radio commercial will precede the speech and will not exsede thirty seconds.

_____

3. Roberto succeeded in convincing his family to prosede with their camping trip.

_____

4. The man with the receeding hairline conceded that he hopes to buy a hairpiece.

_____

5. The latest curfew rule will supercede all preceding ones.

_____

6. Although the gymnast conseded defeat in the semifinal tournament, she proceeded to practice her routine.

_____

7. The company president acceded to the workers' demand that a preceeding agreement be honored.

_____

8. The princess acceded to the throne, since her attempt to depose the prince succeeded.

_____

9. The lawyer proseeded to intercede in the argument between the defendant and his accusers.

_____

10. The exceedingly talented ballet dancer sucseded in winning the competition.

_____

Number correct _____ (total 10)

Exercise B Put a check by the five correctly spelled words below.

1. accede _____   6. intercede _____

2. excede _____   7. prosede _____

3. precede _____   8. receed _____

4. succede _____   9. secede _____

5. concede _____   10. superseed _____

Number correct _____ (total 10)

The Letter c

When the letter *c* has a *k* sound, it is usually followed by the vowel, *a, o,* or *u,* or by any consonant except *y.*

verti*c*al   *c*ommon   *c*urious   pra*c*ti*c*al

When the letter *c* has an *s* sound, it is usually followed by an *e,* an *i,* or a *y.*

*ce*aseless   turbulen*ce*   bi*c*ycle   *ci*tizen

Exercise A Decide if the *c* in each word below has a *k* or an *s* sound. Write *k* or *s* in the blank.

1. fiction _____
2. apprentice _____
3. particle _____
4. eminence _____
5. emergency _____
6. combustion _____
7. credit _____
8. factor _____
9. drastically _____
10. nuclear _____

11. reluctant _____
12. excess _____
13. college _____
14. precede _____
15. claim _____
16. exclude _____
17. discount _____
18. contented _____
19. resistance _____
20. discard _____

Number correct _____ (total 20)

Exercise B Write the missing letter or letters in each word.

1. c __ ntempt
2. c __ adle
3. forec __ st
4. resilienc __
5. distinc __
6. applic __ ble
7. rec __ de
8. c __ ndition
9. enc __ unter
10. technic __ lly

11. dec __ ased
12. c __ rburetor
13. c __ nvert
14. produc __ ion
15. c __ ntradic __
16. ec __ nomy
17. occ __ sional
18. diligenc __
19. financ __
20. supremac __

Number correct _____ (total 20)

The Letter *g*

When the letter *g* has a hard sound, as in the word *go*, it is usually followed by the vowel *a*, *o*, or *u*, or by any consonant except *y*.

gather   govern   gust   magnify

When the letter *g* has a *j* sound, it is usually followed by an *e*, an *i*, or a *y*.

verge   rigid   biology   gymnasium

Exceptions:

giggle   gill   girl   give

Exercise A Decide if the *g* in each word has a *j* sound or a hard sound, as in the word *go*. Write *j* or *go* in the blank.

1. degenerate   ____   11. ingenious   ____

2. colleague   ____   12. tragic   ____

3. gratitude   ____   13. glossary   ____

4. plunge   ____   14. dislodge   ____

5. digest   ____   15. gesture   ____

6. oregano   ____   16. golden   ____

7. rigorous   ____   17. grain   ____

8. tangible   ____   18. distinguish   ____

9. immigrant   ____   19. gyroscope   ____

10. guard   ____   20. glory   ____

Number correct _____ (total 20)

Exercise B Write the missing letter or letters in each word.

1. portag __   8. trag __ dy   15. reg __ lar

2. elig __ ble   9. converg __   16. colleg __

3. grudg __   10. dilig __ nce   17. g __ neration

4. g __ ther   11. g __ ilty   18. g __ ssip

5. exceeding __ y   12. g __ laxy   19. sing __ e

6. g __ nuine   13. mytholog __   20. cong __ eg __ tion

7. bellig __ rent   14. eng __ g __

Number correct _____ (total 20)

Spelling Review

Exercise A Add the prefix or suffix indicated, and write the word.

1. *dis-* + engage = _____

2. collect + *-ion* = _____

3. amaze + *-ment* = _____

4. *ad-* + mire = _____

5. external + *-ize* = _____

6. *in-* + possible = _____

7. *ex-* + ficient = _____

8. rely + *-able* = _____

9. remote + *-ness* = _____

10. *pre-* + tense = _____

11. *re-* + serve = _____

12. express + *-ive* = _____

13. *ad-* + commodate = _____

14. *com-* + vert = _____

15. define + *-ed* = _____

16. *in-* + regular = _____

17. transmit + *-ion* = _____

18. *fore-* + cast = _____

19. time + *-ly* = _____

20. *ex-* + ponent = _____

Number correct _____ (total 20)

Exercise B Three of the words in each row follow the same spelling pattern. Circle the word that does not follow the pattern.

1. propelled   transmitting   committal   elitist

2. remoteness   ceasing   operation   diversity

3. congratulate   intangible   rigor   single

4. explain   eloquent   exceed   exhaust

234

5. typifies   applying   reliance   preliminarily

6. collection   distinct   particle   diligence

7. proceed   concede   recede   accede

8. compromise   surprise   rationalize   devise

9. apprentice   adapt   adjacent   adhere

10. irregular   illegal   immovable   indebted

Number correct _____ (total 10)

Exercise C Find the misspelled words in these sentences, and spell them correctly on the line after the sentence. There may be more than one misspelled word in a sentence.

1. Curtis monopolyzed the radio for an excedingly long time.

_____

2. The prisoner was placed in total isolateion for a period of three days.

_____

3. Young animals learn surviveal techniques early in their lives.

_____

4. The adsembly hall was filled to maximum capacitie.

_____

5. Dr. Jung specialises in pediatric medicine because she cares about children.

_____

6. It was Lucille's intension to dissregard her brother's teaseing.

_____

7. Joanne wrote a musical composition that requird great skill to perform.

_____

8. The convict told the inpartial judge that he was truely sorry.

_____

9. Switzerland exsports cheese to varyous countries.

_____

10. The robin siting in the maple tree arouseed the curiosity of the nieghbor's cat.

_____

11. The recent inmigrant sucseded because of his perseverance.

_____

12. Exsamine the contents of your suitcase before leaveing on your vacasion.

_____

13. Paula's releif was evident to everyone.

_____

14. There were few obstaclees Mary could not overcome if she was determined.

_____

15. The forcast called for clear skies through the holiday weekend.

_____

16. The pair of butterflys eluded us as they flew into the forest.

_____

17. The teacher provided individualised instrucsion to those students who required additionnal assistance.

_____

18. Eddie comsumed massive quantityes of potato salad at the school picnic.

_____

19. The speaker refered the audience to the charts she had prepared.

_____

20. Mark Twain was a fameous humorist whose writtings are still popular today.

_____

Number correct _____ (total 35)

Number correct in Spelling Handbook _____ (total 455)

Commonly Misspelled Words

abbreviate
accidentally
achievement
all right
altogether
amateur
analyze
anonymous
answer
apologize
appearance
appreciate
appropriate
arrangement
associate
awkward
bargain
beginning
believe
bicycle
bookkeeper
bulletin
bureau
business
calendar
campaign
candidate
certain
changeable
characteristic
column
committee
courageous
courteous
criticize
curiosity
cylinder
dealt
decision
definitely
dependent

description
desirable
despair
desperate
dictionary
different
disappear
disappoint
discipline
dissatisfied
efficient
eighth
eligible
embarrass
emphasize
enthusiastic
environment
especially
exaggerate
exhaust
experience
familiar
fascinating
February
financial
foreign
fourth
fragile
generally
government
grammar
guarantee
guard
gymnasium
handkerchief
height
humorous
imaginary
immediately
incredible
influence

intelligence
knowledge
laboratory
lightning
literature
loneliness
marriage
mathematics
medicine
minimum
mischievous
missile
mortgage
municipal
necessary
nickel
ninety
noticeable
nuclear
nuisance
obstacle
occasionally
occur
opinion
opportunity
outrageous
parallel
particularly
permanent
permissible
persuade
pleasant
pneumonia
politics
possess
possibility
prejudice
privilege
probably
pronunciation
psychology

realize
recognize
recommend
reference
referred
rehearse
repetition
representative
restaurant
rhythm
ridiculous
sandwich
scissors
separate
sergeant
similar
sincerely
sophomore
souvenir
specifically
success
syllable
sympathy
symptom
temperature
thorough
throughout
together
tomorrow
traffic
tragedy
transferred
truly
Tuesday
twelfth
undoubtedly
unnecessary
vacuum
vicinity
village
weird

Commonly Confused Words

The following section lists words that are commonly confused and misused. Some of these words are homonyms, words that sound similar but have different meanings. Study the words in this list and learn how to use them correctly.

accent (ak′sent) n.—emphasis in speech or writing
ascent (ə sent′) n.—act of going up
assent (ə sent′) n.—consent; v.—to accept or agree

accept (ək sept′, ak-) v.—to agree to something or receive something willingly
except (ik sept′) v.—to omit or exclude; prep.—not including

adapt (ə dapt′) v.—to adjust; make fitting or appropriate
adept (ə dept′) adj.—skillful
adopt (ə däpt′) v.—to choose as one's own; accept

affect (ə fekt′) v.—to influence; pretend
affect (af′ekt) n.—feeling
effect (ə fekt′, i-) n.—result of an action
effect (ə fekt′, i-) v.—to accomplish or produce a result

all ready adv. (all) and adj. (ready)—completely prepared
already (ôl red′ē) adv.—even now; before the given time

any way adj. (any) and n. (way)—in whatever manner
anyway (en′ē wā′) adv.—regardless

appraise (ə prāz′) v.—to set a value on
apprise (ə prīz′) v.—to inform

bibliography (bib′lē äg′rə fē) n.—list of writings on a particular topic
biography (bī äg′ rə fē, bē-) n.—written history of a person's life

bazaar (bə zär′) n.—market; fair
bizarre (bi zär′) adj.—odd

coarse (kôrs) adj.—rough; crude
course (kôrs) n.—route; progression; part of a meal; class or unit of instruction in a subject

costume (käs′tōōm, -tyōōm) n.—special way of dressing
custom (kus′təm) n.—usual practice or habit

decent (dē′s'nt) adj.—proper
descent (di sent′) n.—a fall; a coming down
dissent (di sent′) n.—disagreement; v.—to disagree

desert (dez′ərt) n.—dry region
desert (di zʉrt′) v.—to abandon
dessert (di zʉrt′) n.—sweet course served at the end of a meal

device (di vīs′) n.—a tool or machine
devise (di vīz′) v.—to plan

elusive (i lo͞o′siv) adj.—hard to catch or understand
illusive (i lo͞o′siv) adj.—misleading; unreal

emigrate (em′ə grāt′) v.—to leave a country and take up residence
                               elsewhere
immigrate (im′ə grāt′) v.—to enter a country and take up residence

farther (fär′thər) adj.—more distant (refers to space)
further (fʉr′thər) adj.—additional (refers to time, quantity, or degree)

flair (fler) n.—natural ability; knack; sense of style
flare (fler) v.—to flame; erupt; n.—a blaze of light

lay (lā) v.—to set something down or place something
lie (lī) v.—to recline; tell untruths; n.—an untruth

moral (môr′əl, mär′-) n.—lesson; adj.—relating to right and wrong
morale (mə ral′, mô-) n.—mental state of confidence, enthusiasm

personal (pʉr′s′n əl) adj.—private
personnel (pʉr′sə nel′) n.—persons employed in an organization

precede (pri sēd′) v.—to go before
proceed (prə sēd′, prō-) v.—to advance; continue

profit (präf′it) v.—to gain earnings; n.—financial gain on investments
prophet (präf′it) n.—predictor, fortuneteller

quiet (kwī′ ət) adj.—not noisy; n.—a sense of calm; v.—to soothe
quit (kwit) v.—to stop
quite (kwīt) adv.—very

step (step) n.—footfall; dance movement; one of a series of acts; v.—to move
                         the foot as in walking
steppe (step) n.—large, treeless plain

team (tēm) n.—group of people working together on a project
teem (tēm) v.—to swarm or be full of

than (*th*an, *th*en; *unstressed th*ən, *th*′n) conj.—word used in comparison
then (*th*en) adv.—at that time; next in order of time; n.—that time

thorough (thʉr′ ō, -ə) adj.—complete
through (thro͞o) prep.—by means of; from beginning to end; adv.—in one
                       side and out the other

Glossary

A

abandon (v.) to give up something; desert; p. 69. *Related word:* abandonment; p. 78.

abruptly (adv.) unexpectedly; p. 168. *Related word:* abrupt; p. 176.

accord (n.) mutual agreement, harmony; an informal agreement, as between nations; p. 26.

accurate (adj.) careful and exact; free from error; adhering closely to a standard; p. 26. *Related word:* accuracy; p. 34.

achievement (n.) accomplishment; p. 81. *Related word:* achieve; p. 90.

acquaintance (n.) knowledge (of something) obtained from personal experience or study; a person whom one knows slightly; p.26. *Related word:* acquaint; p. 34.

acquire (v.) to get; come to have as one's own; p. 81. *Related word:* acquisition; p. 90.

adjacent (adj.) bordering; neighboring; p.123.

agent (n.) a person or thing that brings about a certain result; a force or substance that produces an effect; a person, firm, etc., authorized to act for another; a representative of a government agency; p.26.

aide (n.) an assistant; p. 134. *Related word:* aid; p. 141.

aloof (adj.) distant in interest, sympathy; (adv.) apart, at a distance but in view; p. 36. *Related word:* aloofness; p. 43.

application (n.) the act of putting something on or putting something to use; a form to be filled out when requesting employment, membership, etc.; p. 58. *Related word:* apply; p. 65.

apprentice (n.) a person who is being trained by a master craftsman; (v.) to place in or accept such a position; p. 134. *Related word:* apprenticeship; p. 141.

aridity (n.) condition of being dry and barren; p. 168. *Related word:* arid; p. 176.

arrest (v.) to stop or check the motion, course, or spread of; (n.) a taking into custody; p. 168. *Related word:* arresting; p. 176.

artery (n.) a main road; a tube that carries blood away from the heart to the other parts of the body; p. 58. *Related word:* arterial; p. 65.

aspiration (n.) a strong desire; the inhalation of something into the lungs; p. 134. *Related words:* aspire, conspire, expire, inspire; p. 141.

assembly (n.) a group of persons gathered together for the purpose of instruction, worship, etc.; a fitting together of parts; p. 69. *Related words:* assemblage, assemble, disassembly; p. 78.

associate (v.) to join together; bring someone in as a partner; (n.) a friend, partner, or fellow worker; (adj.) accompanying; p. 14. *Related word:* association; p. 23.

attest (v.) to declare to be true; certify; p. 179.

attitude (n.) a manner of acting, feeling, or thinking; posture; p. 134.

austerely (adv.) harshly; severely; p. 168. *Related words:* austere, austerity; p. 176.

B

bankrupt (adj.) broke; out of money; (v.) to cause to become bankrupt; p. 14. *Related word:* bankruptcy; p. 23.

barbaric (adj.) uncivilized, primitive; wild, crude, and without control; p. 36. *Related word:* barbarian; p. 43.

belated (adj.) delayed; overdue; p. 158.

belligerent (adj.) warlike; quarrelsome; inclined to show hostility or aggressiveness; (n.) a belligerent person or nation; p. 158.

benefit (n.) advantage; payments made by an insurance company, employer, public agency, etc. during sickness, retirement, or unemployment; a public performance to raise money for a cause; (v.) to do good for, aid; receive an advantage; p. 134.

bough (n.) a branch of a tree, esp. a main branch; p. 36.

bound (adj.) confined by (or as by) being tied; destined; obliged; going, headed; (v.) to limit, confine; serve as a boundary to; (n.) *usually plural:* limits, boundaries; p. 36.

bounteous (adj.) provided in abundance; plentiful; p. 158.

briskly (adv.) energetically; p. 123. *Related word:* briskness; p. 131.

burrow (n.) a hole or tunnel dug by an animal; (v.) to dig a tunnel; search; p. 112.

C

carburetor (n.) the part of an internal-combustion engine that blends air and gas to make an explosive mixture; p. 179.

casually (adv.) happening by chance; slightly or superficially; informally, relaxed; p. 36.

cease (v.) to stop; p. 168. *Related word:* ceaseless; p. 176.

chaos (n.) disorder; p. 168. *Related word:* chaotic; p. 176.

clarity (n.) the quality or condition of being clear; p. 26. *Related word:* clarify; p. 34.

colleague (n.) fellow worker; p. 112.

combustion (n.) the act or process of burning; p. 179. *Related word:* combustible; p. 188.

communion (n.) a sharing of one's thoughts and emotions; a close relationship; p.26. *Related words:* commune, community; p. 34.

component (n.) an ingredient; (adj.) serving as one of the parts of something; p. 112. *Related words:* opponent, proponent; p. 119.

condition (n.) situation; provision; requirement; state of health; (v.) to bring into a desired state of health; p. 134. *Related word:* conditional; p. 141.

considerable (adj.) large; important; p. 69. *Related words:* consider, considerate; p. 78.

consume (v.) to use up; eat or drink; destroy; waste; p. 58. *Related word:* consumer; p. 65.

contemptuous (adj.) scornful; p. 158.

contend (v.) to compete; clash; p. 58. *Related word:* contention; p. 65.

contented (adj.) satisfied; p. 123.

converge (v.) to come together at a point; p. 69.

convey (v.) to take from one place to another, transport; serve as a channel or a medium; to make known, communicate; transfer to another person; p. 123.

corrosion (n.) a wearing away by the action of chemicals; a substance, such as rust, formed by corroding; p. 58. *Related words:* corrode, corrosive; p. 65.

counsel (v.) to advise; recommend; (n.) advice; suggestion; lawyer; p. 134. *Related word:* council; p. 141.

courteous (adj.) well-mannered, polite; considerate of others; p. 36.

curious (adj.) inquisitive; peculiar; p. 123.

D

debt (n.) something owed; p. 69. *Related word:* indebted; p. 78.

decline (v.) to refuse; worsen; (n.) a dip; descent; p. 69. *Related words:* inclination, incline, recline; p. 78.

defect (n.) fault or deficiency; (v.) to abandon a country or cause; p. 81. *Related word:* defective; p. 90.

definitely (adv.) certainly; precisely; p. 69. *Related words:* define, definite; p. 78.

delicately (adv.) daintily; in a way that gives pleasure or delight; softly, lightly; sensitively; p. 123.

dense (adj.) crowded, compact; p. 36.

deport (v.) to carry or send away; force someone to leave a country; p. 158.

desperate (adj.) without hope; p. 81. *Related words:* despair, desperation; p. 90.

despite (prep.) in spite of; not withstanding; p. 69.

destination (n.) goal; p. 69. *Related word:* destiny; p. 78.

devoted (adj.) to set apart for a special use; dedicated to some purpose, activity, or person; p. 14. *Related word:* devotion; p. 23.

diameter (n.) a straight line passing through the center of a circle from one side to the other; p. 58.

diligence (n.) careful, persistent effort; p. 134. *Related word:* diligent; p. 141.

dilution (n.) the thinning down of a mixture by the addition of water or other liquid; p. 112. *Related word:* dilute; p. 119.

dislodge (v.) to remove by force from a position where trapped or hiding; p. 69. *Related word:* lodge; p. 78.

dismay (n.) a loss of courage when faced with trouble or danger; p. 36.

distinct (adj.) different; not alike; individual; easily seen or heard; unmistakable; p. 179. *Related words:* distinction, distinctive; p. 188.

distributor (n.) a device that dispenses electric current to the spark plugs of a gasoline engine; a person or business that divides and hands something out; p. 179. *Related words:* distribute, distribution; p. 188.

diverse (adj.) dissimilar; p. 14. *Related word:* diversity; p. 23.

domestic (adj.) of one's home country; of the home or housekeeping; (n.) a servant; p. 58.

drastic (adj.) extreme; harsh; p. 14.

duplicate (v.) to correspond exactly; copy; (adj.) same or alike; (n.) an exact copy; p. 81. *Related word:* duplication; p. 90.

E

economical (adj.) thrifty; p. 58. *Related word:* economy; p. 65.

effective (adj.) having an effect; producing the desired result; making a striking impression; p. 112. *Related word:* effectively; p. 119.

efficiently (adv.) producing a desired effect with the least effort or waste; competently; p. 58. *Related words:* efficiency, efficient; p. 65.

eligible (adj.) qualified; p. 81. *Related words:* eligibility, ineligible; p. 90.

elite (adj.) choice, superior, select; (n.) a group regarded as best, the finest, etc.; p. 179. *Related word:* elitist; p. 188.

elusive (adj.) fugitive; hard to find or grasp; p. 69. *Related word:* elude; p. 78.

emission (n.) something that is given forth or discharged; p. 179. *Related word:* emit; p. 188.

emotional (adj.) showing strong feeling; p.14. *Related words:* emotion, unemotional; p.23.

employment (n.) work; occupation; job; p. 134.

encounter (n.) a meeting; conflict; (v.) to meet; experience; p. 179.

endear (v.) to make dear or beloved; p. 158.

energetic (adj.) vigorous, forceful; p. 36. *Related word:* energize; p. 43.

exclusive (adj.) restrictive; belonging to a select group; p. 81. *Related words:* exclude, include; p. 90.

existence (n.) being; p. 58. *Related word:* exist; p. 65.

exotic (adj.) foreign; strangely beautiful, attractive; (n.) a foreign or imported thing; a plant that is not native; p. 179. *Related word:* exotically; p. 188.

expression (n.) a putting into words; a particular word or phrase; a showing of feeling or character; a look, intonation, etc., that shows meaning or feeling; p. 26. *Related word:* express; p. 34.

external (adj.) on the outside; p. 179.

extract (v.) to pull out; remove metal from ore; (n.) something removed or pulled out; p. 69. *Related word:* extraction; p. 78.

F

factor (n.) an element or ingredient; p. 112.

falter (v.) to stumble; hesitate; p. 81.

federal (adj.) having to do with the central government of the United States or another union of states; p. 134. *Related word:* federation; p. 141.

fictional (adj.) imaginary; of a literary work with imaginary characters or events; p. 14. *Related words:* fiction, nonfiction; p. 23.

financial (adj.) having to do with money matters; p. 81. *Related words:* finance, financier; p. 90.

fixture (n.) anything firmly in place; p. 69.

flair (n.) a natural talent or ability; a sense of what is stylish; p. 14.

flamboyant (adj.) flashy; extravagant; p. 14.

flounder (v.) to struggle awkwardly; act with confusion and hesitation; (n.) a flatfish caught for food; p. 158.

G

generation (n.) a single stage in the history of a family; the act of producing offspring; all of the people born at about the same time; p. 179. *Related word:* generate; p. 188.

gesture (n.) a movement made with some part of the body to emphasize or express an idea or feeling; anything said or done to communicate one's wishes or feelings; (v.) to express through gestures or movements; p. 123.

gratitude (n.) a feeling of thankful appreciation; p. 26.

grave (adj.) solemn; important, weighty; serious, threatening; dignified; p. 26.

H

habitat (n.) region where a plant or animal naturally lives; p. 112. *Related words:* inhabit, inhabitant; p. 119.

hesitate (v.) to pause or delay in acting; falter; p. 123. *Related word:* hesitation; p. 131.

humanitarian (n.) a person who is actively concerned with promoting human welfare; philanthropist; (adj.) helping humanity; of humanism or the humanities; p. 14.

humorist (n.) a person skilled at telling jokes and funny stories; p. 14. *Related word:* humorous; p. 23.

I

immigrate (v.) to settle in a new country; p. 134. *Related words:* immigrant, migrate; p. 141.

immunity (n.) freedom from something unpleasant; resistance to a particular disease; exemption; p. 112. *Related word:* immune; p. 119.

inanimate (adj.) without life; dull; p. 36. *Related words:* animate, animated, animation, animator, animosity; p. 43.

individualistic (adj.) unique; nonconforming; unusual; p. 14. *Related word:* individualist; p. 23.

industry (n.) any large-scale business activity; hard work; skill; p. 134.

injection (n.) an introduction of a missing quality; the forcing or driving of (a liquid) into something; the act of forcing liquid into a part of the body by means of a hypodermic needle; p. 58. *Related words:* dejected, eject, inject, project, reject; p. 65.

innovation (n.) something newly introduced; p. 58.

inquisitive (adj.) questioning; curious; prying; p. 14. *Related words:* inquire, inquiry, require, uninquisitive; p. 23.

instinctive (adj.) of, or having the nature of, an inborn ability, talent, or tendency; p. 26.

intangible (adj.) vague; not easily defined; (n.) something vague; p. 168. *Related word:* tangible; p. 176.

integrity (n.) the condition of being complete; wholeness; strong, stable condition; uprightness, honesty; p. 26.

intently (adv.) with strong concentration; p. 123. *Related word:* intention; p. 131.

interior (n.) the inside of a room or building; (adj.) inner; p. 14. *Related word:* exterior; p. 23.

internal (adj.) having to do with the inside; p. 179.

intimate (adj.) very close; familiar; private or personal; suggesting privacy, romance; p. 26. *Related word:* intimacy; p. 34.

isolate (v.) to set apart from others; p. 58. *Related word:* isolation; p. 65.

J

jostle (v.) to bump or push, as in a crowd; (n.) a rough bump or shove; p. 168.

jubilant (adj.) joyful, elated; p. 158. *Related word:* jubilee; p. 166.

K

keen (adj.) sharp; quick in seeing, hearing, thinking; acute; p. 36.

L

languid (adj.) without vigor or vitality; drooping; listless; sluggish; p. 36. *Related word:* languor; p. 43.

lethal (adj.) deadly; fatal; p. 112.

long (v.) to feel a strong yearning; wish for; (adj.) not short or brief; p. 36.

M

maintenance (n.) the work of keeping something in good repair; p. 81. *Related word:* maintain; p. 90.

mason (n.) a person who builds with brick and stone; p. 134. *Related word:* masonry; p. 141.

materialize (v.) to give physical form to; develop into something real; appear; p. 123. *Related word:* material; p. 131.

memento (n.) a reminder or souvenir; p. 158.

memorable (adj.) worth remembering; notable; p. 14. *Related word:* memorize; p. 23.

merit (v.) to deserve; (n.) the state, fact, or quality of deserving well or ill; worth; value; something deserving reward; p. 179. *Related word:* meritorious; p. 188.

methodically (adv.) in an orderly fashion; systematically; p. 123. *Related words:* method, methodical; p. 131.

metropolitan (adj.) designating or of a population area made up of a central city and smaller surrounding communities; p. 179.

monopolize (v.) to get full possession or control of; dominate completely; p. 81. *Related word:* monopoly; p. 90.

multiple (adj.) having many parts; (n.) a number that is a product of some specific number and another number; p. 112.

N

nucleus (n.) the center of something, around which other things are grouped or collected; p. 158.

O

obstacle (n.) anything that gets in the way or hinders; a barrier; p. 58.

obviously (adv.) clearly; evidently; p. 69. *Related word:* obvious; p. 78.

occasional (adj.) infrequent; p. 123.

offensive (adj.) attacking, aggressive; unpleasant, disgusting; insulting; p. 36. *Related word:* offend; p. 43.

operative (adj.) capable of being used; (n.) a worker; p. 158.

outlook (n.) viewpoint; perspective; p. 81.

P

particular (adj.) distinct; specific; (n.) an item or fact; p. 112.

passive (adj.) acted upon without acting in return; submissive; offering no resistance; p. 134.

patronizing (adj.) to treat in a helpful but haughty or snobbish way; being a regular customer of; p. 36. *Related word:* patron; p. 43.

pedestrian (adj.) commonplace, uninteresting; (n.) a person who walks; p. 81.

peer (n.) one that has the same value, rank, etc.; a noble; (v.) to look closely; p. 123.

perseverance (n.) patient effort; persistence; p. 134.

physical (adj.) of nature and all matter, natural; of, or produced by the forces of, physics; of or concerned with the body as opposed to the mind; p. 26. *Related word:* physics; p. 34.

poise (v.) to balance; keep steady; (n.) ease and dignity of manner; p. 168.

populate (v.) to supply with inhabitants; inhabit; p. 69. *Related word:* population; p. 78.

portion (n.) a fraction or part of something; p. 69.

position (n.) the manner in which a person or thing is placed; one's attitude or opinion on a subject; a location or condition that gives one an advantage; a person's rank or status; a person's job; (v.) to put in a particular position; place; p. 36.

possess (v.) to own; have as a characteristic, quality, etc.; p. 26. *Related words:* possession, possessive; p. 34.

poverty (n.) the condition of being poor; inadequacy; smallness in amount; p. 134.

preliminary (adj.) preparatory; leading up to the main action; p. 112.

private (adj.) of or concerning only one particular person or group; not open or controlled by the public; away from public view; secret; confidential; (n.) an enlisted person of either of the two lowest ranks in the U.S. Army; p. 134.

procedure (n.) the order of steps to be followed; process, course; p. 58. *Related word:* proceed; p. 65.

profitable (adj.) moneymaking; beneficial; p. 158. *Related word:* profit; p. 166.

prominent (adj.) noticeable; widely and favorably known; p. 81. *Related word:* prominence; p. 90.

prompt (v.) to urge; (adj.) quick to act; on time; p. 112. *Related word:* promptness; p. 119.

propel (v.) to set in motion; push, drive, or make go forward; p. 179. *Related word:* propeller; p. 188.

properly (adv.) appropriately; correctly; respectably; p. 123.

proportion (n.) a part or share of the whole; (v.) to arrange the parts into harmony or balance; p. 112. *Related word:* proportional; p. 119.

propose (v.) to put forth for consideration; plan; present as a toast; nominate for office, membership; offer marriage; p. 112. *Related words:* dispose, impose, imposter, proposal; p. 119.

prosper (v.) to succeed; flourish; p. 158.

purity (n.) the quality or condition of being pure; cleanness; clearness; innocence or chastity; p. 26.

pursue (v.) to chase, follow, or go on with; aim at; p. 14. *Related word:* pursuit; p. 23.

Q

quality (n.) any of the features that make something what it is; characteristic; the degree of excellence that a thing possesses; superiority; p. 26.

quietude (n.) calmness; p. 168.

quip (n.) a witty or sarcastic remark; (v.) to make a witty or sarcastic remark; p. 158.

R

random (n.) aimless or unplanned movement; now only in *at random,* without careful choice, aim, or plan; (adj.) haphazard; p. 158.

realistic (adj.) tending to face facts and be practical; depicting things, people, or events in a lifelike way; p. 36. *Related word:* reality; p. 43.

recede (v.) to go or move back; lessen; p. 123. *Related word:* precede; p. 131.

refinery (n.) a plant or establishment where a raw material, such as sugar cane, is made fine or pure; p. 58. *Related words:* refine, refinement; p. 65.

relish (v.) to enjoy thoroughly; (n.) a distinctive flavor; zest; pickles, olives, etc., served with a meal to add flavor; p. 81.

reluctant (adj.) hesitant; unwilling; p. 36. *Related word:* reluctance; 43.

remote (adj.) isolated; distant; p. 168. *Related word:* remoteness; p. 176.

repose (n.) rest; sleep; composure; calm; (v.) to lie at rest; p. 168.

requirement (n.) necessity; something obligatory; a condition; p. 81. *Related word:* require; p. 90.

resilient (adj.) bouncing or springing back into original shape or form; p. 168. *Related word:* resilience; p. 176.

resistance (n.) the act of withstanding or opposing; p. 112.

responsibility (n.) duty; obligation; a person or thing that one is taking care or in charge of; p. 26. *Related words:* irresponsible, responsible; p. 34.

responsive (adj.) answering; reacting quickly and easily; p. 123.

revert (v.) to return to a former practice, opinion, or state; p. 158. *Related words:* controversy, convert, divert, invert, reverse; p. 166.

revolutionize (v.) to make a complete and basic change in; effect political change; p. 179. *Related words:* revolt, revolution; p. 188.

rigid (adj.) not bending or flexible; p. 168. *Related word:* rigidity; p. 176.

rodent (n.) a family of mammals that includes mice, rats, squirrels, etc.; p. 112.

rural (adj.) of or like the country; rustic; p. 14.

S

scour (v.) to go over quickly and thoroughly, as in searching or hunting; to clean and polish by hard rubbing; p. 69.

sheer (adj.) extremely steep; very thin, fine enough to be seen through (said of textiles); pure; absolute; p. 69.

simplicity (n.) the fact of being not complicated, not difficult; the condition of being plain, not fancy; a sincere or natural quality; p. 26.

somnolent (adj.) sleepy, drowsy; causing drowsiness; p. 168.

specialist (n.) expert; p. 134.

spirit (n.) a frame of mind or disposition; life principle or soul; liveliness; courage; an apparition; (adj.) of ghosts or spirits; (v.) to encourage; carry away; p. 168. *Related word:* spiritual; p. 176.

sponsor (v.) to support or promote; vouch for; guarantee; (n.) a patron or benefactor; company or individual that pays the cost of a radio or television program in exchange for advertising; p. 134.

stray (v.) to wander from a given place; (adj.) having wandered; lost; (n.) a person or thing that is lost; esp. a domestic animal wandering at large; p. 123.

sufficient (adj.) as much as is needed; enough; p. 26. *Related words:* insufficient, suffice; p. 34.

sullenness (n.) the condition of being silent and keeping to oneself because of anger, bitterness, hurt, etc.; p. 36. *Related word:* sullen; p. 43.

supremacy (n.) highest power or authority; p. 179. *Related words:* supreme, supremely; p. 188.

surge (n.) any sudden strong increase or rush; a large wave of water; (v.) to move in a surge; p. 36.

survive (v.) to continue to live after or in spite of something; outlive; p. 69. *Related word:* survivor; p. 78.

sympathize (v.) to share the feelings or ideas of another; to express pity or compassion for another; p. 158. *Related word:* sympathy; p. 166.

system (n.) network; method; scheme; p. 58. *Related word:* systematic; p. 65.

T

tariff (n.) a tax placed by a government on exports or imports; (v.) to set a tax on; p. 158.

technically (adv.) according to specific principles or rules; in terms of a specific art, science, or technology; p. 134. *Related word:* technique; p. 141.

technological (adj.) of technology; resulting from the progress in the use of machinery and automation; p. 58.

temperament (n.) disposition; p. 112.

terminal (n.) a depot; a device through which a user communicates with a computer; (adj.) occurring at the end of a series; final; of or in the final stages of a fatal disease; p. 58.

thesis (n.) theory; essay or dissertation; p. 179.

toxin (n.) poison; p. 112. *Related words:* nontoxic, toxic; p. 119.

trace (n.) a very small amount; (v.) to sketch; follow the course of; p. 69.

tragedy (n.) disaster; a serious play; having a sad or unfortunate ending; p. 14. *Related word:* tragic; p. 23.

transfer (v.) to carry or move from one place or position to another; (n.) a thing or person that is transferred; p. 123. *Related words:* confer, defer, infer, refer; p. 131.

transform (v.) to convert; revolutionize; p. 14. *Related word:* transformation; p. 23.

travail (n.) very hard work; intense pain; (v.) to toil or work hard; p. 168.

treacherous (adj.) seemingly safe, but not really so; not loyal; betraying or likely to betray; p. 26.

trend (n.) the general tendency or direction of events; a current style; p. 179.

turbulent (adj.) wild; stormy; p. 168. *Related word:* turbulence; p. 176.

typical (adj.) normal; having the characteristic qualities of a group or class; p. 81. *Related words:* atypical, typify; p. 90.

U

unique (adj.) one and only; p. 14. *Related word:* uniqueness; p. 23.

universal (adj.) occurring everywhere or in all things; p. 81. *Related word:* universe; p. 90.

unpretentious (adj.) modest and simple; p. 158. *Related words:* pretense; pretentious; p. 166.

utterly (adv.) extremely; p. 123. *Related word:* utter; p. 131.

V

vagabond (adj.) moving from place to place with no fixed home; (n.) a wanderer; p. 81.

venom (n.) the poison secreted by some snakes, spiders, insects, etc.; p. 112.

verge (n.) the edge or brink of something; (v.) to be on the brink of; to bend or incline to or toward; p. 168.

vertical (adj.) upright; perpendicular to the horizon; (n.) an upright position; p. 168.

veto (n.) the power to prevent a bill from becoming a law; (v.) to reject or forbid; p. 81.

virtually (adv.) practically; in effect though not in fact; p. 179. *Related word:* virtual; p. 188.

volume (n.) a quantity, bulk; mass, or amount; a book; p. 58.

W

warrant (v.) to justify or deserve; (n.) assurance; guarantee; p. 158. *Related word:* warranty; p. 166.

wistfully (adv.) thoughtfully yearning; p. 123. *Related word:* wistful; p. 131.

Pronunciation Key

Symbol	Key Words
a	ask, fat, parrot
ā	ape, date, play
ä	ah, car, father
e	elf, ten, berry
ē	even, meet, money
i	is, hit, mirror
ī	ice, bite, high
ō	open, tone, go
ô	all, horn, law
o͞o	ooze, tool, crew
o͝o	look pull, moor
yo͞o	use, cute, few
yo͝o	united, cure, globule
oi	oil, point, toy
ou	out, crowd, plow
u	up, cut, color
ur	urn, fur, deter
ə	a in ago e in agent i in sanity o in comply u in focus
ər	perhaps, murder

Symbol	Key Words
b	bed, fable, dub
d	dip, beadle, had
f	fall, after, off
g	get, haggle, dog
h	he, ahead, hotel
j	joy, agile, badge
k	kill, tackle, bake
l	let, hellow, ball
m	met, camel, trim
n	not, flannel, ton
p	put, apple, tap
r	red, port, dear
s	sell, castle, pass
t	top, cattle hat
v	vat, hovel, have
w	will, always, swear
y	yet, onion, yard
z	zebra, dazzle, haze
ch	chin, catcher, arch
sh	she, cushion, dash
th	thin, nothing, truth
th	then, father, lathe
zh	azure, leisure
ŋ	ring, anger, drink
′	able (aʹ b'l)
′ ′	expedition (ekʹ spə dishʹ ən)

Inventory Test

These are all the target words in the book. Why not see how many you think you already know . . . or don't know?

- If you're sure *you know the word*, mark the **Y** *("yes") circle.*
- If *you think you* might *know it*, mark the **?** *(question mark) circle.*
- If *you have* no idea *what it means*, mark the **N** *("no") circle.*

Y	?	N	
O	O	O	abandon
O	O	O	abruptly
O	O	O	accord
O	O	O	accurate
O	O	O	achievement
O	O	O	acquaintance
O	O	O	acquire
O	O	O	adjacent
O	O	O	agent
O	O	O	aide
O	O	O	aloof
O	O	O	application
O	O	O	apprentice
O	O	O	aridity
O	O	O	arrest
O	O	O	artery
O	O	O	aspiration
O	O	O	assembly
O	O	O	associate
O	O	O	attest
O	O	O	attitude
O	O	O	austerely
O	O	O	bankrupt
O	O	O	barbaric
O	O	O	belated
O	O	O	belligerent
O	O	O	benefit
O	O	O	bough
O	O	O	bound
O	O	O	bounteous
O	O	O	briskly
O	O	O	burrow
O	O	O	carburetor
O	O	O	casually
O	O	O	cease
O	O	O	chaos
O	O	O	clarity
O	O	O	colleague
O	O	O	combustion
O	O	O	communion

That's the first 40.

Y	?	N	
O	O	O	component
O	O	O	condition
O	O	O	considerate
O	O	O	consume
O	O	O	contemptuous
O	O	O	contend
O	O	O	contented
O	O	O	converge
O	O	O	convey
O	O	O	corrosion
O	O	O	counsel
O	O	O	courteous
O	O	O	curious
O	O	O	debt
O	O	O	decline
O	O	O	defect
O	O	O	definitely
O	O	O	delicately
O	O	O	dense
O	O	O	deport

You're making good progress.

Y	?	N	
O	O	O	desperate
O	O	O	despite
O	O	O	destination
O	O	O	devoted
O	O	O	diameter
O	O	O	diligence
O	O	O	dilution
O	O	O	dislodge
O	O	O	dismay
O	O	O	distinct
O	O	O	distributor
O	O	O	diverse
O	O	O	domestic
O	O	O	drastic
O	O	O	duplicate
O	O	O	economical
O	O	O	effective
O	O	O	efficiently
O	O	O	eligible
O	O	O	elite

Y	?	N	
O	O	O	elusive
O	O	O	emission
O	O	O	emotional
O	O	O	employment
O	O	O	encounter
O	O	O	endear
O	O	O	energetic
O	O	O	exclusive
O	O	O	existence
O	O	O	exotic
O	O	O	expression
O	O	O	external
O	O	O	extract
O	O	O	factor
O	O	O	falter
O	O	O	federal
O	O	O	fictional
O	O	O	financial
O	O	O	fixture
O	O	O	flair
O	O	O	flamboyant
O	O	O	flounder
O	O	O	generation
O	O	O	gesture
O	O	O	gratitude
O	O	O	grave
O	O	O	habitat
O	O	O	hesitate
O	O	O	humanitarian
O	O	O	humorist
O	O	O	immigrate
O	O	O	immunity
O	O	O	inanimate
O	O	O	individualistic
O	O	O	industry
O	O	O	injection
O	O	O	innovation
O	O	O	inquisitive
O	O	O	instinctive
O	O	O	intangible

Take a break!

Y	?	N		Y	?	N		Y	?	N	
O	O	O	integrity	O	O	O	possess	O	O	O	specialist
O	O	O	intently	O	O	O	poverty	O	O	O	spirit
O	O	O	interior	O	O	O	preliminary	O	O	O	sponsor
O	O	O	internal	O	O	O	private	O	O	O	stray
O	O	O	intimate	O	O	O	procedure	O	O	O	sufficient
O	O	O	isolate	O	O	O	profitable	O	O	O	sullenness
O	O	O	jostle	O	O	O	prominent	O	O	O	supremacy
O	O	O	jubilant	O	O	O	prompt	O	O	O	surge
O	O	O	keen	O	O	O	propel	O	O	O	survive
O	O	O	languid	O	O	O	properly	O	O	O	sympathize
O	O	O	lethal	O	O	O	proportion	O	O	O	system
O	O	O	long	O	O	O	propose	O	O	O	tariff
O	O	O	maintenance	O	O	O	prosper	O	O	O	technically
O	O	O	mason	O	O	O	purity	O	O	O	technological
O	O	O	materialize	O	O	O	pursue	O	O	O	temperament
O	O	O	memento	O	O	O	quality	O	O	O	terminal
O	O	O	memorable	O	O	O	quietude	O	O	O	thesis
O	O	O	merit	O	O	O	quip	O	O	O	toxin
O	O	O	methodically	O	O	O	random	O	O	O	trace
O	O	O	metropolitan	O	O	O	realistic	O	O	O	tragedy
O	O	O	monopolize	O	O	O	recede				*Only 20 more.*
O	O	O	multiple	O	O	O	refinery	O	O	O	transfer
			Half the alphabet.	O	O	O	relish	O	O	O	transform
O	O	O	nucleus	O	O	O	reluctant	O	O	O	travail
O	O	O	obstacle	O	O	O	remote	O	O	O	treacherous
O	O	O	obviously	O	O	O	repose	O	O	O	trend
O	O	O	occasional	O	O	O	requirement	O	O	O	turbulent
O	O	O	offensive	O	O	O	resilient	O	O	O	typical
O	O	O	operative	O	O	O	resistance	O	O	O	unique
O	O	O	outlook	O	O	O	responsibility	O	O	O	universal
O	O	O	particular	O	O	O	responsive	O	O	O	unpretentious
O	O	O	passive	O	O	O	revert	O	O	O	utterly
O	O	O	patronizing	O	O	O	revolutionize	O	O	O	vagabond
O	O	O	pedestrian	O	O	O	rigid	O	O	O	venom
O	O	O	peer	O	O	O	rodent	O	O	O	verge
O	O	O	perseverance	O	O	O	rural	O	O	O	vertical
O	O	O	physical	O	O	O	scour	O	O	O	veto
O	O	O	poise				*This list will end soon.*	O	O	O	virtually
O	O	O	populate	O	O	O	sheer	O	O	O	volume
O	O	O	portion	O	O	O	simplicity	O	O	O	warrant
O	O	O	position	O	O	O	somnolent	O	O	O	wistfully

Congratulations!

That was 240 words. How many of them *don't* you know? Highlight any words you marked **N**, write them on the Personal Vocabulary Log pages provided (beginning on page 267), and pay special attention to them as you work through the book. You'll soon know them all!

Pretest Strategies

Use What You Already Know

There are many ways to get information about what an unfamiliar word might mean.

- It may contain a familiar **whole word.**
- It may be a **compound** of familiar words put together.
- You may recognize the **root.**
- You may recognize a **prefix** or **suffix.**
- There may be **context clues** to the meaning.

Try Everything

When you see an unfamiliar word, use every trick you can think of. You may be surprised to discover how useful what you already know can be. Take a look at how this can work with the word *malodorous* in the sentence "What a malodorous plant!"

	THOUGHT PROCESS	
malodorous	It describes a plant. Must be an adjective.	**a context clue**
mal•*odorous*	What does *mal-* do? Let's see. A malfunction is bad. Malnutrition is bad. So *mal-* is probably "bad."	**thought process**
mal•<u>odor</u>•ous	I see odor in there.	**a whole word**
malodor•<u>ous</u>	I've seen *-ous* at the end of lots of words, like *famous.* Hmm . . . *fame, famous . . . humor, humorous.*	**a familiar suffix**
	Adjective. Bad. Odor. . . . What a <u>bad-smelling</u> plant!	

Try It Yourself

_____ 1. replicate (think about <u>re</u>consider and <u>duplicate</u>)
      a. to push   b. to repeat   c. to sympathize

_____ 2. biped (think about <u>bi</u>cycle and <u>ped</u>al or <u>ped</u>estrian)
      a. two-sided   b. two-eyed   c. two-footed

_____ 3. breakneck (think about <u>break</u> and <u>neck</u>)
      a. dangerous   b. ridiculous   c. not qualified

_____ 4. antiquity (think about <u>antique</u> and activ<u>ity</u>)
      a. great age   b. sturdiness   c. charm or grace

_____ 5. benevolence (think about <u>bene</u>fit and <u>vol</u>unteer)
      a. jealousy   b. kindliness   c. sleepiness

UNIT 1 Test Yourself

Part A Matching Definitions

Match each word on the left with its definition on the right. Write the letter of the appropriate definition in the blank.

_____ 1. associate   a. showing strong feelings

_____ 2. humorist   b. someone who works for the good of others

_____ 3. rural   c. not all alike; involving differences

_____ 4. unique   d. a natural skill or a good sense of style

_____ 5. memorable   e. someone who tells or writes funny stories

_____ 6. devoted   f. willing to give time or energy for a special purpose

_____ 7. humanitarian   g. so unusual as to be one of a kind

_____ 8. flair   h. to think of together

_____ 9. emotional   i. having to do with the country

_____ 10. diverse   j. easy to recall; worth remembering

Part B Synonyms

Write the letter of the word that is closest in meaning to the capitalized word.

_____ 11. BANKRUPT: (A) safe   (B) stuck   (C) damaged   (D) penniless

_____ 12. PURSUE: (A) chase   (B) mix   (C) suspect   (D) find

_____ 13. DRASTIC: (A) silly   (B) dangerous   (C) extreme   (D) unknown

_____ 14. FICTIONAL: (A) new   (B) interesting   (C) made-up   (D) broken

_____ 15. TRANSFORM: (A) change   (B) reverse   (C) cross   (D) create

_____ 16. FLAMBOYANT: (A) proud   (B) showy   (C) bouncy   (D) angry

_____ 17. INQUISITIVE: (A) selfish   (B) hidden   (C) mistaken   (D) questioning

_____ 18. TRAGEDY: (A) sorrow   (B) explosion   (C) disaster   (D) confusion

_____ 19. INDIVIDUALISTIC: (A) lonely   (B) unusual   (C) selfish   (D) admirable

_____ 20. INTERIOR: (A) inside   (B) worse   (C) secret   (D) surface

---

Score Yourself!   *The answers are on page 265.*   Number correct: _____   Part A: _____   Part B: _____

UNIT 2   Test Yourself

Part A   Applying Meaning

Write the letter of the best answer.

_____ 1. If the <u>purity</u> of water is important to you, you want the water to be very
a. clean.   b. cold.   c. deep.   d. bubbly.

_____ 2. A person you would be likely to describe as an <u>acquaintance</u> would be one of your
a. siblings.   b. classmates.   c. parents.   d. best friends.

_____ 3. Someone with <u>integrity</u> is most likely to be
a. funny.   b. attractive.   c. shy.   d. honest.

_____ 4. Something that is often referred to as <u>treacherous</u> is
a. wisdom.   b. thin ice.   c. friendship.   d. a flower garden.

_____ 5. An action often used to express <u>accord</u> is a
a. yawn.   b. nod.   c. raised fist.   d. bow.

_____ 6. To show a feeling of <u>gratitude</u>, a person would be likely to say,
a. "Help!"   b. "Please."   c. "Thank you."   d. "Be quiet."

_____ 7. An <u>intimate</u> relationship is one in which people often tell each other
a. secrets.   b. jokes.   c. lies.   d. what to do.

_____ 8. If you <u>possess</u> something, you
a. want it.   b. hate it.   c. give it up.   d. own it.

Part B   Matching Definitions

Match each word on the left with its definition on the right. Write the letter of the
appropriate definition in the blank.

_____ 9. grave

a. correct; careful and exact

_____ 10. communion

b. having to do with the body rather than the mind or emotions

_____ 11. agent

c. known or felt since birth; completely natural; not learned

_____ 12. clarity

d. enough; as much as necessary

_____ 13. responsibility

e. the fact of being easy, not complicated, or not fancy

_____ 14. expression

f. the quality of being clear

_____ 15. instinctive

g. a sharing of feelings or thoughts; closeness

_____ 16. accurate

h. a saying or a way of saying something

_____ 17. physical

i. something that produces an effect; a representative

_____ 18. sufficient

j. whatever makes something what it really is; characteristic

_____ 19. simplicity

k. serious; having to do with important things

_____ 20. quality

l. a willingness to do what one is expected or required to do;
   duty

Score Yourself!   *The answers are on page 265.*   Number correct: _____   Part A: _____   Part B: _____

UNIT 3 Test Yourself

Part A Recognizing Meaning

Write the letter of the word or phrase that is closest in meaning to the word in italics.

_____ 1. a *courteous* man
a. nosy
c. mannerly
b. strange
d. short-tempered

_____ 2. to *long* to be successful
a. wait
c. work
b. pretend
d. strongly desire

_____ 3. an *energetic* effort
a. weak
c. foolish
b. powerful
d. successful

_____ 4. a *dense* forest
a. dark
c. peaceful
b. thick
d. dangerous

_____ 5. a *barbaric* ruler
a. cruel
c. strict
b. intelligent
d. unlucky

_____ 6. to be *reluctant* to go
a. happy
c. not able
b. impatient
d. unwilling

_____ 7. an *inanimate* object
a. lovely
c. not living
b. expensive
d. not necessary

_____ 8. his obvious *sullenness*
a. bad manners
c. gloomy silence
b. loneliness
d. lack of skill

_____ 9. water that *surges*
a. rushes
c. rises
b. freezes
d. leaks

_____ 10. an *offensive* remark
a. loud
c. unpleasant
b. scolding
d. unnecessary

_____ 11. to remain *aloof*
a. silent
c. ready
b. not involved
d. exhausted

_____ 12. an unusual *position*
a. chance
c. feeling
b. delay
d. situation

_____ 13. a *realistic* request
a. hopeful
c. small
b. reasonable
d. important

_____ 14. a *keen* desire
a. intense
c. angry
b. sudden
d. foolish

Part B Applying Meaning

Write the letter of the best answer.

_____ 15. You would be most likely to behave in a <u>languid</u> way if you felt
a. lazy.　b. jealous.　c. shy.　d. excited.

_____ 16. A person would act in a <u>patronizing</u> way if he or she felt
a. surprised.　b. superior.　c. embarrassed.　d. grateful.

_____ 17. Someone who is <u>bound</u> for home is
a. going home.　b. leaving home.　c. stuck at home.　d. happy at home.

_____ 18. What is often found on a <u>bough</u>?
a. a wheel　b. a puddle　c. a nest　d. a chimney

_____ 19. You could express a feeling of <u>dismay</u> by saying,
a. "Thanks!"　b. "Go for it!"　c. "Well, maybe."　d. "Oh, no!"

_____ 20. If you do something <u>casually</u>, you do it in a way that is
a. rude.　b. kind or friendly.　c. dishonest.　d. easy and relaxed.

Score Yourself!　*The answers are on page 265.*　Number correct: _____　Part A: _____　Part B: _____

UNIT 5 Test Yourself

Part A Synonyms

Write the letter of the word that is closest in meaning to the capitalized word.

_____ 1. CORROSION: (A) crime   (B) decay   (C) meaning   (D) problem

_____ 2. TERMINAL: (A) amount   (B) essay   (C) room   (D) station

_____ 3. INNOVATION: (A) entrance   (B) building   (C) book   (D) invention

_____ 4. CONTEND: (A) fight   (B) measure   (C) satisfy   (D) win

_____ 5. ISOLATE: (A) choose   (B) delay   (C) separate   (D) waste

_____ 6. VOLUME: (A) appearance (B) quantity   (C) arrangement (D) wish

_____ 7. EXISTENCE: (A) presence   (B) death   (C) thought   (D) excitement

_____ 8. PROCEDURE: (A) path   (B) agreement (C) method   (D) selection

_____ 9. ECONOMICAL: (A) plain   (B) thrifty   (C) amusing   (D) greedy

_____ 10. CONSUME: (A) use   (B) argue   (C) erase   (D) cover

Part B Matching Definitions

Match each word on the left with its definition on the right. Write the letter of the appropriate definition in the blank.

_____ 11. system   a. a main road or channel

_____ 12. injection   b. a place where a raw material is made pure

_____ 13. diameter   c. a group of parts working together; method or plan

_____ 14. application   d. in a way that wastes little

_____ 15. technological   e. having to do with one's home or own country

_____ 16. obstacle   f. having to do with practical science or the use of machinery

_____ 17. artery   g. something that gets in the way

_____ 18. domestic   h. the distance across a circle, through the center

_____ 19. refinery   i. the forcing of a liquid into something

_____ 20. efficiently   j. the act of putting on or using [something]

UNIT 6 Test Yourself

Part A Recognizing Meaning
Write the letter of the word or phrase that is closest in meaning to the word in italics.

_____ 1. during the *assembly*
   a. speech   c. election
   b. gathering   d. agreement

_____ 2. to *abandon* the town
   a. clean   c. leave
   b. decorate   d. move to

_____ 3. a *considerable* effort
   a. polite   c. large
   b. simple   d. careless

_____ 4. a *portion* of the building
   a. roof   c. window
   b. section   d. covering

_____ 5. if they *survive*
   a. live   c. tip over
   b. bloom   d. get better

_____ 6. no *trace* to be found
   a. peace   c. trouble
   b. comfort   d. remaining bit

_____ 7. to *decline* with a smile
   a. say no   c. whisper
   b. express joy d. turn around

_____ 8. will *definitely* go
   a. sadly   c. surely
   b. quickly   d. probably

_____ 9. a large *debt*
   a. gift   c. spot or stain
   b. problem   d. something owed

_____ 10. to *scour* the house
   a. damage   c. repair
   b. pay for   d. search through

_____ 11. to *extract* a nail
   a. take out   c. use
   b. run into   d. firmly pound

_____ 12. to *populate* an area
   a. like   c. live in
   b. mess up   d. go away from

_____ 13. where rivers *converge*
   a. flood   c. come together
   b. flow   d. become wide

_____ 14. a *sheer* side
   a. tall   c. thick
   b. smooth   d. very steep

Part B Applying Meaning
Write the letter of the best answer.

_____ 15. A <u>fixture</u> found in most kitchens is a
   a. sink.   b. pitcher.   c. frying pan.   d. refrigerator.

_____ 16. To have a picnic <u>despite</u> rainy weather means to have it
   a. later.   b. anyway.   c. canceled.   d. because of the rain.

_____ 17. When you leave home to go shopping, your <u>destination</u> could be
   a. a mall.   b. a car.   c. a credit card.   d. new clothes.

_____ 18. A dog that is being <u>elusive</u> will usually
   a. growl.   b. run away.   c. cry or howl.   d. wag its tail.

_____ 19. Someone is <u>obviously</u> sleepy when he or she is
   a. yawning.   b. grouchy.   c. up late.   d. wide awake.

_____ 20. In order to <u>dislodge</u> a root, you would
   a. plant it.   b. poison it.   c. dig it up.   d. measure it.

Score Yourself!   *The answers are on page 265.*   Number correct: _____   Part A: _____   Part B: _____

UNIT 7   Test Yourself

Part A   Matching Definitions

Match each word on the left with its definition on the right. Write the letter of the appropriate definition in the blank.

_____ 1. desperate   a. to become uncertain; pause; stumble

_____ 2. maintenance   b. a ruler's refusal to allow a law to pass

_____ 3. achievement   c. the work of keeping something in good shape

_____ 4. typical   d. extremely serious; having a great need; hopeless

_____ 5. eligible   e. normal; regular; having the characteristics of a group

_____ 6. exclusive   f. belonging to only a small or chosen group

_____ 7. veto   g. present everywhere

_____ 8. universal   h. having to do with money

_____ 9. financial   i. something that has been done successfully

_____ 10. falter   j. having the necessary characteristics; fit to be chosen

Part B   Synonyms

Write the letter of the word that is closest in meaning to the capitalized word.

_____ 11. DUPLICATE: (A) copy   (B) repair   (C) trick   (D) divide

_____ 12. OUTLOOK: (A) top   (B) wish   (C) view   (D) doorway

_____ 13. ACQUIRE: (A) like   (B) get   (C) know   (D) save

_____ 14. DEFECT: (A) imperfection (B) discovery   (C) truth   (D) strength

_____ 15. VAGABOND: (A) unclear   (B) clever   (C) poor   (D) wandering

_____ 16. REQUIREMENT: (A) product   (B) question   (C) need   (D) concern

_____ 17. RELISH: (A) use   (B) enjoy   (C) finish   (D) create

_____ 18. PEDESTRIAN: (A) slow   (B) interesting   (C) ordinary (D) dangerous

_____ 19. MONOPOLIZE: (A) choose   (B) control   (C) dislike   (D) join

_____ 20. PROMINENT: (A) loud   (B) careful   (C) patient   (D) important

UNIT 9 Test Yourself

Part A Applying Meaning

Write the letter of the best answer.

_____ 1. A person who wanted a <u>rodent</u> for a pet might choose a
a. kitten. b. hamster. c. parakeet. d. goldfish.

_____ 2. Which of the following animals is a source of <u>venom</u>?
a. bees b. cows c. sheep d. rats

_____ 3. One animal that is known for making <u>burrows</u> is the
a. mole. b. beaver. c. robin. d. honeybee.

_____ 4. If a doctor were talking about a <u>colleague</u>, the conversation would be about
a. a hospital. b. a patient. c. a medicine. d. another doctor.

_____ 5. If a fire is referred to as being <u>lethal</u>, that means that it
a. spread. b. was put out. c. was deliberate. d. killed someone.

_____ 6. A <u>component</u> for a car is a
a. driver. b. gas station. c. steering wheel. d. truck.

Part B Matching Definitions

Match each word on the left with its definition on the right. Write the letter of the appropriate definition in the blank.

_____ 7. toxin

_____ 8. prompt

_____ 9. dilution

_____ 10. particular

_____ 11. multiple

_____ 12. preliminary

_____ 13. temperament

_____ 14. propose

_____ 15. factor

_____ 16. habitat

_____ 17. proportion

_____ 18. effective

_____ 19. immunity

_____ 20. resistance

a. the area where a plant or animal can be found in nature

b. one's usual frame of mind; one's nature; disposition

c. a condition that brings about a result

d. the act of thinning or weakening something by adding a liquid

e. specific or special; distinct

f. having, or made up of, many parts

g. a part, fraction, or share of a whole

h. a poison

i. to present for consideration

j. useful; producing the desired result

k. leading up to the main event; done as a preparation

l. to urge or encourage an action or response

m. the act of working against or opposing something

n. the ability to be unaffected by something dangerous or unpleasant

UNIT 10 Test Yourself

Part A Recognizing Meaning

Write the letter of the word or phrase that is closest in meaning to the word in italics.

_____ 1. a *curious* statue
    a. small   c. famous
    b. strange   d. poorly made

_____ 2. to be *utterly* happy
    a. briefly   c. mildly
    b. foolishly   d. completely

_____ 3. the *adjacent* houses
    a. expensive   c. empty
    b. neighboring d. newest

_____ 4. water that *recedes*
    a. goes back   c. dribbles
    b. pours out   d. soaks in

_____ 5. a *contented* family
    a. large   c. wildly happy
    b. wealthy   d. happy enough

_____ 6. if you *hesitate*
    a. ask   c. pause
    b. guess   d. make a mistake

_____ 7. to touch *delicately*
    a. lightly   c. sadly
    b. lovingly   d. with pleasure

_____ 8. her *occasional* smiles
    a. warm   c. fake
    b. not often   d. pleased

_____ 9. to do the work *methodically*
    a. cheerfully   c. for free
    b. right away   d. carefully

_____ 10. to suddenly *materialize*
    a. change   c. show up
    b. disappear   d. seem important

_____ 11. likely to *stray*
    a. be rude   c. break
    b. wander away d. get tired

_____ 12. to do it *properly*
    a. partly   c. now and then
    b. sadly   d. the right way

_____ 13. clean it *briskly*
    a. quickly   c. soon
    b. completely   d. cheerfully

_____ 14. to make a *gesture*
    a. gift   c. motion
    b. threat   d. mistake

Part B Applying Meaning

Write the letter of the best answer.

_____ 15. In order to <u>peer</u>, you use your
    a. nose.   b. eyes.   c. hands.   d. ears.

_____ 16. Something that could be used to <u>transfer</u> groceries is a
    a. cart.   b. shelf.   c. farm.   d. cash register.

_____ 17. A sound that is usually made <u>wistfully</u> is a
    a. growl.   b. whimper.   c. purr.   d. scream.

_____ 18. To look at something <u>intently</u>, you might
    a. peek.   b. glance.   c. stare.   d. blink.

_____ 19. To be <u>responsive</u> to a comment someone makes is to
    a. ignore it.   b. forget it.   c. react to it.   d. hear it.

_____ 20. If you wanted someone to <u>convey</u> a message, you would want that person to
    a. answer it.   b. pass it on.   c. keep it secret.   d. give it back.

Score Yourself!   *The answers are on page 265.*   Number correct: _____   Part A: _____   Part B: _____

UNIT 11 Test Yourself

Part A Synonyms

Write the letter of the word that is closest in meaning to the capitalized word.

_____ 1. SPECIALIST: (A) soldier   (B) worker   (C) expert   (D) solution

_____ 2. AIDE: (A) gift   (B) boss   (C) tool   (D) helper

_____ 3. COUNSEL: (A) enjoy   (B) advise   (C) protect   (D) communicate

_____ 4. BENEFIT: (A) help   (B) teach   (C) cure   (D) give

_____ 5. ASPIRATION: (A) hope   (B) skill   (C) education   (D) happiness

_____ 6. INDUSTRY: (A) school   (B) government   (C) business   (D) pollution

_____ 7. DILIGENCE: (A) laziness   (B) intelligence   (C) persistence   (D) speed

_____ 8. EMPLOYMENT: (A) job   (B) question   (C) skill   (D) allowance

Part B Matching Definitions

Match each word on the left with its definition on the right. Write the letter of the appropriate definition in the blank.

_____ 9. immigrate   a. not owned by the government; the opposite of *public*

_____ 10. poverty   b. according to certain rules; in terms of a specific science or art

_____ 11. attitude   c. a way of looking at life or a situation; outlook; manner

_____ 12. technically   d. a person learning a job from an experienced worker

_____ 13. sponsor   e. not reacting or fighting back; the opposite of *active*

_____ 14. apprentice   f. the condition of not having enough money

_____ 15. passive   g. the state or shape someone or something is in; situation

_____ 16. condition   h. to help or support

_____ 17. diligence   i. to move to and live in a new country

_____ 18. federal   j. a person who builds things with stone

_____ 19. private   k. careful, lasting effort

_____ 20. mason   l. having to do with the central government rather than local government

---

Score Yourself!   *The answers are on page 265.*   Number correct: _____   Part A: _____   Part B: _____

UNIT 13 Test Yourself

Part A Recognizing Meaning

Write the letter of the word or phrase that is closest in meaning to the word in italics.

_____ 1. its *belated* appearance
    a. tardy   c. gradual
    b. strange   d. expected

_____ 2. a small *memento*
    a. idea   c. souvenir
    b. period   d. flash of light

_____ 3. a *jubilant* noise
    a. loud   c. necessary
    b. joyful   d. frightening

_____ 4. to be *belligerent*
    a. happy   c. attractive
    b. thoughtless d. ready to fight

_____ 5. a lower *tariff*
    a. tax   c. salary
    b. score   d. expectation

_____ 6. to *warrant* a response
    a. copy   c. offer
    b. deserve   d. often repeat

_____ 7. an *unpretentious* remark
    a. funny   c. critical
    b. whispered d. not stuck-up

_____ 8. to *revert* to the plan
    a. go back   c. look back
    b. approach d. make changes in

_____ 9. the *bounteous* fish
    a. largest   c. active
    b. plentiful d. most desirable

_____ 10. to *sympathize* with her
    a. meet   c. disagree
    b. spend time d. share feelings

Part B Matching Definitions

Match each word on the left with its definition on the right. Write the letter of the appropriate definition in the blank.

_____ 11. operative   a. full of disrespect or scorn

_____ 12. flounder   b. a clever, witty, or sarcastic remark

_____ 13. endear   c. not planned beforehand

_____ 14. prosper   d. to send away; force someone to leave a country

_____ 15. quip   e. put into action or use; in effect

_____ 16. deport   f. to do well; succeed

_____ 17. random   g. the center around which a group gathers

_____ 18. nucleus   h. to make dear or beloved

_____ 19. profitable   i. to plunge about; struggle awkwardly

_____ 20. contemptuous j. producing a gain or benefit

UNIT 14 Test Yourself

Part A Synonyms

Write the letter of the word that is closest in meaning to the capitalized word.

_____ 1. REMOTE: (A) still   (B) lovely   (C) faraway   (D) convenient

_____ 2. ARREST: (A) halt   (B) accuse   (C) discover   (D) accept

_____ 3. JOSTLE: (A) amuse   (B) shake   (C) fight   (D) drop

_____ 4. VERGE: (A) edge   (B) meadow   (C) decision   (D) assistant

_____ 5. RIGID: (A) sad   (B) smooth   (C) unbending   (D) pure

_____ 6. CHAOS: (A) danger   (B) balance   (C) foolishness   (D) confusion

_____ 7. TRAVAIL: (A) motion   (B) fear   (C) doubt   (D) labor

_____ 8. CEASE: (A) sleep   (B) grab   (C) notice   (D) discontinue

_____ 9. SPIRIT: (A) cloud   (B) chance   (C) mood   (D) movement

_____ 10. AUSTERELY: (A) harshly   (B) repeatedly   (C) loudly   (D) helpfully

_____ 11. REPOSE: (A) sorrow   (B) faith   (C) answer   (D) relaxation

_____ 12. ABRUPTLY: (A) painfully   (B) suddenly   (C) calmly   (D) cruelly

Part B Applying Meaning

Write the letter of the best answer.

_____ 13. One place where you would expect to find aridity is a
a. hospital.   b. desert.   c. library.   d. greenhouse.

_____ 14. An extremely resilient material is
a. sand.   b. steel.   c. rubber.   d. glue.

_____ 15. To measure the vertical size of something would be to measure its
a. weight.   b. height.   c. width.   d. distance around.

_____ 16. An intangible idea is one that's hard to
a. define.   b. remember.   c. forget.   d. like.

_____ 17. Which kind of song encourages a feeling of quietude?
a. a theme song   b. a march   c. a national anthem   d. a lullaby

_____ 18. You would expect to find a turbulent group of people at a
a. riot.   b. theater.   c. funeral.   d. dinner party.

_____ 19. When you feel somnolent, you are likely to
a. giggle.   b. yawn.   c. blush.   d. shiver.

_____ 20. In order to poise, you would need to
a. smile.   b. make a decision.   c. keep steady.   d. tell the truth.

Score Yourself!   *The answers are on page 265.*   Number correct: _____   Part A: _____   Part B: _____

UNIT 15 Test Yourself

Part A   Matching Definitions

Match each word on the left with its definition on the right. Write the letter of the appropriate definition in the blank.

_____ 1. trend   a. actually; nearly; practically

_____ 2. internal   b. something given forth; discharge

_____ 3. generation   c. to change completely

_____ 4. elite   d. a general direction of events; tendency

_____ 5. virtually   e. having to do with the inside

_____ 6. thesis   f. limited to a few of the finest or best; very special

_____ 7. metropolitan   g. a person or thing that divides and gives out something

_____ 8. emission   h. an idea not yet proven to be true; theory

_____ 9. combustion   i. the act or process of burning

_____ 10. revolutionize   j. all the people born at about the same time

_____ 11. carburetor   k. having to do with a city and its close surroundings

_____ 12. distributor   l. an engine part that blends air and fuel to create an explosion

Part B   Recognizing Meaning

Write the letter of the word or phrase that is closest in meaning to the word in italics.

_____ 13. a *distinct* difference
    a. small   c. new
    b. obvious   d. major

_____ 14. for *external* use
    a. careful   c. frequent
    b. lasting   d. on the outside

_____ 15. to *propel* the boat
    a. push   c. protect
    b. tip over   d. quickly stop

_____ 16. to achieve *supremacy*
    a. happiness   c. lasting peace
    b. total safety   d. highest position

_____ 17. to *merit* a good grade
    a. earn   c. notice
    b. hope for   d. take pride in

_____ 18. actions that *attest* feelings
    a. deny   c. substitute for
    b. disprove   d. show to be true

_____ 19. to *encounter* trouble
    a. avoid   c. run into
    b. ask for   d. fail to see

_____ 20. to eat *exotic* foods
    a. expensive   c. unfamiliar
    b. unhealthy   d. very filling

Score Yourself!

Unit 1	Unit 2	Unit 3	Unit 5	Unit 6	Unit 7
Part A	*Part A*	*Part A*	*Part A*	*Part A*	*Part A*
1. h	1. a	1. c	1. B	1. b	1. d
2. e	2. b	2. d	2. D	2. c	2. c
3. i	3. d	3. b	3. D	3. c	3. i
4. g	4. b	4. b	4. A	4. b	4. e
5. j	5. b	5. a	5. C	5. a	5. j
6. f	6. c	6. d	6. B	6. d	6. f
7. b	7. a	7. c	7. A	7. a	7. b
8. d	8. d	8. c	8. C	8. c	8. g
9. a	*Part B*	9. a	9. B	9. d	9. h
10. c	9. k	10. c	10. A	10. d	10. a
Part B	10. g	11. b	*Part B*	11. a	*Part B*
11. D	11. i	12. d	11. c	12. c	11. A
12. A	12. f	13. b	12. i	13. c	12. C
13. C	13. l	14. a	13. h	14. d	13. B
14. C	14. h	*Part B*	14. j	*Part B*	14. A
15. A	15. c	15. a	15. f	15. a	15. D
16. B	16. a	16. b	16. g	16. b	16. C
17. D	17. b	17. a	17. a	17. a	17. B
18. C	18. d	18. c	18. e	18. b	18. C
19. B	19. e	19. d	19. b	19. a	19. B
20. A	20. j	20. d	20. d	20. c	20. D

Unit 9	Unit 10	Unit 11	Unit 13	Unit 14	Unit 15
Part A	*Part A*	*Part A*	*Part A*	*Part A*	*Part A*
1. b	1. b	1. C	1. a	1. C	1. d
2. a	2. d	2. D	2. c	2. A	2. e
3. a	3. b	3. B	3. b	3. B	3. j
4. d	4. a	4. A	4. d	4. A	4. f
5. d	5. d	5. A	5. a	5. C	5. a
6. c	6. c	6. C	6. b	6. D	6. h
Part B	7. a	7. C	7. d	7. D	7. k
7. h	8. b	8. A	8. a	8. D	8. b
8. l	9. d	*Part B*	9. b	9. C	9. i
9. d	10. c	9. i	10. d	10. A	10. c
10. e	11. b	10. f	*Part B*	11. D	11. l
11. f	12. d	11. c	11. e	12. B	12. g
12. k	13. a	12. b	12. i	*Part B*	*Part B*
13. b	14. c	13. h	13. h	13. b	13. b
14. i	*Part B*	14. d	14. f	14. c	14. d
15. c	15. b	15. e	15. b	15. b	15. a
16. a	16. a	16. g	16. d	16. a	16. d
17. g	17. b	17. k	17. c	17. d	17. a
18. j	18. c	18. l	18. g	18. a	18. d
19. n	19. c	19. a	19. j	19. b	19. c
20. m	20. b	20. j	20. a	20. c	20. c

Acknowledgments

- Virginia Barber Literary Agency, Inc.: For an excerpt from "Red Dress," from *Dance of the Happy Shades* by Alice Munro; copyright © 1968 by Alice Munro. Published by Penguin Books.

- Little, Brown & Company: For an excerpt from *The Incredible Journey: A Tale of Three Animals* by Sheila Burnford; copyright © 1960, 1961 by Sheila Burnford, reprinted by permission of Little, Brown and Company in association with The Atlantic Monthly Press.

- Macmillan Publishing Company: For an excerpt from "A Mother in Mannville," from *When the Whippoorwill* by Marjorie Kinnan Rawlings; copyright © 1940 Marjorie Kinnan Rawlings; copyright renewed © 1968 Norton Baskin. Reprinted by permission of Charles Scribner's Sons, an imprint of Macmillan Publishing Company.

Every effort has been made to trace the ownership of all copyrighted material and to obtain permission.

Cover Art

Butterflies, 1950, M.C. ESCHER. National Gallery of Art, Washington, D.C., Cornelius Van S. Roosevelt Collection.

Photographs/Illustrations

- *Mark Twain*, 1897, photographer unknown. The Bettmann Archive, New York. p. 17
- *Fox Island Cabin*, ROCKWELL KENT. Rockwell Kent Legacies. p. 29
- UPI/The Bettmann Archive, New York. p. 38
- © Don Klumpp/The Image Bank. p. 61
- Michael Roytek/Courtesy Boy Scouts of America. p. 72
- The Granger Collection, New York. p. 87
- © Karl H. Maslowski, The National Audubon Society Collection/Photo Researchers, Inc. p. 115
- © MCMLXIII Walt Disney Productions/Photofest. p. 126
- © Robert Landau/Westlight. p. 137
- *Acadian Expulsion*, Edward Austin Abbey (1852-1911.) From "Poetical Works of Henry Wadsworth Longfellow" published by Houghton, Osgood & Co., Boston, 1879. North Wind Picture Archives. p. 161
- © 1991 David Muench. p. 171
- Dover Publications p. 182

Personal Vocabulary Log

Use the following pages to keep track of the unfamiliar words you encounter in your reading. Write brief definitions and pronunciations for each word. This will make the words part of your permanent vocabulary.

_____

_____

_____

_____

_____

_____

_____

_____

_____

_____

_____

_____

_____

_____

_____

_____

_____

_____

_____

_____

_____

_____

_____

_____

Personal Vocabulary Log

Personal Vocabulary Log

Personal Vocabulary Log

Personal Vocabulary Log

Personal Vocabulary Log

Personal Vocabulary Log

Personal Vocabulary Log